Volatility in Indian Stock Markets

Prashant Joshi

Associate Professor,
Shrimad Rajchandra Institute of
Management and Computer Application,
Tarsadi.

First Edition : 2011

Himalaya Publishing House

MUMBAI • NEW DELHI • NAGPUR • BENGALURU • HYDERABAD • CHENNAI • PUNE • LUCKNOW • AHMEDABAD • ERNAKULAM • BHUBANESWAR • INDORE • KOLKATA • GUWAHATI

First Edition : 2011

Published by : Mrs. Meena Pandey for **Himalaya Publishing House Pvt. Ltd.**, "Ramdoot", Dr. Bhalerao Marg, Girgaon, **Mumbai - 400 004.** Phone: 022-23860170/23863863, Fax: 022-23877178 **E-mail: himpub@vsnl.com; Website: www.himpub.com**

Branch Offices :

New Delhi : "Pooja Apartments", 4-B, Murari Lal Street, Ansari Road, Darya Ganj, New Delhi - 110 002. Phone: 011-23270392, 23278631; Fax: 011-23256286

Nagpur : Kundanlal Chandak Industrial Estate, Ghat Road, Nagpur - 440 018. Phone: 0712-2738731, 3296733; Telefax: 0712-2721215

Bengaluru : No. 16/1 (Old 12/1), 1st Floor, Next to Hotel Highlands, Madhava Nagar, Race Course Road, Bengaluru - 560 001. Phone: 080-32919385; Telefax: 080-22286611

Hyderabad : No. 3-4-184, Lingampally, Besides Raghavendra Swamy Matham, Kachiguda, Hyderabad - 500 027. Phone: 040-27560041, 27550139; Mobile: 09848130433

Chennai : No. 85/50, Bazullah Road, T. Nagar, Chennai - 600 017. Phone: 044-28144004/28144005

Pune : First Floor, "Laksha" Apartment, No. 527, Mehunpura, Shaniwarpeth (Near Prabhat Theatre), Pune - 411 030. Phone: 020-24496323/24496333

Lucknow : Jai Baba Bhavan, Church Road, Near Manas Complex and Dr. Awasthi Clinic, Aliganj, Lucknow - 226 024. Phone: 0522-2339329, 4068914; Mobile: 09305302158, 09415349385, 09389593752

Ahmedabad : 114, "SHAIL", 1st Floor, Opp. Madhu Sudan House, C.G. Road, Navrang Pura, Ahmedabad - 380 009. Phone: 079-26560126; Mobile: 09327324149, 09314679413

Ernakulam : 39/104 A, Lakshmi Apartment, Karikkamuri Cross Rd., Ernakulam, Cochin - 622011, Kerala. Phone: 0484-2378012, 2378016; Mobile: 09344199799

Bhubaneswar : 5 Station Square, Bhubaneswar (Odisha) - 751 001. Mobile: 09861046007

Indore : Kesardeep Avenue Extension, 73, Narayan Bagh, Flat No. 302, IIIrd Floor, Near Humpty Dumpty School, Narayan Bagh, Indore - 452 007 (M.P.). Mobile: 09301386468

Kolkata : 108/4, Beliaghata Main Road, Near ID Hospital, Opp. SBI Bank, Kolkata - 700 010, Phone: 033-32449649, Mobile: 09910440956

Guwahati : House No. 15, Behind Pragjyotish College, Near Sharma Printing Press, P.O. Bharalumukh, Guwahati - 781009. (Assam). Mobile: 09883055590, 09883055536

DTP by : HPH, Editorial Office, Bhandup (Shilpa R. Patil)

Printed by : Shri Krishna offset Press Delhi-93

PREFACE

Analysis of stock market for the assessment of the risk has assumed greater significance in India after liberalization. Usefulness of efficient stock market in mobilizing resources is well-known among policy makers and investors. Volatility in the prices of stock adversely affects individual earnings and health of the economy. Volatility in the price of stock market can arise because of several reasons. It creates atmosphere of uncertainty and thus it hampers productive investment. Volatility is inherent feature of stock markets. It should be known to those who are concerned directly and indirectly with stock markets.

Volatility of stock prices refers to the frequency with which changes in stock prices over a given period of time. The volatility can also be understood as the frequency or relative rate at which the price of a security moves up and down. Volatility is found by calculating the annualized standard deviation of daily change in price. Standard deviation of return is widely used as a measure of total risk of a financial asset. If a stock is highly volatile, there is risk of losing capital and thus investors tend to avoid investing in these stocks.

Stock markets across the world are not insulated. The recent rapid growth in emerging markets could be attributable to various measures initiated by various developing countries such as adoption of the more market oriented policies, restructuring of the corporate sector, opening of the different sectors of economy to foreign investors, privatization of state-owned enterprises etc. One of the great barriers to investing in emerging markets is that they are generally prescribed as highly volatile and informationally inefficient compared to the developed stock markets (Chowdhury and Iqbal, 2005). The emerging stock markets generally suffer from these problems due to inferior infrastructure, tendency of institutional investors to participate only in good companies, lack of appropriate regulations, inadequate accounting information disclosure standards and the like. Inefficient markets provide the opportunity to technical traders and managers to construct strategies to make high returns.

While there is a public perception that increases in volatility is bad, it is difficult to establish link between volatility and economic activity or economic welfare. Economic growth is essential for improving the quality of life. Standard classical and neo-classical theories emphasize the role of investment in enhancing economic growth. Monetary and financial sectors play a key role in mobilizing resources. Financial stability is crucial for promoting investment. In a situation of financial stability, financial institutions and markets are able to efficiently mobilize savings, provide liquidity and allocate investment. The growing role of the financial sector in the efficient allocation of resources at appropriate prices could significantly enhance the efficiency with which our economy functions. If financial markets work well, they will direct resources to their most productive uses. Risks will be more accurately priced and will be borne by those who have appetite for absorbing risks. Real economic activity with higher investments, in both quantity as well as quality, would result in growth with macroeconomic stability and fewer financial uncertainties. A stable financial system facilitates efficient transmission of monetary policy initiatives.

Uncertainty plays an important role in economic theory. Many economic models assume that the variance as a measure of uncertainty is constant through time. However, it is not supported by empirical evidence. Financial time series such as stock returns or exchange rates exhibit volatility clustering where large returns of either sign are expected to follow large returns and small returns of wither sign to follow small return. Prediction of financial asset volatility is now considerably improved due to advanced modeling technique that is capable of estimating time varying volatility. The book makes a modest attempt to investigate the nature and pattern of volatility of stock market prices in India and its relation with developing and developed stock markets of the world.

— Prashant Joshi

ACKNOWLEDGEMENT

The research work done in the book would not have been possible without the benign guidance and assistance of number of persons and organizations without whom, it would neither have been worthwhile nor possible to undertake this work.

I have been fortunate enough to be blessed by our Sadgurudev Swami Shri Abhiramdastyagiji. I wish to express my sincere thanks to Dr. Kiran Pandya for being the best mentor I could have ever had during the years of my education. I appreciate what I have learned from him, not only the broad knowledge, sharp scientific instinct and creative ideas, but also the optimistic and friendly attitude. He introduced to me stimulating and challenging areas of econometrics. His understanding, encouraging and personal guidance provided good basis for the book. I am especially indebted to him for his guidance in both professional development and personal growth. I wish to express my deep sense of gratitude to his family members. I would like to thank Ba, Archanben, Prita and Lekha for providing a loving, affectionate and encouraging environment for me.

I am thankful to Dr. Bankim Patel, Director, SRIMCA for providing me all possible facilities at the college to complete this book. He constantly kept me motivated by taking account of it from time to time. Thanks are also due to my other colleagues in SRIMCA for their cooperation at various stages of the study. I am grateful to office bearers of BPKM especially Shri Bhagubhai Patel, Chairman, Shri Kiritbhai Patel, Secretary and Dr. D. R. Shah, Campus Director for providing me continuous encouragement and institutional support to complete the study.

I express my gratitude to Dr. Neeraj Hatekar, then Director of ICSSR, Western Region who awarded of ICSSR Study Grant Scheme. I was able to get access to libraries of some of the top-level institutes of India like Indira Gandhi Institute of Development and Research, Mumbai, Gokhale Institute of Politics and Economics, Pune, and Mumbai University. He also provided expert comments on my econometric analysis. I was fortunate to interact with him at different stages of my study. Thanks are also due to Dr. Kamiaha, Professor and Head, Department of Economics, University of Hyderabad and Dr. Nilanjan Banik, IFMR for their insightful comments on VAR analysis used in my study. I am grateful to Dr. Kaushik Bhattachrya, IIM Kolkata and Dr. Rajendra Vaidya, IGIDR for their valuable suggestions into some methodological aspects and analysis of time series data.

During the course of research work, I interacted with some scholars working abroad and their comments and quick response helped me to grasp certain intricate issues. I thank Dr. Chris Brooks, Professor in Finance and Director of Research, ICMA, UK for his excellent comments on volatility spillover analysis undertaken in my study. I am grateful to Dr. Carol Alexander, Chair, Financial Risk Management, Henley Business School, UK for her insightful suggestions in volatility analysis. Thanks are also due to Dr. Walter Enders, Professor, Department of Economics, University of Alabama and Dr. Ruey Tsay, Alexander Professor of Econometrics and Statistics, The University of Chicago Booth School of Business for their valuable comments and suggestions in time series analysis.

I am fortunate to have the words of wisdom from Dr. Vikas Chitre and Dr. Nilkant Rath for improving quality of my doctoral work. I had benefits of interactions with Prof. Dilip Nachane, Director,

IGIDR on volatility and VAR analysis. I am thankful to Dr. Umesh Naik, Mr. Kishore Parikh, Dr. P. Marvania, Dr. K. Shanmugum and Mr. Jignashu Yagnik for their encouragement, support and valuable comments.

I thank Mr. Deshpande, librarian of Gokhale Institute, Pune and Mr. G. K. Manjunath, Chief librarian, IGIDR for their support.

I must thank the members of my KP research group. I am grateful to Smruti Bulsari for her valuable help. She took efforts in reading and providing me with valuable suggestions on chapters of my book that helped me in my work. She deserves special appreciations for the excellent help of improving the quality of presentation of my book. Thanks are also due to Jayesh Desai, Gaurang Rami, Krishnaraj Chudasama and Madhusudan Raj for providing intellectually stimulating environment and that maintained the tempo for quickly finishing the research work in time.

I express my gratitude to faculty members of Department of Research Methodology and Interdisciplinary Studies in Social Sciences. Special thanks to Dr. D G Thakore, Co-ordinator of MHRD programme for permitting me to use infrastructure and resources of the department.

Thanks are due to Manish Patel, Librarian of Department of Research Methodology and Interdisciplinary Studies in Social Science for giving all facilities for referencing, reading and photocopying. Helps extended by Siba and Kishore, Office Assistants, Department of Research Methodology and Interdisciplinary Studies in Social Science are admirable. They always showed their readiness to work even till late hours in the department. I am grateful to the Department for the support it has extended throughout my study. The department has not only purchased the softwares for econometric analysis I needed for my data analysis but also taken special care to train me in the area of my research.

During my work, I have received assistance and encouragement from a large number of people. I would like to thank Dr. Rakesh Desai, Dr. Satyakam Joshi and Mr. Kaushikbhai for their support, guidance and motivation.

I express my gratitude towards Mr. S. Shrivastava and Mr. Anuj Pandey of Himalaya Publications for readily agreeing to publish and enthusiastically pursuing the writing of this book. Their suggestions are very useful to keep the contents of the book focused.

I would like to thank my mom; her love and support have kept me strong even during the most difficult days. I am also grateful to my dad for his unreserved support in my life. Special acknowledgement for my wife Hetal, for giving me encouragement, for being full of love and support and making my life so colorful and for always having bigger dreams for me. When she needed me the most, I was not available. What a great devotion! I express my thanks to elder son Bhavesh and little naughty son Chhayanshu who relieved me of incessant work with their lovely company. I thank my brother, his wife and their son-Labhesh for their love. I would not have achieved anything without their whole-hearted love. I have been fortunate enough to have my parents-in-law's help and for their moral support. My special gratitude to Mr. Milind Joshi and Mrs. Deval Rawal for their support. I want to express my extreme gratitude to them for their continuous and unselfish love.

— Prashant Joshi

CONTENTS

BRIEF CONTENTS

1 CHAPTER
Introduction

Analysis of stock market for the assessment of the risk has assumed greater significance in India after liberalization. Usefulness of efficient stock market in mobilizing resources is well-known among policy makers and investors. Volatility in the prices of stock adversely affects individual earnings and health of the economy. Volatility in the price of stock market can arise because of several reasons. It creates atmosphere of uncertainty and thus it hampers productive investment. Volatility is inherent feature of stock markets. It should be known to those who are concerned directly and indirectly with stock markets.

Volatility of stock prices refers to the frequency with which changes in stock prices over a given period of time. The volatility can also be understood as the frequency or relative rate at which the price of a security moves up and down. Volatility is found by calculating the annualized standard deviation of daily change in price. Standard deviation of return is widely used as a measure of total risk of a financial asset. If a stock is highly volatile, there is risk of losing capital and thus investors tend to avoid investing in these stocks.

Stock markets across the world are not insulated. The recent rapid growth in emerging markets could be attributable to various measures initiated by various developing countries such as adoption of the more market oriented policies, restructuring of the corporate sector, opening of the different sectors of economy to foreign investors, privatization of state-owned enterprises etc. One of the great barriers to investing in emerging markets is that they are generally prescribed as highly volatile and informationally inefficient compared to the developed stock markets (Chowdhury and Iqbal, 2005). The emerging stock markets generally suffer from these problems due to inferior infrastructure, tendency of institutional investors to participate only in good companies, lack of appropriate regulations, inadequate accounting information disclosure standards and the like. Inefficient markets provide the opportunity to technical traders and managers to construct strategies to make high returns.

While there is a public perception that increase in volatility is bad, it is difficult to establish link between volatility and economic activity or economic welfare. Economic growth is essential for improving the quality of life. Standard classical and neo-classical theories emphasize the role of investment in enhancing economic growth. Monetary and financial sectors play a key role in mobilizing resources. Financial stability is crucial for promoting investment. In a situation of financial stability, financial institutions and markets are able to efficiently mobilize savings, provide liquidity and allocate investment. The growing role of the financial sector in the efficient allocation of resources at appropriate prices could significantly enhance the efficiency with which our economy functions. If financial markets work well, they will direct resources to their most productive uses. Risks will be more accurately priced and will be borne by those who have appetite for absorbing risks. Real economic activity with higher investments, in both quantity as well as quality, would result in growth with macroeconomic stability and fewer financial uncertainties. A stable financial system facilitates efficient transmission of monetary policy initiatives.

Uncertainty plays an important role in economic theory. Many economic models assume that the variance as a measure of uncertainty is constant through time. However, it is not supported by empirical evidence. Financial time series such as stock returns or exchange rates exhibit volatility clustering where large returns of either sign are expected to follow large returns and small returns of wither sign to follow small return. Prediction of financial asset volatility is now considerably improved due to advanced modeling technique that is capable of estimating time varying volatility. Present study attempts to investigate the nature and pattern of volatility of stock market prices in India and its relation with developing and developed stock markets of the world.

1.1 Rationale of the Study

United States of America experienced stock market price crisis recently. It impacts on the other stock markets economy of other countries, financial institutions and individual investors. The great, sudden and unexpected crash of the stock prices has also affected the psychology and expectations of participants.

The study of financial assets volatility is important to academics, policy makers, and financial market participants for several reasons. First, prediction of financial market volatility is important to economic agents because it represents a measure of risk exposure in their investments. Second, a volatile stock market is a serious concern for policy makers because instability of the stock market creates uncertainty and thus adversely affects growth prospects. Recent evidence shows that when markets are perceived as highly volatile, it "may act as a potential barrier to investing" (Poshakwale and Murinde, 2001, Raju, M.T., Ghosh and Anirban, 2004).

Third, the stock market volatility causes reduction in consumer spending (Garner, 1988). He found that the stock market crash in 1987 brought about a reduction in the consumer spending in the U.S. Fourth, pricing of derivative securities and pricing of call option is a function of volatility. Finally, stock return forecasting is in a sense volatility forecasting, and this has created new job opportunities for the professionals those who are experts in volatility forecasting. Thus it can be seen that the study of stock market volatility is very important and can be helpful for the formulation of economic policies and framing rules and regulations related to stock market volatility.

Volatility in equity market has become a matter of major concern in recent years for investors, regulators and brokers. Stock return volatility hinders economic performance through consumer spending. Gertler and Hubbard (1989) found that Stock Return Volatility affects business investment spending. Further the extreme volatility could disrupt the smooth functioning of the financial system and lead to structural or regulatory changes.

However, increase in volatility per se is not a problem. Increased volatility reflects underlying problems in fundamental forces affecting economic activities and expectations about them. In fact the more quickly and accurately prices reflect the available information; the more efficient would be pricing of securities and thereby allocation of resources. A market in which prices fully reflect available information is called "efficient" where share prices fluctuate randomly around their "intrinsic" values. The stock market in India has had its fair share of crisis engendered by excessive speculation resulting in excessive volatility. Undoubtedly, the confidence of investors in the early 1990's to some extent has been eroded by excessive volatility of the Indian Stock Markets. The wide spread concern of the exchange management, brokers and investors alike has realized the importance of being able to measure and predict stock market volatility.

Volatility of stock returns in the developed countries has been studied extensively using different variants of ARCH (Autoregressive Conditional Heteroscedasticity) and GARCH (Generalized Autoregressive Conditional Heteroscedasticity) models. There is relatively less empirical research on stock return volatility in emerging markets.

High levels of volatility in a stock market can lead to a general erosion of investors' confidence and an outflow of capital from stock markets, volatility has become a matter of concern for government, management, brokers and investors. It is, therefore, necessary to explore a model of stock market volatility that can measure and estimate volatility in Indian stock markets.

Deregulation and market liberalization measures, rapid development in communication technology and computerized trading systems and increasing activities of multinational corporations have accelerated the growth of Indian capital market which is now slowly moving towards global financial integration. From 1999 onwards, Indian firms are raising capital from offshore markets. The growing international integration of financial markets has prompted several empirical studies to examine the mechanism through which stock market movements are transmitted around the world. These studies examine how stock returns in one national stock market influence the returns of other stock markets.

The present study attempts to examine the interactions of Indian stock market with developing and developed stock markets of India, Hong Kong, China and USA using Vector Autoregression (VAR). It also attempts to analyze return and volatility spillover effects using Multivariate Generalized Autoregressive Conditional Heteroscedasticity (MGARCH) models.

1.2 Chapter Scheme

The book is organized in seven chapters. Chapter Two (Risk, Return and Stock market volatility: Conceptual and Analytical Frameworks) presents various measures of risk and return. It attempts to identify issues involved in volatility measurement. It discusses advanced time varying volatility models referred as ARCH/GARCH (Autoregressive/ Generalized autoregressive conditional heteroscedasticity) used in modeling of volatility in stock markets. It further explains Multivariate GARCH (MGARCH) model used to analyze return and volatility spillover across the stock markets.

Chapter Three (Indian Capital Market: An Overview) presents the structure of Indian financial system. It discusses the empirical studies focusing on the relationship between financial system and economic growth. The chapter explains working of primary and secondary markets. It also discusses recent trends and reforms in Capital markets.

Chapter Four (Review of Literature) critically examines relevant literature on the subject of present study. The chapter presents review of studies volatility into three categories. First category includes the studies focusing on extent of volatility and its determinants. The second category includes review of studies on the econometric modeling of volatility and last category includes studies focusing on transmission mechanism of return and volatility among different stock markets of the world. The methodology and results of the studies are critically examined. The chapter tries to identify the gaps in existing literature and summarize by providing a conceptual framework for undertaking this study. It also discusses in detail the methodology adopted in the present study. The chapter begins with the objectives. The chapter provides description of sample used in the present study and sources of the data. The chapter includes the discussion on unit root test and Vector Autoregression (VAR) model which is used to examine interaction effects among the stock markets.

Chapter Five (Stock Market Volatility: An Empirical Investigation) is organized into three sections:

The first section presents descriptive statistics of returns of Indian stock markets. The section estimates mean equation and time varying volatility models for Indian stock markets for a period of more than 8 years from January 3, 2000 to July 3, 2008. It tries to find out leverage effect in the stock markets using asymmetric GARCH models. The section identifies a suitable model to capture nature and characteristics of time varying volatility. The results suggest that the volatility exhibits persistent and clustering.

The second section analyzes the interdependence structure of S&P 500 of American, SSE of Chinese, Hang Seng of Hong Kong, NSE and BSE of Indian stock markets. Granger Causality test was performed on returns of stock markets under study after using appropriate methodology. Later on VAR analysis is performed on the full sample. VAR analysis includes impulse response and variance decomposition analysis on stock market returns.

The third section examines return and volatility spillover among the stock markets using Multivariate GARCH (MGARCH) volatility models. It also examines asymmetric responses to negative shocks in all the stock market indices using MGARCH.

Chapter Six (Summary and Policy Recommendations) presents the summary of the study and makes policy recommendation for Indian stock markets with a view to controlling excessive volatility for the benefit of participants of stock markets. The chapter also highlights the area for further research in stock market volatility.

* * *

CHAPTER 2

Risk, Return and Stock Market Volatility: Conceptual and Analytical Framework

Financial markets are becoming highly sophisticated in pricing, isolating and transferring risks. Tools such as derivatives and securitisation not only contribute to this process, but they pose their own risks. The failure of accounting and other regulations introduce additional risks. Practical applications-including risk limits, trader performance-based compensation, portfolio optimization and capital calculations-all depend on the measurement of risk. In the absence of appropriate measure of risk, it is unclear what exactly, such measurements reflect (Knight, 2004).

Investments can be broadly classified into two categories. Investments in financial assets namely shares, debentures, post office savings certificates, insurance policies etc. and the second category of investment like buying plants, buildings, machinery etc. are known as investment in physical assets. Returns in both these assets vary with their risk.

Investors' main objective is to maximize returns on their investments. Returns from investing in equity comprise of dividends and capital gains or losses. The return from debt consists of fixed interest payment and maturity value. Capital gains or losses arising from stock price movements constitute the major component of returns. Investors generally diversify their investment portfolio by holding multiple securities with the intention to minimize risk. Investors could be risk lover, risk avert or risk neutral. The risk may relate to loss of capital, delay in repayment of capital, non repayment of interest or variability of returns. This chapter presents conceptual frame of risk and return and also discusses various models of volatility.

The chapter is organized in seven sections: Section 2.1 defined risk and its various classifications. Section 2.2 discusses returns and its definitions. Section 2.3 provides discussion on measurement of risk. It also discusses issues concerning volatility and its measurements. Section 2.4 provides theoretical discussion on various advanced time varying volatility models. Section 2.5 explains the importance of Multivariate GARCH (Generalized Autoregressive Conditional Heteroscedasticity) models to study volatility and return spillover effects. Section 2.6 explains short-term and long-term factors affecting volatility. Section 2.7 summarizes.

2.1 Risk Defined

The most appropriate definition of risk is that provided by Frank Knight (1921). According to him, "To preserve distinction between measureable uncertainty and an unmeasureable one, we may use the term "risk" to designate the former and the term "uncertainty" for the latter (p.233)". Harry Markowitz (1952) developed portfolio theory to describe how investors may balance risk and reward in constructing investment portfolios. It is interesting that Markowitz offered no definition of risk in his article on "Portfolio Selection". He simply proposed the following rule:

....that the investor does (or should) consider expected return a desirable thing and variance of return an undesirable thing (p.77).

"The concepts "yield" and "risk" appear frequently in financial writings. Usually if the term "yield" were replaced by "expected yield" or "expected return" and "risk" by "variance of return" little change of apparent meaning would result.(p.89)" This statement suggests that variance of return might be used as a proxy for risk.

An individual expects to get some return from the investment in the future. The future expected return is uncertain because of uncertain future. It is this uncertainty associated with the returns from an investment that introduces an element of risk into an investment. The investor makes the investment decision based on the expected return from the investment. The actual return realized from the investment may not correspond to the expected return. This possibility of variation of the actual return from the expected return is termed as risk. When realized and expected returns are same, there would be no risk.

Factors which cause variations in the returns from an investment represent the elements of risk. The total risk can be divided into systematic risk and unsystematic risk. The factors that cause systematic risk are external to a company, uncontrollable and affect a large number of securities simultaneously. They affect the entire market. Examples are inflation, growth rate of economy, interest rate etc. Unsystematic risk is internal and unique to the companies. It is controllable to a great extent. The examples of the factors are fluctuations in the sales, shortage of parts, labour strikes, fixed cost etc. Total risk is composed of systematic and unsystematic risks. More discussion on two types of risk shall be provided in the ensuing sections.

2.1.1 Systematic Risk

Constant changes in Economic, political and social systems have influences on the performance of companies and thereby on their stock prices in varying degree. Economic recession or financial crisis will have negative influence on corporate profitability and thereby on stock prices. The impacts of such factors are system wide causing variability in security return. The impact caused by them is referred to as systematic risk. Systematic risk comprises of interest rate risk, market risk and purchasing power risk.

2.1.1.1 Interest Rate Risk

It affects debt securities like bonds and debentures. A bond or debenture normally has a fixed coupon rate of interest. Subsequent to the issue, the market interest rate may change but the coupon rate remains constant till the maturity of the instrument. The change in market interest rate relative to the coupon rate of a bond causes changes in its market price. There exists the inverse relationship between the interest rate and price of debt instruments. This variation in bond prices caused due to the variation in the interest rates is known as interest rate risk.

2.1.1.2 Market Risk

It connotes to movement and variability of stock prices due to external factors known as market wide factors. The alternating movements of share prices can be easily seen in the movement of share price indices such as the Bombay Stock Exchange's BSE Sensitivity Index, S &P CNX Nifty etc. indices of Indian stock market. Business cycles are considered to be a major determinant of the timing and extent of the bull and bear phases of the market (Kevin, 2004). Business cycle expansion and contraction brings about variation in stock prices which in turns induces market risk.

2.1.1.3 Purchasing Power Risk

It refers to the variation in investor returns caused by inflation. Inflation results in variation in the purchasing power of money and investment. This is known as purchasing power risk and its impact is uniformly felt on all securities in the market. There are two important sources of inflation known as cost-push caused by rising costs of production and demand-pull inflation contributed by excess demand for goods and services in relation to their supply. These inflations cause fluctuations in investor returns form an investment.

2.1.2 Unsystematic Risk

It is originated from certain factors like raw material scarcity, labour strike, and management inefficiency etc are firm specific. When variability of returns occurs because of such factors unique to companies, it is known as unsystematic risk. The major sources of unsystematic risk are the operating environment of the company and the financing pattern adopted by the company. These two types of unsystematic risk are known as business risk and financial risk respectively.

2.1.2.1 Business Risk

Business risk is a function of the operating conditions faced by a company. It is the variability in revenue caused by the operating conditions of the company. The operating environment consists of internal environment within the firm and external environment outside the firm. The impact of these operating affect the operating costs of the company divided into fixed and variable costs. If the total revenue of such a company declines because of sudden change in demand condition or by other reasons, there would be a fall in its operating profits leading to a business risk.

2.1.2.2 Financial Risk

Financial risk is related to a financial leverage which is the use of debt in the capital structure. The presence of debt in the capital structure creates obligatory fixed payments in the form of interest irrespective of profit or loss. This fixed interest payment creates more variability in the earnings per share (EPS) available to equity share holders.

This variability in EPS due to the presence of debt in the capital structure of a company is referred to as financial risk. This is specific to each company and forms part of its unsystematic risk. A company can avoid the financial risk by financing its activities without the use of debt in its capital structure.

2.2 Return

The goal of investment is to make profit. The revenue from investing or the loss in the case of negative revenue depends upon both the change in prices and the amounts of the assets being held. Return is the primary motivating force that drives investment. It represents the reward for undertaking the investment. Most financial studies focus on returns, instead of prices, of assets. Campbell, Lo and MacKinlay (2006) give two main reasons for using returns. First, for average investors, return of an asset is a complete and scale-free summary of the investment opportunity. Second, return series are easier to handle than price series because the former have more attractive statistical properties.

There are, however, several definitions of an asset return. We discuss here some widely used definitions of returns.

2.2.1 One-Period and Multiperiod Simple Return

Let Pt be the price of the asset at date t, the simple net return, Rt, on the asset between dates t-1 to t would result in a simple net return which is denoted as:

$$R_t = (P_t - P_t - 1) \; / \; P_{t-1}$$

Equation 2.1

Equation 2.1 is used to calculate the rate of return. The simple gross return on the asset is just one plus the net return, $1+R_t$(Campbell, Lo and Mackinaly,2006).The numerator,(P_t-P_{t-1}), in the above equation is the revenue or profit during the holding period with a negative profit meaning a loss. The denominator P_{t-1} was the initial investment at the start of the holding period. Therefore, the net return can be viewed as the relative profit or revenue rate. The revenue here is obtained by multiplying the initial

Multiperiod (k-period) simple gross return is just the product of the k one period simple gross returns involved. This is called a compound return(Tsay, 2005).

2.2.2 Continuous Compounded Return

The natural logarithm of the simple gross return of an asset is called the continuously compounded return or *log return*:

$$R_t = \log(1+R_t) = \ln (P_t/P_{t''1}) = \ln (p_t) - \ln (p_{t''1})$$

Equation 2.2

The continuously compounded returns R_t enjoy some advantages over the simple net returns and Multiperiod returns. First, the continuously compounded multiperiod return is simply the sum of continuously compounded one-period returns involved. Second, statistical properties of log returns are more tractable (Campbell, Lo and MacKinlay,1996,Tsay, 2005, Mills & Markellos, 2008).

Distributional properties of returns provide valuable insights on their future values. The analysis can be carried over two frameworks. The static (historical) approach consists of computing marginal moments such as the marginal mean and variance from a sample of past returns and using these statistics as indicators of future patterns. The dynamic approach concerns the conditional distribution and conditional moments, such as the conditional mean and variance. These are assumed to vary in time, so that at each date t, new estimates need to be computed conditional on past observations. The condition is necessary whenever there are reasons to believe that the present returns, to some extent, are determined by past values. By the same argument, future returns depend on present and past returns as well, and their values can be used for forecasting.

2.2.3 Historical Approach

The historical approach explores the marginal distribution of returns. Let us consider the series of returns on a single asset y = R(t,t + 1). The expected return is evaluated from the data

on past returns by, $E(Y_t) = 1/T \sum_{t\,1}^{t} = \bar{y}_t$ *whereas the*

variance of the return is approximated by $V_{Yt} = 1/T \sum_{t-1}^{r} (Y_t - \overline{Y_r})^2$

The historical approach can be refined by applying rolling estimators. Implicitly, this procedure assumes that marginal distributions of returns vary in time. It is implemented by introducing a window of a fixed length K and approximating the expected return at t by rolling average:

$Ey_t = 1/K \sum_{k-0}^{k-1} y_{t-k} = 1/K(y_t + y_{t-1} + ... + y_{t-k+1})$ (Gourieroux Christian and Jasiak Joann (2005).

On the transition from t to t+1, the approximation of the expected return is updated by adding a new observation and deleting the oldest y_{t-K+1}.

2.2.4 Conditional Distribution

The expected values and variances of returns are partly predictable from the past. This suggests that there is a temporal dependence which requires a dynamic approach. It consists of updating the conditional moments by using past information. Generally, the analysis is limited to the first and second order conditional moments.

2.3 Measurement of Risk

Investment decisions require estimates of expected return and risk. Expected return is the mean or central tendency of the probability distribution of one-period returns. Expected risk is measured by the dispersion of the probability distribution of one-period returns.

An investor tries to quantify the risk of an investment that he considers before making the final selection. The quantification of risk is necessary for investment analysis. The most popular measure of risk is the standard deviation of possible returns. It measures the extent of variability of possible returns from the expected return. The standard deviation provides a measure of the total risk associated with a security.

2.3.1 The concept of volatility

Volatility is the measure of risk. It can be used to measure the risk of a single instrument or an entire portfolio of investments. Volatility of an asset can be defined as variability or randomness of its returns. Theoretically, a change in the volatility of either future cash flows or discount rates causes a change in the volatility of share prices (Schwert, 1989). In day-to-day practice, volatility is calculated for all sorts of random financial variable such as stock prices, interest rates, exchange rates, the market value of portfolio etc.

In finance literature, there are a number of alternative methods to measure volatility (Beckers, 1983). The most commonly used measure of volatility in financial analysis is standard deviation. The standard deviation of return (R) from a sample of n observations is the square root of the average squared deviation of returns from the average in the sample. It is defined as:

$$\sigma = \sqrt{\frac{1}{n-1}\sum_{t-1}^{n}(R_t - \overline{R})^2}$$

Equation 2-3

Where Average return in the sample, n= number of observation in the sample

The standard deviation of the return describes an asset's volatility and risk. The variance of return is the square of standard deviation. Daily returns are identified as the difference in the natural logarithm of the closing index or asset value for the two consecutive trading days. It can be presented as:

$$R_t = log(P_t/P_{t-1}) \text{ or } R_t = log(P_t) - log(P_{t-1})$$

Equation 2-4

Where R_t is logarithmic daily return at time t. P_{t-1} and P_t are daily prices of an asset at two successive days, t-1 and t respectively.

2.3.2 Issues concerning Volatility and its measurement

The first issue to be tackled is whether to measure volatility of the stock prices or stock returns. Time series of asset prices display a growing tendency in the long run. Occasionally, however, price series may switch from upward to downward movements and vice-versa in the short or middle run. For this reason, prices of the same asset sampled at different periods of time may exhibit unequal means. Since this feature greatly complicates statistical inference, it needs to be eliminated. A simple approach consists in transforming the prices into returns, which empirically displays more stationary behaviour with a stable mean which is a basic requirement while measuring dispersion around an average value (Campbel, Lo and Mackinlay, 2006; Gourieroux & Jasiak 2005). In order to symmetrically treat upward and downward movement of stock prices, returns are calculated as the logarithmic difference of closing prices at the beginning (Pt-1) and end (Pt) of one measurement period as shown in equation 2.4. The change in the log of the stock price index yields continuously compounded series. Some scholars (Bollerslev, 1986; Schewert, 1989; Engle and Patton, 2001; Harvinder Kaur, 2002; M.Karmakar, 2005) have also used this kind of transformation of the price series in their studies.

The econometric challenge is to specify how the information is used to forecast the mean and variance of the return, conditional on the past information. While many specifications have been considered for the mean return and have been used in efforts to forecast future returns, virtually no methods were available for the variance before introduction of ARCH models. The primary description tool was the rolling standard deviation. This is a standard deviation calculated using a fixed number of the most recent observations. It assumes that the variance of tomorrow's return is an equally weighted average of the squared residuals from the previous days. The assumption of equal weights seems unattractive, as one would think that the more recent events would be more relevant and therefore should have higher weights. Furthermore the assumption of zero weights for observations more than one month old is also unattractive (Engle, 2001). The ARCH model proposed by Engle (1982) allows the data to determine the best weights to use in forecasting the variance. A useful generalization of this model is the GARCH introduced by Bollerslev (1986). This model is also a weighted average of past squared residuals, but it has declining weights that never go completely to zero. It gives models that are easy to estimate and has proven successful in predicting conditional variances (Engle, 2001).

Stock returns are characterized by statistical distributions. Most high frequency financial time series are found deviating from normality. One of the key assumptions of the ordinary regression is that variance of the errors is constant throughout the sample which is known as homoscedasticity. Violation of this assumption indicates the problem of heteroscedasticity. Findings of heteroscedasticity in stock return are well documented by Fama (1965), Engle (1982) and Bollerslev (1986). These studies have found that stock return data is typically characterized by following empirical regularities:

I. Serial Correlation in the Returns

Serial correlation is a measure of relationship between successive errors. Serial correlation in the returns indicates that successive returns are not independent.

II. Thick Tails

Skewness and Kurtosis measure the shape of a probability distribution. Skewness measures the degree of asymmetry, with symmetry implying zero skewness. Positive skewness indicates a relatively long right tail compared to the left tail and negative skewness indicates the opposite. By the tails of a distribution is meant the regions far from the center. Kurtosis indicates the extent to which probability is concentrated in the center and especially and especially at the tail of the distribution rather than in the shoulders which are the regions between center and the tails. Every normal distribution has skewness equal to 0 and Kurtosis of 3. Kurtosis in excess of 3 indicates heavy tails, an indicator of leptokurtosis. Asset returns tend to be leptokurtotic i.e. too many values near the mean and in the tails of the distribution when compared with the normal distribution. The documentation of this empirical regularity is presented in Mandelbrot (1965).

III. Volatility Clustering

Large changes tend to be followed by large changes, of either sign and small changes tend to be followed by small changes (Engle, 1982) and (Bollerslev, 1986). This is known as volatility clustering. Statistically, volatility clustering implies a strong autocorrelation in squared returns.

IV. Leverage Effect

Volatility seems to react differently to a big price increase or a big price drop. These properties, known as "leverage effect", play an important role in the development of volatility models. The negative asymmetry in the distribution of return questions the assumption of an underlying normal distribution. The so-called "leverage effect" first observed by Black (1976) refers to the tendency for stock prices to be negatively correlated with changes in stock volatility. A firm with outstanding debt and equity typically becomes more highly leveraged when value of the firm falls. This raises the equity return volatility.

V. Forecastable Events

Forecastable releases of important information are associated with high volatility. For example, Cornell (1978) and Patell and Wolfson (1981)show that individual firms' stock returns volatility is high around earnings announcements. Similarly, Harvey and Huang (1991) find that fixed income and foreign exchange volatility is higher during periods of heavy trading by central banks or when macroeconomic news is being released.

There are also important predictable changes in volatility across the trading day. For example, volatility is typically much higher at the open and close of stock trading than during the middle of the day. This pattern has been documented by Harris (1986), Gerity and Mulherin (1992) and Baillie and Bollerslev (1991) among others.

Volatility clustering is modelled as an Autoregressive Conditional Heteroscedastic (ARCH) process. Robert Engle (1982) in his seminal work on inflation in the UK first introduced the idea of ARCH effect. Bollerslev (1986) generalized the model by introducing the Generalized-ARCH (GARCH) model. Many variants of the GARCH models have been proposed in the literature thereafter. ARCH and GARCH models assume conditional heteroscedasticity with homoscedastic unconditional error variance. That is, the changes in variance are a function of the realizations of preceding errors and these changes represent temporary and random departure from a constant unconditional variance. The advantage of GARCH model is that it captures the tendency in financial data for volatility clustering. It, therefore, enables us to make the connection between information and volatility explicit since any change in the rate of information arrival to the market will change the volatility in the market. Thus, unless information remains constant, which is hardly the case, volatility must be time varying even on a daily basis. We discuss various time varying volatility models in the following section.

2.4 Volatility Models

Markov Switching approaches have attracted much attention in financial and economic modeling in recent years, due to business cycle characteristics highlighted in macroeconomics and monetary economics and a changing business and investment environment featured by bull and bear market alternations in financial studies. Collectively, these cyclical movements can be termed as regime shifts common to most modern market economies. As markov switching model clearly defines two or more states or regimes, it can vividly reveal the dynamic process of variables in concern and provide the researcher and policy maker with a clue of how these variables evolved in the past and how they may change in the future. Nevertheless, the implementation and execution of a Markov switching model may be technically difficult as it is sensitive to the choice of initial values and other settings such as the lag length and even the data sample.

A dynamic system can be described by changes in the state of its components. The variables concerned which are observable, are represented as dynamic functions of these components, which are unobservable. The unobservable component also called state variables, transit form ne state to another or evolve according to certain rules which are not easily applied to observed variables themselves. This kind of dynamic modeling is called the state space method. It explains the behavior of externally observed variables by examining the internal, dynamic and systematic properties of the unobserved components. Therefore, this modeling strategy if applied properly may reveal the nature and cause of dynamic movement of variables in an effective and fundamental way.

State space models can be estimated using the Kalman filter named after Kalman (1963) which was originally for and is still widely used in automatic control and communications. There are growing applications of the Kalman Filter in state space models but the number is small relative to GARCH. One of the reasons is that state space models are not easy to implement. On one hand, most of the econometric software packages either do not have Kalman Filter procedures or have procedures which are too basic to be of practical use and on the other hand estimates of parameters are rather sensitive to the choice of initial values and other settings of the filter.

Conventional econometric analysis assumes the variance of the disturbance terms as constant over time. The assumption is very limiting for analyzing financial series because of volatility clustering. The models capable of dealing with variance of the series are required. The researchers engaged in forecasting time series such as stock prices and foreign exchange rates observed autocorrelation in the variance ó2 at t with its values lagged one or more periods. If the error variance is related to the squared error term in the previous term, such autocorrelation is known as autoregressive conditional heteroscedasticity (ARCH).

The ARCH model developed by Engle (1982) that allows that conditional variance to be time varying, while unconditional variance is constant (a model with conditional heteroscedasticity, but unconditional homoscedasticity). If mean, variance or covariance of a time series are time-varying, then the series is non-stationary. One might assume that a series with conditional heteroscedasticity is non-stationary. But when we are defining 'non-stationarity', we are actually referring to the long-run or unconditional movements of the series. A time series with conditional heteroscedasticity can still be stationary, as long as its unconditional moments are constant. The properties of a time series with conditional and unconditional moments are explained in section 2.4.1.

2.4.1 Conditional and Unconditional Moments

Before presenting the alternative ARCH type models, we will briefly review the difference between conditional and unconditional moments. Let us assume that yt is generated by the following (first order autoregressive (AR)) process:

$$y_t = py_{t-1} + \varepsilon_t$$

Equation 2-5

The current values of variable y_t depends on the last period's value y_{t-1}, plus a disturbance term, the latter encapsulating all other random influences. It is assumed that this disturbance term comprises T random numbers drawn from a normal distribution with mean equal to 0 and variance σ^2. Statistically, it indicates white noise process.

In equation 2.5 if $\rho=1$, the y_t will be non-stationary and it is possible to rearrange and accumulate y_t for different periods, starting with the initial value of y_0 to obtain:

$$y_t = y_0 + \sum_{t-1}^{T} \varepsilon_1$$

Equation 2-6

That is, the current value of y_t depends on its initial value and all disturbances cumulating between i=1 and T.

2.4.2 Unconditional Moments

When r=1, y_t will be non-stationary. The AR process is said to have unit root. Then the equation 2.6 becomes

$$y_t = y_{t-1} + \varepsilon_t$$

Equation 2-7

which is called random walk model without drift. If it starts at at time 0, its value at time t is given by. If the expectations are taken at time 0, the expected value at any future time t is independent of t and is equal to y_0, but the variance is given by:

$$\sigma^2_\varepsilon = \sigma^2_\varepsilon + ... + \sigma^2_\varepsilon = t\sigma^2_\varepsilon$$

Mean of the series $E(y_t)$ is equal to its initial or starting value , which is constant, but as t increases, its variance $V(y_t)$ increases indefinitely violating the condition of stationarity.

Thus, 's unconditional mean and variance are given below.

1. $E(y_i) = y_0$
2. $V(y_t) = t\,6^2$

Thus for random walk with drift, the mean as well as the variance increases over time, again violating the condition stationarity. If mean, variance or covariance is time varying, the series is said to be non-stationary.

However, if $|\rho|<1$, then yt will be stationary and it is possible to rearrange and accumulate y_t for different time period, starting from the initial value of y_0, to obtain:

$$y_t = p^T y_0 + \sum_{i=0}^{T-1} p^i \varepsilon_{t-i}$$

Equation 2-9

Since $|\rho|$ <1, as , equation 2.9 reduces to yt being determined solely by a finite moving average (MA) process of order n with most weight being placed on the first elements of the disturbance term. Thus, when yt is stationary, it has constant mean and variance and covariance that are independent of time.

Thus when yt process is determined by equation 2.8, then it has zero mean and a variance of. Thus it is possible to conclude that a stochastic process is (weakly) stationary if:

1. E (y_t) =constant for all t.
2. $\text{Van}(y_t) = (\sigma^2 / 1 - p) =$ constant for all t and
3. $\text{Covan(Yt,+n)} = \sigma^2 \varphi \, \text{IhI} / 1 - \varphi^2) =$ constant for all t.

Thus, a stationary AR (1) has a constant unconditional mean and variance while random walk model i.e. ρ=1, has a constant unconditional mean but a time varying unconditional variance.

In addition to the long-run unconditional moments of a time series, we can also calculate the conditional moments (the mean, variance and covariance at time t conditional on the actual values taken by the series in previous periods).

2.4.3 Conditional Moments

The conditional mean of y_t in the equation 2.5 refers to the mean of y_t, conditional on information available at time t-1. Let Ω_{t-1} is information set representing the nformation available at time t-1. Assuming that y_t is generated by equation 2.5, the conditional mean of y_t is given by:

$$E(y_t / \Omega_{t-1}) = py_{t-1}$$

Equation 2-10

And the conditional variance of y_t is given by:

$$\text{Van}(y_t / \Omega_{t-1}) = E(\Sigma^{t2} \Omega_{t-1}) = \sigma^2$$

Equation 2-11

In this case, clearly the conditional mean of y_t is time varying, but unconditional mean is not time varying.

2.4.4 Time-Varying Volatility Models

We may associate the variance of the rate of return on the stock with the rate of arrival of new information because new information may lead investors to revise their assessment of intrinsic value. The rate of arrival of new information is time varying. Consequently, we should expect the variance of the rates of return on stocks to be time varying.

When we consider time-varying return distribution, we must refer to the conditional mean, variance and covariance, that is, the mean, variance, or covariance conditional on currently available information. In 1982, Robert Engle published the study of U.K.inflation rates that measured their time-varying volatility. He has introduced Autoregressive Conditional Heteroscedasticity Model (ARCH) to model the time-varying volatility.

Today, the most widely used model to estimate the conditional (hence time-varying) variance of stock and stock-index returns is the generalized autoregressive conditional Heteroscedasticity (GARCH) model. The model uses rate of return history as the information set used to form our estimate of variance. Various ARCH types of models like Threshold GARCH(T-GARCH),ARCH in Mean(ARCH-M) and Exponential GARCH (EGARCH) models are used to capture much of the time varying volatility. Time varying volatility is observed and was initially concerned with an economic phenomenon-time-varying and autoregressive variance of inflation (Engle 1982). The data availability and strong empirical research interest in finance encouraged the application and facilitated the development of these models and their variations which are explained below.

2.4.4.1 The ARCH and GARCH Models

The ARCH (q) model is commonly written with the conditional variance function

$$h_t = a_0 + \sum_{j=1}^{q} aj\varepsilon^2 t - j$$

Equation 2-12

With to ensure that the conditional variance is positive. The effect of return shock i periods ago on current volatility is governed by the parameter a_i. For i>j, a_i>a_j, that is, the older the news, the less effect it has on current volatility. In an ARCH (q) model, old news arrived at the market more than q period ago has no effect on current volatility at all.

In the ARCH model, the variance of the current error is an increasing function of the magnitude of lagged errors, irrespective of their sign. ARCH model implies that a large (small) variance tends to be followed by a large (small) variance. The ARCH model has many apparent advantages but has some weaknesses. First the model assumes that positive and negative shocks have the same effects on volatility because it depends on the square of the previous shock. Second, ARCH model hardly provides any new insight for understanding the source of variations of a financial time series. It only provides the mechanical way of describing the behavior of the conditional variance. Third, ARCH model is rather restrictive. For instance, a12 of an ARCH (1) model must be in the interval [0, 1/3] if series to have finite fourth moment. The constraint becomes complicated for high order ARCH models. Finally, it over predicts the volatility because it responds slowly to large isolated shocks in time series data (Tsay, 2002).

In empirical applications it is often difficult to estimate models with large number of parameters, say ARCH (q). To circumvent this problem, Bollerslev (1986) proposed the Generalized ARCH or GARCH (p,q) models. The conditional variance of the GARCH (p,q) process is specified as

$$h_t = a + \sum_{j=1}^{q} a_j \varepsilon^2_{t-j} + \sum_{i=1}^{p} \beta_i h_{t-i}$$

Equation 2-13

With to ensure that conditional variance is positive. In GARCH process, unexpected returns of the same magnitude (irrespective of their sign) produce same amount of volatility. But Engle and Ng(1993) argue that if a negative return shock causes more volatility than a positive return shock of the same magnitude, the GARCH model under-predicts the amount of volatility following bad news and over-predicts the same amount of volatility following good news.

Stationarity and Persistence

The GARCH (p, q) above defined as stationary when $(\alpha_1 + \alpha_2 + \ldots\ldots + \alpha_q) + (\beta_1 + \beta_2 + \ldots\ldots + \beta_p) < 1$. The large GARCH lag coefficients β_p indicate that shocks to conditional variance takes a long time to die out, so volatility is 'persistent.' Large GARCH error coefficient α_q means that volatility reacts quite intensely to market movements and so if α_q is relatively high and α_q is relatively low, then volatilities tend to be 'spiky'.

If $(\alpha + \beta)$ is close to unity, then a shock at time t will persist for many future periods. A high value of it implies a 'long memory.' Nonnegativity constraints on α_q, β_p and α_0 can create difficulties in estimating GARCH models. Furthermore those non-negativity constraints imply that increasing ε_t^2 in any period increases h_{t+m} for all ruling out the random oscillatory behaviour in the ht process. To overcome such weaknesses in the GARCH model, Nelson (1991) proposed the EGARCH model.

2.4.4.2 EGARCH Model

GARCH models successfully capture thick tailed returns, and volatility clustering, but they are not well suited to capture the "leverage effect" since the conditional variance is a function only of the magnitudes of the lagged residuals and not their signs.

In the exponential GARCH (EGARCH) model of Nelson (1991) σ_t^2 depends upon the size and the sign of lagged residuals. The specification for the conditional variance is:

$$\sigma_t^2 = \alpha + \sum_{j-1}^{q} \beta_j \sigma_{t-j}^2 + \sum_{i-1}^{p} \alpha_i \varepsilon_{t-j}^2 + \sum_{h-1}^{y} y_h \varepsilon_{t-h}^2 d_{t-h}$$

Equation 2-14

Note that the left-hand side is the log of the conditional variance. This implies that the leverage effect is exponential, rather than quadratic, and that forecasts of the conditional variance are guaranteed to be nonnegative thus eliminating the need for parameter restrictions to impose non-negativity as in the case of ARCH and GARCH models. The presence of leverage effects can be tested by the hypothesis that The impact is asymmetric if $y_{h \neq} 0$.

2.4.4.3 Threshold-GARCH Model

In ARCH/GARCH models both positive and negative shocks of same magnitude will have exactly same effect in the volatility of the series. T-GARCH model helps in overcoming this restriction. TARCH or Threshold GARCH model was introduced independently by Zakoin (1994) and Glosten, Jaganathan and Runkle (1993). The generalized specification for the conditional variance is given by:

$$\sigma_t^2 = \alpha + \sum_{j=1}^{q} \beta_j \sigma_{t-j}^2 + \sum_{i=1}^{p} \alpha_i \varepsilon_{t-j}^2 + \sum_{h-1}^{y} y_h \varepsilon_{t-h}^2 d_{t-h}$$

Equation 2-15

Where d_t=1 if ε <0 and zero otherwise.

In this model, good news, and bad news, have differential effect on the conditional variance; good news has an impact of while bad news has an impact of If , bad news increases volatility, and we say that there is a leverage effect for the i-th order. If ¹0, the news impact is asymmetric. The main target of this model is to capture asymmetries in terms of positive and negative shocks.

2.4.4.4 GARCH-M Model

The return of a security may depend on its volatility. To model such a phenomenon, one may consider the GARCH-M model, where M stands for GARCH in mean. A simple GARCH (p, q)-M model can be specified as,

$$Y_t = \rho Y_{t-1} + \gamma \sigma_t^2 + \varepsilon_t$$

Equation 2-16

$$h_t = \alpha_0 + \sum_{j-1}^{q} \alpha_j \varepsilon_{t-j}^2 + \sum_{i-1}^{p} \beta_i h_{t-1}$$

Equation 2-17

GARCH-M models allow conditional mean to depend on its on conditional variance. Another variant of GARCH-M uses the log of conditional variance in place of variance in the above equation. It can be represented as:

$$Y_t = \rho Y_{t-1} + \gamma \log(\sigma_t^2) + \varepsilon_t$$

Equation 2-18

The formulation of the GARCH-M model in the above equations implies that there are serial correlations in the return series Yt. These serial correlations are introduced by those in the volatility process. The existence of risk premium is, therefore, another reason that some historical stock returns have serial correlations. If coefficient of variance is statistically significant then it can be said that there is strong relationship between stock returns and volatility.

The growing international integration of financial markets has prompted several empirical studies to examine the mechanism through which stock market movements are transmitted around the world. Multivariate GARCH models have been used to study return and volatility spillover across the different stock markets of the world. Multivariate GARCH models are very similar to their univariate counterparts except that the former specify equations for how the covariances move over time. Several different multivariate GARCH formulations have been proposed in the literature, including the VECH, the diagonal VECH and BEKK model. Each of these is discussed in the ensuing section.

2.5 Multivariate GARCH model

The MGARCH (multivariate GARCH) models are used in the study of the relations between the volatilities and co-volatilities of several markets. Is the volatility of a market leading the volatility of other markets? Is the volatility of an asset transmitted to another asset directly (through its conditional variance) or indirectly (through its conditional covariances)? Does a shock on a market increase the volatility on another market, and by how much? Is the impact the same for negative and positive shocks of the same amplitude? A related issue is whether the correlations between asset returns change over time. Are they higher during periods of higher volatility (sometimes associated with financial crises)? Are they increasing in the long run, perhaps because of the globalization of financial markets? Such issues can be studied directly by using a multivariate model, and raise the question of the specification of the dynamics of covariances or correlations. In a slightly different perspective, MGARCH models have been used to assess the impact of volatility in financial markets.

The following model is used to examine the joint process relating to the share price indices under study.

$$Y_t = \alpha + \Gamma Y_{t-1} + \varepsilon_t,$$

$$\varepsilon_t / I_{t-1} \approx N(0, H_t)$$

Equation 2-19

Where Y_t is a vector of daily returns at time t and is a 5 5 matrix for parameters associated with the lagged returns. The diagonal elements in matrix , measure the effect of own past returns while the off-diagonal elements, captures the relation in terms of returns across the markets, also known as return spillover. The vector of random error,, is the innovation for each market at time t and has a conditional variance-covariance matrix, Ht. The market information available at time t-1 is represented by the information set It-1. The vector of a represents the constants. Bollerslev et al. (1988) propose that Ht is a linear function of the lagged squared errors and cross products of errors and lagged values of the elements of Ht as follows: The variance-covariance matrix Ht is presented below:

$$\text{vech}(H_t) = \text{vech}(C) + \sum_{i-1}^{q} A_i \text{vech}(\varepsilon_{t-1}\varepsilon_{t-i}) + \sum_{i-1}^{p} G_i \text{vech}(H_{t-i}) + \sum_{i-1}^{p} D_i \text{vech}(H_{t-i})$$

Equation 2-20

Where is the operator that stacks the lower triangular portion of a symmetric matrix into a vector. The problems with this formulation are that the number of parameters to be estimated is large and restrictions on the parameters are needed to ensure that the conditional variance matrix is positive definite. Engle and Kroner (1995) propose the following new parameterization for Ht, i.e. the BEKK model, to overcome the above two problems.

$$H_t = C'C + A'S'_{t-1}\varepsilon_{t-1}A + G'H_{t-1}G$$

Equation 2-21

The BEKK model provides cross-market effects in the variance equation parsimoniously and also guarantees positive semi-definiteness by working with quadratic forms. Kroner and Ng (1998) propose to extend the BEKK model to allow for the asymmetric responses of volatility, i.e. stock volatility tends to rise more in response to bad news than positive shocks, in variance-covariances.

$$H_t = C'C + A'\varepsilon'_{t-1}\varepsilon_{1-1}A + G'H_{t-1}G + D'\varepsilon'_{t-1}\varepsilon_{t-1}D$$

Equation 2-22

where ε_t is defined as ε_t if ε_t is negative and zero otherwise. The last term on the right-hand side captures the asymmetric property of time varying variance-covariance. The notion used in the equation is as follows:

C is 5x5 lower triangular matrix of constants while A, G and D are 5×5 matrices. The diagonal parameters of matrices A and G measures the effects of own past shocks and past volatility of market i on its conditional variance, while diagonal parameter in matrix D measure the response of market i on its own past negative shocks. The off-diagonal parameters in matrices A and G, a_{ij} and g_{ij}, measure the cross-market effects of shock and volatility, also known as volatility spillover, while off-diagonal parameters d_{ij}, measures the response of market i on the negative shocks i.e. bad news of other markets, to be called the cross-market asymmetric responses.

The BEKK systems can be estimated using maximum likelihood method. The log likelihood function of the joint distribution is the sum of all the log likelihood functions of the conditional distributions, i.e. the sum of the logs of multivariate-normal distribution. Letting Lt be the log likelihood of observation t, n be the number of stock exchanges and L be the joint log likelihood which gives,

$$L = \sum_{i=1}^{T} L_t L_t = n/2\ln(2\pi/ - \frac{1}{2}\ln|H| - \frac{1}{2}\varepsilon'_t H_t^{-1}\varepsilon_t$$

Equation 2-23

Conditional volatility plays a key role in various financial activities. Volatility in the prices of stock adversely affects individual earnings and health of the economy. It creates atmosphere of uncertainty and thus it hampers productive investment. Several factors have been held responsible for the behaviour of financial prices. These include trading and non-trading days in asset returns (Fama, 1965), financial and economic crisis (Schwert, 1989).When prices of securities move together across the markets, a common set of factors influencing the markets have also been found to produce temporal variation in the variance of return distribution (Mohanty and Kamaiah, 2000). It is necessary to know the factors which influence volatility. It enables market participants to understand nature and characteristic of volatility. It also helps them to take investment decisions wisely. The regulators can design sound policy on the basis of the knowledge to curb excessive volatility in the stock market. The factors that affect the volatility have been discussed in the following section.

2.6 Factors Affecting Volatility

The factors that affect short-term and long-term volatility are considered to be different. These are discussed in the following sections.

Several economic factors may cause slow changes in stock market volatility. These factors include corporate leverage, comprising financial leverage and operating leverage, personal leverage and the condition of the economy (Schewert, 1989 & 1990).

2.6.1 Corporate Leverage

Financial and operating leverage effect the volatility of stock returns. Financial leverage indicates the use of debt financing to increase the expected return and risk of equity capital. The use of fixed assets to increase the expected profitability and risk of production and marketing activities is known as operating leverage. The standard deviation of stock returns of all equity firms simply equals the standard deviation of the returns to its assets. If the firm issue debt to buy back its share, the volatility of its stock returns will increase because the stockholders still have to bear most of the risk. Similarly, large amounts of operating leverage will make the value of the firm more sensitive to economic conditions. When a demand for the company's products falls off unexpectedly, the profits of a firm with large fixed costs will fall more than the profits of a firm that avoids large capital investments causing higher stock return volatility. Schwert (1989) has shown that aggregate financial leverage is correlated with stock return volatility, a finding that is in conformity with the financial leverage theory. He has also demonstrated that Stock Return Volatility is higher during economic recessions, as recognized under operating leverage theory. Further evidence indicates that stock return volatility increases after a large drop in stock prices. Because a drop in stock prices relative to bond prices increases financial leverage, this evidence also supports the theory that leverage affects stock volatility.

2.6.2 Personal Leverage

Personal leverage refers to the use of personal debt to increase the expected return and risk of an individual's investment portfolio. Following the US stock market crash of 1929, the Congress and the public became concerned that personal debt used to finance purchases of common stock had caused or exacerbated the magnitude of the crash. (Schwert,1988). Much recent debate has focused on the effects of margin requirements on the volatility of aggregate stock prices. Other research, however, shows at best only a weak relation between margin regulation and stock return volatility (Hsieh and Miller,1990).

2.6.3 Business Conditions

There is strong evidence that stock volatility increases during economic recessions. Evidence (Schwert, 1990) shows that the Great Depression was a period of extremely high volatility. This relationship may in part reflect operating leverage, as recessions are typically associated with excess capacity and unemployment. Fixed costs for the economy would have the effect of increasing the volatility of stock returns during periods of low demand.

2.6.4 Trading Volume & Trading Halts

It has been argued that increased trading activity and stock return volatility occur together (Karpoff, 1987). With high trading volume, prices fluctuate rapidly causing volatility.Stock exchanges apply market-wide or scrip-specific trading halts for providing a "cooling-off" period that allows the investors to re-evaluate market information and to re-formulate investment strategy. A trading halt may be applied in the form of a circuit breaker or a circuit filter. Circuit filters are also referred to as "price limits" since these are applied whenever the stock price change exceeds certain preset percentage limit in either direction. There is no theoretical basis for determining whether the imposition of circuit breakers will have the desired effect of reducing stock market volatility. But it is believed that they will pacify volatility.The Hong Kong stock exchange halted trading for a week following the October19,1987 crash. Stock prices fell more in Hong Kong than in most other countries as of the end of October 1987(Roll, 1988).

2.6.5 Computerized Trading

The sophistication in information technology have made it much easier for larger number of people to learn about and react to information very quickly thereby increasing liquidity. The liquidity of organized securities market plays an important part in supporting the value of traded securities allowing to change price quickly. This will induce variation in price causing the volatility.

2.6.6 Noise Trading

Noise is contrasted with Information. Noise trading is trading on noise as if it were Information. People who trade on noise are willing to trade even though they would be better off not trading. Noise trading is essential to the existence of liquid markets. It provides the essential missing ingredient (Black,1986). The more noise trading there is, the more liquid the markets will be in the sense of having frequent trades that allows us to observe prices. But noise trading actually puts noise into the prices. The price of a stock reflects both the information that information traders trade on and the noise that noise traders trade on. Black(1986) claims that the further away stocks get from their fundamental values the more aggressive the noise traders become which creates more volatility in the market.

2.6.7 International Linkages

There is a trend to the increasing internationalization of security markets. The stocks of leading Indian companies can be quoted on foreign stock markets. The movements of Indian stock prices are influenced by the movements of stock prices on other overseas markets and vice versa. Due to greater integration of stock markets of the world, international developments like recent Financial crisis of United States of America, Iraq and Crisis in European countries like Greece, Ireland would have varying degree of impacts on the Indian stock markets and other stock markets of the world.

2.6.8 Other factors

The extensive coverage of stock market news by media indicates that the newspapers are an important source of information and comment upon the stock market. The news in the news paper and television channels, expert advise etc. bring about change in investors' buying and selling decisions thereby affecting the price of the stock market. This in turns creates volatility.

2.7 Summary

The chapter presented various measures of risk, return and stock market volatility. It has offered discussions on issues concerning volatility and its measurement. The discussion is provided on empirical regularities of return data. The chapter includes detail discussion on time varying volatility models like ARCH/GARCH models and their variants used to capture and model time varying volatility. The chapter reviews some of the most common multivariate GARCH models like VECH and BEKK. The chapter explains how MGARCH models are used to study return and volatility spillover effects across the stock markets. The final section focused on the factors affecting volatility. It explains factors that affect short-term and long-term volatility.

The discussion on overview of capital market is presented in the next chapter.

* * *

CHAPTER 3

Indian Capital Market: An Overview

A financial system plays a vital role in the economic growth of a country. It facilitates the flow of funds between those who save a part of their income to those who invest in productive assets. It mobilizes and usefully allocates scarce financial resources of a country.

The economic development of any country depends upon the existence of well-organized financial system(Levine and Zevos, 1996). A financial system is a complex, well-integrated set of sub-system of financial institutions, markets, instruments and services, which facilitates the transfer, and allocation of funds, effectively and efficiently. It is the financial system which supplies the necessary financial inputs for the production of goods and services which ultimately helps to promote the well-being and standard of leaving of the people of a country.

Development of financial sector is considered to play a major role in stimulating and stabilizing the growth of an economy. An efficient financial sector mobilizes savings and allocates them efficiently to different sectors in the economy. Developed countries have sound financial systems which deliver services that contribute to the prosperity of their economies. The importance of finance in the growth of the economy is due to three key areas (a) mobilizing savings; (b) allocating capital funds and (d) transforming risk (Longjam, 2002). Therefore, it is considered that the financial systems of developing countries must function effectively and provide the full range of financial services to promote higher economic growth and provide a stable macro-economy. Empirical studies show that countries with better financial systems tend to grow faster than countries with less developed financial system. There are many works that show the positive relationship between the financial sector development and economic growth (Goldsmith, 1969; King and Levine, 1993). Financial systems are of crucial significance to capital formation. It needs no reiteration that adequate capital formation is crucial to a speedy and sound economic development (Khan, 2005).

The chapter is organized in twelve sections. Section 3.1 covers the structure of Indian Financial System. Section 3.2 discusses the relationship between financial system and economic growth and presents some empirical evidences. Section 3.3 studies financial system in India. Section 3.4 provides detail discussion of financial markets in India. Section 3.5 presents history of the Indian capital market. Section 3.6 and section 3.7 present regulatory framework and importance of capital market. Section 3.8 discusses functions of primary market and section 3.9 provides discussion on secondary markets including major stock indices of India and the world. Section 3.10 presents recent trends in Indian capital market. Section 3.11 discusses various reforms taken in capital market and section 3.12 summarizes.

3.1 Structure of Indian Financial System

The financial system or the financial sector of any country consists of (a) specialized and non-specialized financial institutions, (b) organized and unorganized financial markets, and (c) financial instruments and services which facilitate transfer of funds. Procedures and practices adopted in the markets, and financial interrelationships are parts of the system. The word "system", in the term "financial system" implies a set of complex and closely connected or intermixed institutions, agents, practices, markets, trans-actions, claims, and liabilities in the economy. The financial system is concerned about money, credit, and finance—the terms intimately related but somewhat different from each other. Money refers to the current medium of exchange or means of payment.

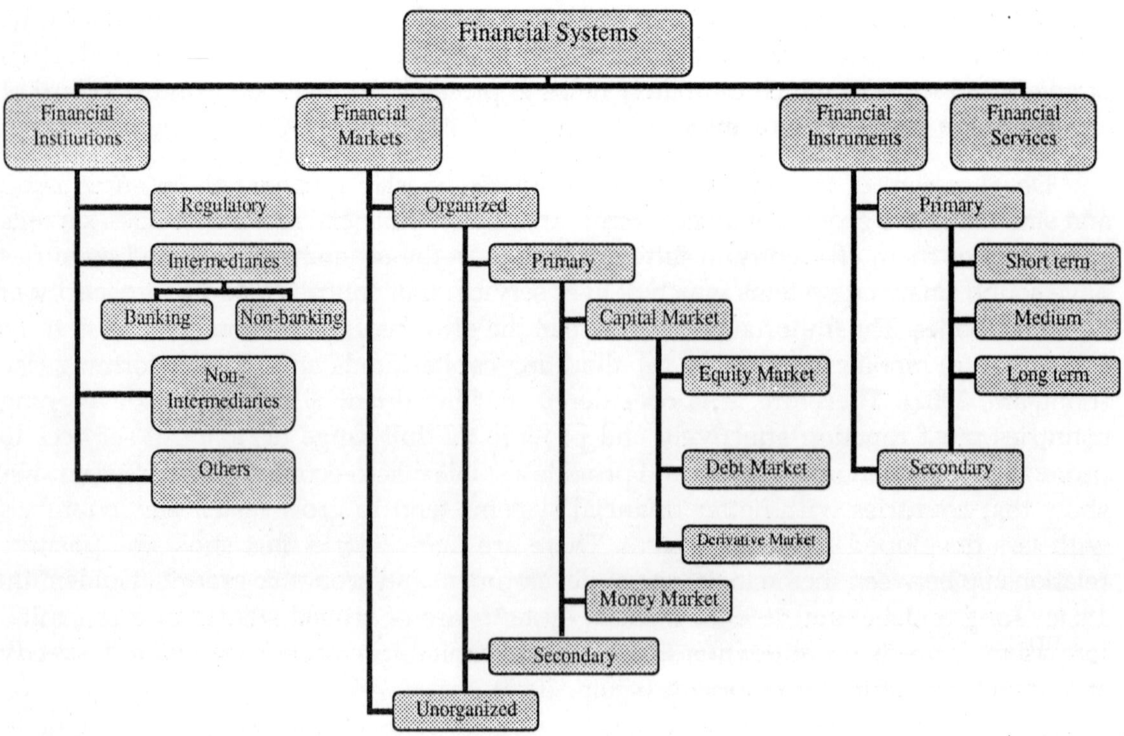

Credit or loan is a sum of money to be returned normally with interest; it refers to a debt of economic unit. Finance is monetary resources comprising debt and ownership funds of the State, company or person. Figure 3-1 presents a typical structure of financial system in any economy. It is adapted from (Bhole L. M., (2005), *Financial Institutions and Markets-structure, growth and innovations,* Tata McGraw-Hill Publishing Company Limited, New Delhi, p.1.4).

Indian financial system can be broadly classified into the formal (organized) financial system and the informal (unorganized) financial system. The formal financial system comes under the purview of the Ministry of Finance (MOF), Reserve Bank of India, Securities and Exchange Board of India (SEBI) and other regulatory bodies. The organized financial system includes an organized institutional and regulated system which caters to the financial needs of the modern spheres of economy; the informal financial system is an unorganized, non-institutional and non-regulated system dealing with the traditional rural spheres of the economy.

The informal financial system consists of:

(i) Individual moneylenders such as relatives, landlords, traders, storeowners, and so on.

(ii) Groups of persons operating as "funds' or "associations". These groups functions under as system of their own rules. These groups use names such as "fixed fund", "association" and "credit society" and so on.

(iii) Partnership firms consisting of local bankers and non-bank financial intermediaries such as finance, investment and chit-fund companies.

3.1.1 Components of the formal Financial System

The formal financial system consists of four segments or components as shown in figure 1. These are financial institutions, financial markets, financial instruments, and financial services.

1. Financial Institutions

Financial institutions mobilize savings and facilitate the allocation of funds in an efficient manner. Financial institutions can be classified as banking and non-banking financial institutions. Banking institutions are generators of credit while non-banking financial institutions are suppliers of credit. In India, non-banking financial institutions, namely, the Developmental Financial Institutions (DFIs), Non-Banking Financial Companies (NBFC) and housing finance companies (HFCs) are the major institutions for purveyors of credit.

Financial institutions like Industrial Development Bank of India (IDBI), Industrial Credit and Investment Corporation of India (ICICI), Industrial Financial Corporation of

India (IFCI), Small Industries Development Bank of India (SIDBI) and Industrial Investment Bank of India (IIBI) can be classified as term-finance institutions.

Specialized financial institutions like Export Import Bank of India (EXIM), tourism Finance Corporation of India (TFCI), ICICI Venture, Infrastructure Development Finance Company (IDFC) and National Bank for Agricultural and Rural Development (NABARD) and National Housing Bank (NHB) and investment institutions in the business of mutual funds (UTI, Public Sector and Private Sector Mutual Funds) and Insurance activity (LIC, GIC and its subsidiaries) are classified as financial institutions.

There are state level financial institutions such as the State Finance Corporations (SFCs) and State Industrial Development corporations (SIDCs) which are owned and managed by the State governments. Banks have undertaken non-bank activities and financial institutions are planning to undertake banking functions. Most of the financial institutions now recourse to financial markets for raising their funds. Thus, differences are getting narrowed.

2. Financial Markets

They are an important component of the financial system. A financial market is a mechanism for the exchange of financial products under a policy framework. The participants in the financial markets are the borrowers (issuers of securities), lenders (buyers of securities), and financial intermediaries.

Financial market comprises of two distinct types of markets:

(a) Money Market

(b) Capital Market

(a) Money Market

A money market is a market for short-term debt instruments having maturity below 1 year. It is a highly liquid market wherein securities are bought and sold in large denominations to reduce transaction costs. Call money market, certificates of deposit, commercial paper and treasury bills are the major instruments/segments of the money market.

The functions of the money market are,

(i) To serve as an equilibrating force that redistributes cash balances in accordance with the liquidity needs of the participants;

(ii) To form a basis for the management of liquidity and money in the economy by monetary authorities;

(iii) To provide a reasonable access to the users of short-term money for meeting their requirements at a realistic prices.

As it facilitates the conduct of monetary policy, a money market constitutes a very important segment of the financial system.

(b) Capital Market

A capital market is a market for long-term securities (equity market and debt). The purpose of capital market is to:

(i) Mobilize long-term savings to finance long-term investments;

(ii) Provide risk-capital in the form of equity to entrepreneurs;

(iii) Encourage broader ownership of productive assets;

(iv) Provide liquidity with a mechanism enabling the investor to sell financial assets;

(v) Lower the costs of transactions and information; and

(vi) Improve the efficiency of capital allocation through a competitive pricing mechanism.

A capital market is further divided into primary and secondary markets. The primary market is the meant for new issues and secondary market provides liquidity through the marketability of these instruments. The secondary market is also known as the stock market.

3. Financial Instruments

It is a claim against the person or an institution for the payment at a future date assume of money and/or a periodic payment in the form of interest or dividend.

Financial securities are primary or secondary securities. Primary securities are termed as direct securities such as equity shares and debentures as they are directly issued by the ultimate borrowers of funds to the ultimate savers. Secondary securities are also referred as indirect securities, as they are issued by the financial intermediaries to the ultimate savers. Banks deposits, mutual fund units and insurance policies are secondary securities.

Financial instruments differ in terms of marketability, liquidity, return, risk, types of options and transaction costs. Financial instruments help financial markets and the financial intermediaries to perform the important role of channelizing funds from lenders to borrowers.

4. Financial Services

Financial intermediaries provide key financial services such as merchant banking, leasing, hire purchase, credit rating and so on. Financial services bridge the gap between lack of knowledge on the part of investors and increasing sophistication of financial instruments and markets. These financial services are vital for creation of firms, industrial expansion and economic growth.

Before investors lend money, they need to be reassured that it is safe to exchange securities for funds. This reassurance is provided by the financial regulators who regulate the conduct of market and intermediaries to protect the investors' interest. The Reserve Bank of India regulates money market and Securities and Exchange Board of India regulates capital market.

3.1.2 Relationship among the Components of Financial System

These four sub-systems do not function in isolation. They are interdependent and interact continuously with each other. Their interactions lead to the development of a smoothly functioning financial system through mobilizing savings by issuing different types of financial instruments which are traded in financial markets. They facilitate the credit allocation process and render specialized financial services like merchant banking, loan syndication etc.

Financial intermediaries have close links with the financial markets in the economy. Financial institutions acquire, hold and trade financial securities which help not only in credit-allocation process but also make the financial markets larger, more liquid, stable and diversified. Financial intermediaries rely on financial markets to raise funds. Financial markets have also made an impact on the functioning of financial intermediaries such as banks and financial institutions. Moreover, liquid and broad markets make financial instruments a more attractive savings, and financial services may encourage further savings if the net returns available to investors are raised or increased.

3.2 Relationship between the Financial System and Economic Growth: Some Empirical Evidence

An efficient financial system facilitates economic activity and growth. The three major functions of financial system namely mobilization of savings, allocation of capital and provision of risk management vehicles are crucial to the process of economic growth. Financial Markets, institutions and instruments are the prime movers of economic growth. The financial system of a country diverts the country's savings towards more productive uses. It helps to increase the output of the economy.

The financial systems around the world differ with respect to the mechanism through which they perform the functions. It may function through banks or through financial markets. Accordingly, economists have categorized financial systems as being bank-based or market-based. The economies of Germany and Japan represent bank-based financial system while that of England and the U.S. are the outstanding examples of market-based system where securities market play a vital role in performing the function of financial system.

Financial system also helps accelerate the volume and rate of savings by providing diversified range of financial services and financial instruments through intermediaries. This results in increased competition in the financial system, which channelizes resources towards the highest-return investment for a given degree of risk. This lowers financial intermediation costs and stimulates economic growth.

A sophisticated financial system makes innovation least costly and most profitable, thereby enabling faster economic growth. Financial markets represents deep end of financial system, which helps in bringing stability and resiliency in the system. A well-developed money and government securities market help central bank to conduct monetary policy effectively with the use of market-based instruments. Well-developed financial markets are required for creating a balanced financial system in which financial markets and financial institutions play important roles.

The domestic financial system when linked to the international financial system increases capital flow with the help of financial markets. This link reduces risk through portfolio diversification and helps in accelerating economic growth. The evidence of relationship between financial system and economic growth can be traced to observations by Gurley and Shaw (1955) and Goldsmith (1969) which indicated that economic development paved the way for debt finance and equity markets for raising external finance. Their studies suggest that the needs of the users and providers of financial services change as economies develop. The studies find that informal finance becomes less important and self financed capital investment first gives way to bank-intermediated debt finance and later to the emergence of equity markets as additional instruments for raising external funds.

King and Levine (1993) studied the empirical link between a range of indicators of financial development and economic growth. The study constructed four indicators of the level of financial development and four indicators of growth. The indicators of financial development were ratio of (i) liquid liabilities to GDP (ii) claims on the nonfinancial private sector to total domestic credit (Iii) ratio of claims on the nonfinancial private sector to GDP and (iv)deposit money bank domestic credit divided by deposit money bank plus central bank domestic credit. The growth indicators were real per capita GDP growth, the rate of physical capital accumulation, the ration of domestic investment to GDP and residual measure of improvements in the efficiency of physical capital allocation. The study conducted cross country regression analysis for the period ranges from 1960 to 1989 for 80 countries. It included the ratio of trade to GDP, the ratio of government spending to GDP and the average inflation rate to control for other economic phenomena. The study found that indicators of levels of financial development are strongly correlated with the growth, the rate of physical capital accumulation and improvements in the efficiency of capital allocation.

Levine and Zervos (1996) examined whether there exists an association between stock market development and long-run economic growth using data on forty-one countries over the period from 1976 to 1993. The study used size, liquidity and risk diversification of stock markets to examine the association. The size of the stock market is defined as the ratio of market capitalization divided by GDP. Stock market liquidity measured either in terms of value of stock trading relative to the size of the market and the value of trading relative to the size of the economy. It used a multifactor International Arbitrage Pricing Model (IAPM) to measure stock market integration to analyze ability of stock markets to diversity risk.. The IAPM implies that the expected excess return on each asset is linearly related to a linear combination of benchmark portfolios. In a perfectly integrated stock markets, the intercept in a regression of any asset's excess return should be zero. Levine and Zervos constructed an index called STOCK by averaging the means-removed values of the market capitalization ratio, the total value traded ratio, the turnover ratio, and the IAPM pricing model as a measure of stock market integration. They evaluated whether this index 'Stock' is strongly linked to long-run economic growth. The method of pooled cross-countries time series growth regressions[1] was used to conduct an analysis. The dependent variable growth was real per capita growth rate. It used set of control variables which include initial income (the logarithm of initial real per capita GDP), initial education (the logarithm of the initial secondary school enrollment rate), the ratio of government consumption expenditures to GDP, the inflation rate and the black market exchange rate premium to control for a variety of factors that may be associated with economic growth. The study draws on the various secondary sources for necessary data. It obtained the stock market data from the International Finance Corporation's (IFC'S) Emerging Markets Data Base and IMF (various issues). Data on real per capita GDP growth, secondary school enrollment rate, and government consumption ratio, and information on exports and imports are from the World Bank's National Accounts Data Base. Data on the black market exchange rate premium were collected from Picks Currency Yearbook (various issues) and International Currency Analysis Incorporations (various issues). The main findings of the study were as follows:

(1) The stock market development is positively associated with economic growth.

1. Regression results are from pooled, cross-country instrumental variables estimation. The dependent variable is average annual growth rate of per capita GDP. Instruments include the constant term; logarithm of initial real per capita GDP; logarithm of initial secondary school enrollment rate; the number of revolutions and coups; and initial values of the ratio of government consumption expenditures to GDP, the rate of inflation, the black market exchange rate premium, market capitalization, total value traded, the turnover ratios, and the ratio of international trade to GDP. The forty-one economies are Argentina, Australia, Austria, Belgium, Brazil, Canada, Chile, Colombia, Denmark, Finland, France, Germany, Greece, Hong Kong, India, Indonesia, Israel, Italy, Japan, Jordan, the Republic of Korea, Luxembourg, Malaysia, Mexico, the Netherlands, New Zealand, Nigeria, Norway, Pakistan, the Philippines, Portugal, Singapore, Spain, Sweden, Taiwan (China), Thailand, Turkey, the United Kingdom, the United States, Venezuela, and Zimbabwe.

(2) The empirical relationship between stock market development and long run growth remains strong even after controlling for inflation, the size of the government expenditure, the black market exchange premium and the predetermined component of financial depth as measured by the ratio of liquid liabilities of the financial intermediaries to GDP.

The study, however does not study the impact of volatility of stock markets on economic growth.

Levine and Zervos (1998) examined the linkages between stock market and economic growth in emerging market economies. Using monthly data on sixteen countries[2] from 1976 through 1993, they have investigated whether measures of stock market liquidity, size, volatility and integration with world stock markets are correlated with the economic growth, capital accumulation, productivity improvements and savings rates. The main findings of the study are as follows:

(1) Stock market liquidity as measured by value of stock traded relative to the size of the market and the value of trading relative to size of the economy, are positively correlated with the rate of economic growth as measured by Gross Domestic Product.

(2) The other stock market indicators like volatility as measured by standard deviation and market size which is equal to the value of listed shares divided by GDP do not possess link with economic growth.

(3) To compute measures of stock market integration, the study used two asset pricing models: the international capital asset pricing model (ICAPM) and the international arbitrage pricing model (IAPM). The capital asset pricing and arbitrage pricing models imply that the expected return on each asset is linearly related to a benchmark portfolio or linear combination of a group of benchmark portfolios. The study found that the international integration did not help in creating economic growth.

(4) The study does not establish the direction of causality between financial sector development and growth, never the less, it substantiates the view that the services rendered by financial institutions and market are important for long-run growth.

Biswal and Kamaiah(2001) evaluated the behavior of stock market development indicators, namely, market size, liquidity and volatility and examines whether these indicators have exhibited any trend changes after India liberalized its financial policies. The study made use of monthly data collected from different issues of the Stock Exchange Review published by BSE Mumbai. Data for market capitalization and turnover ratio ranged from January, 1991 through December, 1998. Required data to construct volatility

2. The sixteen countries are Argentina, Brazil, Chile, Columbia, India, Jordan, Korea, Malaysia, Mexico, Pakistan, Philippines, Portugal, Taiwan, Thiland, Turkey and Venezuela.

series were collected as the average monthly value of BSE Sensitive Index for the period December, 1983 through December, 1998. Here, size of the stock market was measured by Market Capitalization Ratio(MCR) defined as the value of listed shares divided by GDP. The significance of MCR lies in the fact that it serves as a proxy for market size and it is positively related to the ability to mobilize capital and diversify risk. Market liquidity measured by value traded ratio and turn over ratio. The former defined as the total value of traded shares in the stock market divided by GDP, while the latter is the value of total shares traded divided by market capitalization. These ratios together provide a more comprehensive idea of liquidity of a stock market. Since the total value traded ratio measures the organized trading of the equities as a share of national output, it positively reflects liquidity on an economy wide basis, while turnover ratio measures the trading relative to the size of the stock market. The frequently used indicator of stock market development is volatility, which throws light on the asset price movement in a stock market. Generally, less volatility is believed to be the proxy for greater market efficiency and development. The findings of the study suggest that stock market has become larger and more liquid in the post liberalization period. In respect of volatility, the market does not exhibit any significant change. The findings of the study in line with the findings of the 16 country study of Levine and Zervos(1998) which reported significant change in liquidity and market size after liberalization. However, in case of volatility, the result differ from those of Levine and Zervos(1998) who found volatility to increase after liberali zation.

Though existing literature offers various indicators of financial sector development and also a wide range of stock market development indicators, it is hard to find a 'single indicator', which can directly be applied to measure the development of financial sector or stock market. To this regards, Longjam(2001) aptly raised question:"How do we capture the concept and measure the development in the financial sector in the most appropriate manner?'. Longjam focuses on four indicators to measure financial sector development during the period ranges from 1990 to 1999. They were ratios of (a) Private sector credit to Gross Domestic Product (GDP) (b) Liquid Liabilities of the financial sector to GDP (c) Commercial bank assets to total banking sector assets and (d) stock market capitalization to GDP. Based on the method used in the construction of the Human Development Index' which is basically a conglomerate of the above four financial indicators to compare the level of the financial sector development of the Indian Economy with Argentina, Chile, China, Israel, Korea, Malaysia, Sri Lanka and Thailand. The study found that India's performance has been at moderate level with better performance in the stock market in the last decade. Though cross country analysis showed that India's performances is consistent across all measures of financial sector developments, the figures are much below those of the fast-growing East Asian countries and high-income countries. Thus keeping in view of the current trend of Indian performance in the financial sector, the study called for a greater attention to the development in India's banking and financial sector.

Singh Ajit(1997) came with a new theme of stock markets, which has comparatively remained unnoticed so far but has assumed significance in the context of recent phenomena of liberalization and industrialization in numbers of countries. After providing critical account of debate on stock markets and alternative theoretical paradigms regarding their role in economic development, Singh extensively analyzed the role of Indian Stock Markets in the growth of manufacturing sector of the country. Singh's main contentions were:

1. The fast growth of stock market in India in the 1980s and 1990s is a part of a worldwide trend towards deregulation of financial markets and the greater role of market forces in the allocation of resources.
2. The vast expansion of stock market in India and other industrializing countries in the 1980s and 1990s has a major impact on corporate finance. The new issues on the stock markets have made a significant contribution to corporate growth in the semi-industrial countries.
3. Economies in which stock markets play a central role in mobilizing financial resources find themselves at a competitive disadvantage relative to economies where banks as opposed to stock markets play this role.

From the above important empirical research works, we can summarize that there is a close relationship between the effectiveness of the financial system and the level of economic growth. A shift in the economy from state to private sector bestowed on the stock market the burden of pooling sufficient resources from domestic, regional and international sources and allocating them efficiently for productive uses. Stock markets and banks are likely to play an important role in channeling funds from savings to investments.

3.3 Finance System in India

(a) Pre Reform Phase

Financial system was primitive before the start of economic planning. The financial system in India was not well equipped to meet challenges for industrial investment. Organized credit market was poor or almost absent in rural India. Financial system was not well organized as well as lacked in-depth on the eve of independence.

(b) Financial System During Economic Planning

With the initiation of economic planning, the country took concrete measures for the development of a sound financial system in accordance with our socio-economic objectives. Several new financial institutions were created to cater to the needs of agriculture and industry. This led to the rich growth of financial system both in terms of institutions and diversified financial instruments to raise capital and hedge risk. Following its nationalization, the Reserve Bank of India was entrusted with the major responsibility of developing the institutional infrastructure in the financial system.

Though the financial sector role was to channel resources from the surplus generating unit to deficit spending units, the banking sector suffered from lack of competition, poor technology, bad quality of service, low productivity, inadequate capital and high cost during early 1990s. The Government owned banks were dominated the system. Banks overlooked risk management systems effected poor profitability and asset quality. There was a little competition in insurance sector. The mutual fund industry was protected. It suffered from a lack of completion and was dominated by Unit Trust of India. Though there was a rapid growth of Non-banking financial companies (NBFCs), the regulation on their asset management was absent. The growth of financial markets was impeded by control on pricing of financial assets, high transaction costs, barriers to entry.

The process of financial market development was strengthened by the evolution of an active government securities market after the Government borrowing programme was put through the auction process in 1992-93. The development of a market for Government paper enabled the Reserve Bank to modulate the monetization of the fiscal deficit. The foreign exchange market deepened with the opening up of the economy and the institution of a market-based exchange rate regime in the early 1990s. Although there were occasional episodes of volatility in the foreign exchange market, these were swiftly controlled by appropriate policy measures. The capital market also underwent some metamorphic changes during the 1990s. The development of the financial markets was well supported by deregulation of restrictions in respect of financial institutions, allowing them to operate across markets. This resulted in increased integration among the various segments of the financial markets.

3.4 Financial Markets

A significant component of the Indian financial system is the financial markets. They function as facilitating organizations in the savings-investment process. The financial markets comprise capital/securities market and money market.

The capital market segment of the financial markets represents the institutional source of long-term funds. From a marginal role in the early eighties, the capital market now occupies the centre-stage in the Indian financial system. The capital market aids economic growth by mobilizing savings of the economic sectors and directing the same towards channels of productive uses. This is facilitated through following measures.

(i) Issue of 'primary securities' in the primary market by directing cash flow from the surplus sector to the deficit sectors such as the government and the corporate sector.

(ii) Issue of 'secondary securities' in the primary market by directing cash flow from the surplus sector to financial intermediaries such as banking and non-banking financial institutions.

(iii) 'Secondary Market' transactions in outstanding securities which facilitate liquidity which is an important factor, affecting growth.

The development of a stock market is in the process of development has been well recognized. A developed stock market has been considered crucial to national economic growth as it provides an additional channel along with banks and other financial institutions for encouraging and mobilizing domestic savings and ensures improvements in productivity of investment through effectively allocation of capital. The stock market influences national savings and its allocation and financing decisions of firms before paving the way for economic growth (Biswal and B Kamaiah, 2000). Taking into account the importance of stock market in the process of economic development, a distinguished international study group for the 'World Institute for Development Economics Research' has argued that the developing countries should liberalize their financial markets in order to attract foreign portfolio equity flows. Hence, the development of an efficient capital market is necessary for creating a climate conducive for investment and economic growth.

3.4.1 Classification of Financial Markets

The classification of financial markets in India is shown in Figure 3.2. It is adapted from (Sasidharan and Mathews (2008), *Financial Services and Systems,* The McGraw-Hill Companies, New Delhi, p. 27).

The structure of the securities market consists of the primary market/new issue market and the secondary markets.

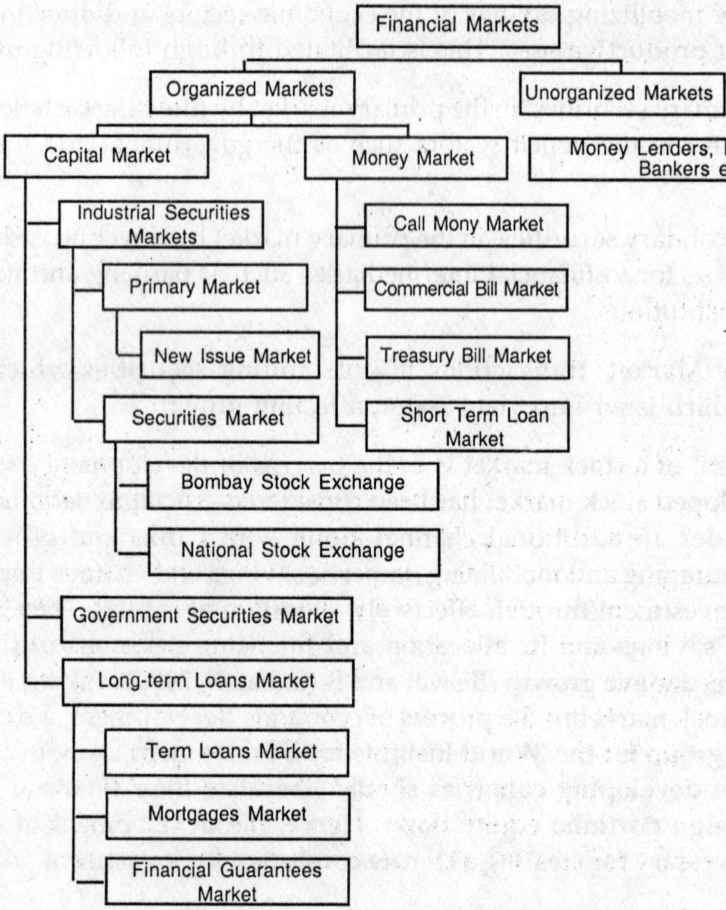

Figure 3 2 Classification of Financial Markets

3.4.1.1 Unorganized Markets

The unorganized financial markets consist of moneylenders, indigenous bankers and traders etc. who lend money to the public. Indigenous bankers accept deposits from the public. There are private finance companies, chit funds etc. whose activities fall outside the regulatory network of the Reserve Bank of India. The RBI has already taken some steps to bring the unorganized sector under the organized fold. They have not been successful fully. The financial instruments in these markets are not standardized.

3.4.1.2 Organized Markets

The organized markets are regulated by regulatory authorities. They are also subject to supervision and control by the Reserve Bank of India or other regulatory bodies like SEBI (Security and Exchange Board of India), SCRA (Securities Contract (Regulation) Act, 1956 etc.

These organized markets can be further classified into two markets. They are:

(i) Capital Market

(ii) Money Market

3.4.1.2.1 Capital Market

The capital market is a market for financial assets which have an indefinite or long maturity more than a year. Capital market is further divided into three namely:

(i) Industrial securities market

(ii) Government securities market

(iii) Long term loans market

(i) Industrial Securities Market

It is a market for industrial securities like equity shares or ordinary shares, preference shares, and debentures or bonds. Here, industrial concerns issue appropriate financial instruments to raise their capital. It can be further subdivided into two. They are:

(i) Primary market or New issue market

(ii) Secondary market or Stock exchange

a. Primary Market

It is a market for new issues or new financial claims therefore it is also called New Issue Market. Primary issues of the corporate sector lead to capital formation. A company can raise capital by four ways namely (i) public issue (ii) rights issue and (iii) private placement (iv) offer for sale.

The most common method of raising capital by new companies is through sale of securities to the public. It is called public issue. When an existing company wants to raise additional capital, securities are then offered to the existing shareholders on a pre-emptive basis. It is called right issue. Private placement is a way of selling securities privately to a small group of investors. We discuss the primary market in detail in section 2.10.

b. Secondary Markets

Secondary market is a market for outstanding securities. Securities are traded on continuous and regular basis on stock exchanges. This market consists of all stock exchanges recognized by Government of India. The stock exchanges in India are regulated under the Securities Contracts (Regulation) Act, 1956. The secondary market facilitates liquidity and marketability of outstanding shares. It helps in most efficient transfer of funds from deficit spending units to surplus generating units thereby promoting economic growth. The Bombay Stock Exchange and National Stock Exchange of India are the principal stock exchanges in India. The participants in this market are registered brokers- both individuals and institutions. They operate through a network of sub-brokers and sub-dealers and are connected through an electronic networking system.

(ii) Government Securities Market

It is called as gilt-edge securities market where government securities are traded. There are two kinds of government securities- short-term and long term. Securities issued by the Central Government, State Corporations, Port Trusts etc. Government securities are generally Stock certificates, promissory notes and Bearer Bonds which can be discounted. Government securities are sold through the Public Debt Office of the RBI while Treasury Bills are sold through auctions. They require to hold substantial portion of these securities to satisfy their Statutory Liquidity Ratio (SLR) requirements.

(iii) Long-term Loans Markets

Development banks and commercial banks play significant role in this market by supplying long-term loans to corporate customers. The market may be classified into:

(i) Term Loan Market

(ii) Mortgages market

(iii) Financial guarantees market

a. Term Loan Market

Industrial financing institutions formed by government like IDBI (Industrial Development Bank of India), IFCI (Industrial Financial Corporations of India), ICICI (Industrial Credit and Investment Corporation of India) and other state financial institution in this market supply long term and medium term loans to corporate customers. They help in identifying investment opportunities, encourage new entrepreneurs and support modernization efforts.

b. Mortgages Market

Mortgage market has primary as well as secondary market. The primary market consists of original extension of credit and secondary market has sales and re-sales of existing mortgages at prevailing prices.

A mortgage loan is a loan against the security of immovable property like real estate. The transfer of interest in a specific immovable property to secure a loan is called mortgage. It may be equitable mortgage or legal one. Equitable mortgage is created by a mere deposit of title deeds to properties as security whereas in the case of a legal mortgage, the title in the property is legally transferred to the lender by the borrower. Legal mortgage is less risky.

In India, Housing and Urban Development Corporation (HUDCO) and the Life Insurance Company (LIC) play a dominant role in financing residential projects. The Land Development Banks provide cheap mortgage loans for the development of lands, purchase of equipment etc. These development banks raise finance through the sale of debentures which are treated as trustee securities.

c. Finance Guarantees Market

A guarantee market is a centre where finance is provided against the guarantee of a reputed person in the financial circle. Guarantee is a contract to discharge the liability of third party default. Here, guarantee act as a security from the creditor's point of view. In case the borrower fails to repay the loan, the liability falls on the shoulders of the guarantor.

The market for guarantees is well organized in India. It relates to deferred payments for imports and exports, medium and long-term loans raised abroad and loans advanced by banks and other financial institutions.

These guarantees are provided by commercial banks, development banks, governments both central and state and other specialized financial institutions like Export Credit Guarantee Corporation (ECGC) and DICGC (Deposit Insurance and Credit Guarantee Corporation).

3.4.1.2.2 Money Market

Money market is a market for dealing with financial assets and securities which have a maturity period of upto one year. It is a market for purely short-term funds. Our primary focus of research is on capital market. We study volatility of Indian Stock Market. The stock market is a component of capital market. We, therefore, do not focus on Money Market in detail.

3.5 Regulatory Framework

The four main legislations governing the securities markets are: (a) the Securities and Exchange Board of India (SEBI) Act, 1992 to protect investors and develop and regulate securities market;(b) the Companies Act, 1956, which sets out code of conduct for the corporate sector in relation to issue, allotment and transfer of securities, and disclosures to be made in the public issues; (c) the Securities Contracts (Regulation) Act, 1956, which provides for regulation of transactions in securities through control over stock exchanges; and (d) The Depositories Act, 1996 which provides for electronic maintenance and transfer of ownership of demat securities.

3.5.1 Regulators

The responsibility for regulating the securities market is shared by Department of Economic Affairs (DEA), Department of Company affairs (DCA), Reserve Bank of India (RBI) and Securities and Exchange Board of India (SEBI). The activities of these agencies are co-ordinated by a high level committee on capital markets. The orders of SEBI under the securities laws are appealable before a Securities Appellate Tribunal (SAT). The regulator ensures that the market participants behave in a desired manner so that securities market continue to be a major source of finance for corporate and government and the interest of investors are protected.

3.6 Secondary Market

Secondary market refers to stock exchanges where existing securities can be regularly purchased and sold. These markets are important elements in mobilization of resources. The existence of these markets fulfills basic needs of investors namely the liquidity. In these markets, holders of securities can easily dispose of their securities and obtain cash. Thus viable secondary markets encourage savers to take risk and make investments in the existing securities by providing marketability to securities. In India, the secondary market consists of recognized stock exchanges operating under rules, by-laws and regulations duly approved by the government. A stock exchange is defined under section 2(3) of the Securities Contracts (Regulation) Act, 1956, as "body of individuals whether incorporated or not, constituted for the purpose of assisting, regulating or controlling the business of buying, selling or dealing in securities.

3.6.1 Stock Market Development in India

The origin of stock market in India dates back to the end of the eighteenth century when long-term negotiable securities were first issued. The real beginning, however occurred in the middle of the nineteenth century, after the enactment of the Companies Act in 1850 which introduced the feature of limited liability companies and generated investors' interest in corporate securities.

The Native Share and Stock Brokers' Association now known as Bombay Stock Exchange(BSE) was formed in Bombay in 1875. This was followed by the formation of exchanges in Ahmedabad(1894), Calcutta (now Kolkata) (1908) and Madras(now Chennai)(1937). In order to promote the orderly development of the stock market, the central government introduced a comprehensive legislation called the Securities Contracts (Regulation) Act, 1956.

The Calcutta Stock Exchange(CSE) was the largest stock exchange in India till the 1960s. In 1961, there were 576 companies listed on CSE and 297 on BSE. Table 1 shows the phenomenal growth in operations of the stock markets in India since 1961.

Table 3-1 Pattern of Growth of Stock Exchanges

Year	1961	1972	1980	1991	2000	2003	2005	2006
Number of stock exchanges	1	8	9	21	23	23	22	22
No. of listed companies	1203	1599	2265	6229	9871	9413	5701	5850
Market Capitalization (Rs. Billion)	12	27	68	1103	11926	6319	27868	45116

Source: Hand Book of Statistics, SEBI, 2007.

It can be seen from the Table that Indian stock market has witnessed positive growth pattern in terms of number of stock exchange, listed companies and market capitalization.

3.6.2 Stock Market Index

The stock market index is the most important of all as it measures overall market segment through a set of stocks that are representative of the market. It reflects the market direction and day-to-day behavior fluctuations in stock prices. A good market index must reflect price movements of typical shares for better market representation. A good market index incorporates a set of scrips which have high market capitalization and high liquidity. Market capitalization is the sum of the market value of all the stocks included in the index. The market value is derived by multiplying the market price of the shares with the number of equity shares outstanding. Liquidity is reflected in the ability to buy or sell scrip at a price close to market price. High liquid market is the market where bid-ask spread is minimum.

3.6.2.1 Major Indices in India

There are two major indices in India: BSE Sensex and NSE Nifty. The BSE sensitivity index is launched in 1986. It comprises 30 shares and its base year is 1978-79. The major criteria for selection of a scrip in the Sensex is large market capitalization. Besides this criteria, other criteria like number of trades, average value of shares traded per day as a percentage of total number of outstanding shares are considered for inclusion in Sensex. The scrip selection is also based on the balanced representation of industry, leadership position in the industry, continuous dividend paying record and the track record of the promoters. Today, BSE has 20 indices representing various sectors like public sector, banking, technology etc.

Another index which has become popular in a short span of time is the S&P CNX Nifty. The National stock exchange began equity trading in November 1994. NSE and

Credit Rating and Information Services of India Limited (CRISIL) undertook a joint venture, wherein they jointly promoted India Index Services and Products Ltd. (), a specialized organization to provide stock index services. This organization developed scientifically devised indices of stock prices in NSE in technical partnership with Standard and Poor(S&P). NSE introduced this index to reflect the market movements more accurately, provide for managers with a benchmark for measuring portfolio performance. The S&PCNX Nifty launched in July 8, 1996, comprises of 50 scrips which are selected on the basis of low impact cost, high liquidity and market capitalization. The impact cost represents the cost of executing the transaction in a given stock. Low impact cost indicates high liquidity of a stock. NSE has introduced 22 indices including Information Technology, Infrastructure, Multinational Corporations, Service Sector, Energy, Pharma etc sectors.

The index on a day is calculated as the percentage of the aggregate market value of the set of scrips incorporated in the index on that day to the average market value of the same scrips during the base period. The BSE Sensex is a weighted average of prices of 30 selected stocks and S&P500 CNX Nifty of 50 selected stocks. The methodology for calculating the index is discussed below:

I. Market Capitalization Weighted

The index is calculated using the "Free-float Market Capitalization" methodology, wherein, the level of index at any point of time reflects the free-float market value of 30 component stocks relative to a base period for Sensex and 50 component stocks relative to Nifty.

a. Free-float market capitalization method

Free-float methodology refers to an index construction methodology that takes into consideration only the free-float market capitalization of a company for the purpose of index calculation and assigning weight to stocks in the index. Free-float market capitalization takes into consideration only those shares issued by the company that are readily available for trading in the market. It generally excludes promoters' holding, government holding, strategic holding and other locked-in shares that will not come to the market for trading in the normal course. In other words, the market capitalization of each company in a free-float index is reduced to the extent of its readily available shares in the market.

b. Price Weighted Index

The price of each stock in the index is summed up which is then equated to an index starting value. Here, each stock influences the index in proportion to its price per share. The value of the index is generated by adding the prices of each of the stocks in the index and dividing them by the total number of stocks. Stocks with a higher price will be given more weight and, therefore, will have a greater influence over the performance of the index.

c. Equal Weighted Index

In this method, each stock's percentage weight in the index is equal and hence all stocks have equal influence on the index movement.

After discussing the various methodologies for calculating the index, we shall discuss some of the major global stock market indices in the following section.

3.9.2.2 Global Stock Market Indices:

1. Dow Jones Industrial Average:

It is the most widely watched and quoted index because of its long existence. The Dow has 30 constituents and it follows the methodology of price-based weightage. Dow is one of several stock market indices created by nineteenth century Wall Street Journal editor and Dow Jones & Company co-founder Charles Dow. Dow compiled the index as a way to gauge the performance of the industrial component of America's stock markets. It is the second oldest continuing U.S. market index, after the Dow Jones Transportation Average, which Dow also created.

2. Nasdaq composite Index:

The index is the market capitalization weightages of prices for all the stock listed in the Nasdaq stock market in USA. It is the largest electronic screen-based equity securities trading market in the United States.

3. S&P500 Index

The S&P 500 is a stock market index containing the stocks of 500 Large-Cap corporations, most of which are American. The index is the most notable of the many indices owned and maintained by Standard & Poor's, a division of McGraw-Hill. S&P 500 is used in reference not only to the index but also to the 500 companies that have their common stock included in the index. The most money managers treat the S&P500 as a proxy for the US stock market The S&P500 covers all major areas of the US economy.

4. FTSE 100

The FTSE 100 Index (Financial Times Stock Exchange Index) is a share index of the 100 most highly capitalised companies listed on the London Stock Exchange. The index began on 3 January 1984 with a base level of 1000; the highest value reached to date is 6950.6, on 30 December 1999. The index is maintained by the FTSE Group, an independent company which originated as a joint venture between the Financial Times and the London Stock Exchange. FTSE 100 companies represent about 80% of the market capitalization of the whole London Stock Exchange. The FTSE 100 is the most widely used UK stock market indicator. Other related indices are the FTSE 250 Index (which lists the next largest 250 companies after the FTSE 100), the FTSE 350 Index (which is the aggregation of the FTSE 100 and 250), FTSE Small Cap Index. The FTSE All-Share aggregates the FTSE 100, FTSE 250 and FTSE Small Cap.

5. Hang Seng Index (HSI)

The Hang Seng Index is a freefloat-adjusted market capitalization-weighted stock market index in Hong Kong. It is used to record and monitor daily changes of the largest forty five companies of the Hong Kong stock market and is the main indicator of the overall market performance in Hong Kong. These 45 companies represent about 67% of capitalization of the Hong Kong Stock Exchange.

HSI was started on November 24, 1969, and is currently compiled and maintained by HSI Services Limited, which is a wholly owned subsidiary of Hang Seng Bank, the largest bank registered and listed in Hong Kong in terms of market capitalisation.

6. Shanghai Stock Exchange

The Shanghai Stock Exchange (SSE) is a Chinese stock exchange based in the city of Shanghai, with a market capitalization of nearly US$3.02 trillion (2007) making it the largest in mainland China. The current exchange was re-established on November 26, 1990 and was in operation on December 19 of the same year. It is a non-profit organization directly administered by the China Securities Regulatory Commission (CSRC). Mainland China has a second, smaller, stock exchange: the Shenzhen Stock Exchange, located in the city of Shenzhen.

3.7 Recent Trends In Indian Capital Market

Economic liberalization, privatization, foreign private participation, disinvestment in public sector and regulatory changes have provided a new impetus to the capital market. macro-economic fundamentals, growth of the manufacturing sector, institutional support led by Foreign Institutional Investors (FIIs) and mutual funds, positive investment climate, sound business outlook, encouraging corporate results and buoyant secondary market induced large number of companies to raise capital resources from primary market. The private sector continued to dominate the primary market activities during 2005-06. There was overwhelming response to most of the public issues reflecting risk appetite of the investors in general and sustained investment activities in particular. Regulatory reforms such as introduction of proportionate allotment and margin requirement for the Qualified Institutional Buyers (QIBs) and special allocation to mutual funds within the QIB category also contributed to brisk activities in the primary market induced large number of companies to raise resources from the primary market. We discuss some recent trends in the section.

3.7.1 Resource Mobilization

Table 3-2 gives a bird's eye view of resources mobilized from the primary market through prospectus, rights and private placements.

The Table 3-2 reflects two distinct trends in resource mobilization from primary market prospectus and right issues. It indicates an increasing trend from 1991-92 to 1994-95 and a decreasing trend from 1995-96 onwards, with unsustained spells of revival in 1998-99. The growth rate of new capital issue was the highest (+232) in the year 1992-93-a year immediately after the reforms were initiated. This growth was partly a result of abolition of the Capital Issue (Control) Act with effect from May 1992 and freeing of the pricing of issues that followed as a consequence. Huge resources were raised in the following two years also.

Table 3-2 Resources Mobilized from the Primary Market through Prospectus and Rights issues*

(Rs. in Crore)

Year	Prospectus and Rights			
	Non gove-rnment	Government Companies	Banks and Fina-ncial institution	Total
1990-91	4,312	-	-	4,312
1991-92	6,193	-	-	6,193 (+44)
1992-93	19,803	430	356	20,589(+232)
1993-94	19,330	819	3,843	23,992(+16.5)
1994-95	26,413	888	425	27,730(+15.6)
1995-96	16,075	1,000	3,465	20,549(-26)
1996-97	10,410	650	4,352	15,412(-25)
1997-98	3,138	43	1,476	4,657(-70)
1998-99	5,013	-	4,352	9,365(+101)
1999-2000	5,153	-	2,551	7,704(-18)
2000-01	4,890	-	1,472	6,362(-17)
2001-02	5,692	350	1,070	7,112(+12)
2002-03	1,878	-	2,989	4,867(-32)
2003-04	3,210	100	3,880	7,190(+48)
2004-05	13,482	2684	5,726	21,892(+204)
2005-06	21,154	373	5,413	26,940(+230)

Note: * including both debt and equity. Figures in the bracket indicate per cent change over the previous year. Source: RBI, Annual Report, various issues.

The primary market has been quite depressed since 1995-96. The overall decline can be attributed to factors operating on demand and supply sides. The scam (M S Shoe, Harshad Mehta & Ketan Parekh) that took place in the secondary market adversely affected the primary market. Many fraudulent promoters cheated investors which led to loss in investor confidence. All these factors drove away investors from the primary market. Moreover, strict disclosure standards and entry point norms prescribed by SEBI and an overall slowdown in the economy and in the industry partly led to deceleration in the primary market. revival of the primary market, which started in 2003-04, gathered momentum in 2004-05 and further invigorated in 2005-06. It can be seen from Table 3-3 that the resource mobilised during these years registered significant increase.

The number of issues made and the amount raised from the market has been phenomenal in the last decade. Table 3-3 shows the capital raised during 2004 to 2006.

Table 3-3 Resource Mobilization

Particulars	2004-05		2005-06		Percentage Share in Total Amount	
	No.	Amount	No.	Amount	2004-05	2005-06
1	2	3	4	5	6	7
Public Issues, ofwhich	34	24,640	103	23,294	87.20	85.07
IPOs	23	12,382	79	10,936	43.82	39.94
FPOs	11	12,258	24	12,358	43.38	45.13
Rights Issues	26	3,616	36	4,088	12.80	14.93
Total	60	28,256	139	27,382	100.00	100.00
Memo Item:						
Offer for Sale	3	3,200	3	278	11.32	1.01

Source: SEBI, Annual Report, various issues.

During 2005-06, 139 companies accessed the primary market through public and rights issues and mobilized Rs.27,382 crore compared to 60 companies raising Rs.28,256 crore in 2004-05 (Table 3-3). While number of issues in 2005-06 was more than twice of that in 2004-05, the amount was marginally lower. Excluding the for sale, the amount raised during 2005-06 stood at Rs.27,104 crore, which was higher than that of Rs.25,056 crore mobilized in the previous year. There were 103 public issues in 2005-06, of which 79 were initial public offerings (IPOs) and 24 were further public offerings (FPOs). The resources mobilized through IPOs and FPOs during -06 were Rs.10, 936 crore and Rs.12,358 , respectively. The average size of the issues was significantly lower at Rs.226 in 2005-06 compared to Rs.725 crore in 2004-05. The number of rights issues during 2005-06 was higher at 36 than that of in 2004-05. The amount mobilized through issues was also higher at Rs.4,088 e in 2005-06 compared to Rs.3,616 crore the previous year.

3.7.2 Private Placement Market

Available data indicates that private placement has become the preferred route for raising resources by both public and private sector companies. This route has gained immense importance during the last few years due to its operational flexibility and attractive pricing.

Table 3-4 Resources Raised by Private Placement Market

Year	Private Sectors	Public Sectors	Total resources raised	%age to total resources in primary market	Year	Private Sectors	Public Sectors	Total resources	%age to total resources in primary market
1995-96	4070	9291	13361	39.1	2001-02	28620	36256	64876	89.6
1996-97	2493	12573	15066	51.2	2002-03	25077	4187	66948	94.5
1997-98	9202	20896	30099	86.8	2003-04	18760	45141	63901	73.3
1998-99	16998	32681	49679	78	2004-05	35794	47611	83405	74.7
1999-00	19404	41856	61259	88.7	2005-06	41205	55164	96368	77.9
2000-01	23106	44731	67836	91.7					

Source: RBI, Annual Report, various issues

Table 3-4 reveals that the amount of resources raised through private placement almost doubled from Rs.15, 000 crore to Rs.30, 098 crore in the year 1997-98. The amount of resources again doubled in the year 1999-00 and 2000-01 from Rs.30, 098 crore to Rs.67,837 crore. The share of resources mobilised through private placement in 2005-06 accounted for nearly 78 percent of the total resources mobilised from the primary market.

3.7.3 Sector-wise Resource Mobilization

Sector-wise classification reveals that private sector garnered Rs.20,199 crore through 131 issues in 2005-06 compared to Rs.17,163 crore raised through 55 issues in 2004-05 (Table 3-5). Most of the non-government public limited companies accessed the primary market mainly due to congenial investment climate prevailing in the , supported by sustained buoyancy in the secondary market. In fact, the share of private sector in the total resource mobilization rose significantly from 60.7 per cent in 2004-05 to 73.8 per cent in 2005-06. During 2005-06, there were 8 issues from the public sector which mobilised Rs.7,183 crore compared to 5 issues which raised Rs.11,094 crore in 2004-05. Out of 8 public sector issues, 6 were from the public sector banks and the remaining two issues from Gujarat State Petronet Corporation . and Infrastructure Development Finance Ltd.

3.7.3 Sector-wise Resource Mobilization

Sector-wise classification reveals that private sector garnered Rs.20,199 crore through 131 issues in 2005-06 compared to Rs.17,163 crore raised through 55 issues in 2004-05 (Table 3-5). Most of the non-government public limited companies accessed the primary market mainly due to congenial investment climate prevailing in the , supported by sustained buoyancy in the secondary market. In fact, the share of private sector in the total resource mobilization rose significantly from 60.7 per cent in 2004-05 to 73.8 per cent in 2005-06. During 2005-06, there were 8 issues from the public sector which mobilised Rs.7,183 crore compared to 5 issues which raised Rs.11,094 crore in 2004-05. Out of 8 public sector issues, 6 were from the public sector banks and the remaining two issues from Gujarat State Petronet Corporation . and Infrastructure Development Finance Ltd.

Table 3-5 Sector-wise Resource Mobilization

Sector	2004-05		2005-06		Percentage share in the total amount	
	No.	Amount	No.	Amount	2004-05	2005-06
1	2	3	4	5	6	7
Private	55	17,163	131	20,199	60.74	73.77
Joint	0	0	0	0	0.00	0.00
Public	5	11,094	8	7,183	39.26	26.23
total	60	28,256	139	27,382	100.00	100.00

Source: SEBI Annual report

3.7.4 Industry wise resource mobilization:

Banks/financial institutions continued to dominate the amount of mobilised from the primary market 2005-06 and raised Rs.12,439 crore through 12 issues. It has been increased four fold from Rs. 3139 crore during the year 2000-01. During 2004-05, there were 12 issues from the banks / financial institutions which raised Rs.11,311 crore. The share of the banks/financial institutions in the total amount raised increased to 45.4 per cent in 2005-06 from .0 per cent in 2004-05. The highest numbers of issues werefrom the information technology sector (15 issues) which was just 5 numbers in the year 2000-01, followed by sector (13 issues). Other sectors which sizeable amount of resources from primary market were power (Rs.2,164 crore), engineering (Rs.1,124 crore), cement and construction (Rs.1,020 crore) and information technology (Rs.902 crore). The share of the power sector, which was 20.7 per cent of the total resource mobilization in 2004-05, declined to 7.9 per cent in 2005-06.

Six public sector banks raised Rs.5,413 crore through equity issues in 2005-06. Apart from the public sector banks, five private banks *viz.*, ICICI Bank Ltd., Yes Bank ., Lakshmi Vilas Bank Ltd., the South Indian Bank Ltd., and United Western Bank Ltd., accessed the primary market for raising resources. As mentioned earlier, the largest issue among the banks/financial institutions was that of ICICI Bank Ltd. which raised Rs.5,101 crore. This was incidentally biggest issue of the financial year. The total capital raised by the various industry has increased from Rs,6,108 crore during the year 2000-01 to 27,382 crore during the year 2005-06.

3.7.5 Size-wise Classification of Resources Mobilised

During 2005-06, the size of the issues was generally smaller than those in the previous year. The average size of the issues 2005-06 was Rs.197 crore compared to Rs.471 crore in 2004-05. This indicates rise in the number of medium and small sized companies accessing the capital market for their financing needs. It also shows a shift in the financing mode from the traditional sources of finance like banks/financial institutions to the capital market. More capital was raised with smaller size issues during 1990-95. In the category of above Rs.500 crore, there were 9 issues which mobilised Rs.15,506 crore compared to 8 such issues which raised .23,431 crore in 2004-05. share of all other size groups witnessed significant improvement except Rs.5 crore to Rs.10 crore categories which recorded marginal decline (SEBI Annual Report, 2007).

3.7.6 Mega Issues Floated by Non-Government Public Limited Company

A record number of mega issues were floated after the reforms. An issue size of Rs.100 crore is a mega issue. A record number of 39 mega issues worth Rs.10,304 crore were issued during the year 1995-96. There were 17 mega issues in 2005-06. The largest issue during 2005-06 was that of ICICI Bank Ltd. (Rs.5,101 crore), followed by Hindalco Industries Ltd. (Rs.2,227 crore) and Bank of Baroda (Rs.1,633 crore). During 2005-06, the largest IPO was issued by Suzlon Energy Ltd., which raised Rs.1,496 crore. It shows investors confidence in the primary market to mobilize their resources. (SEBI, Annual Report, Various Issues)

3.7.7 Resource mobilization by Mutual Funds

The mutual funds have proved to be important conduits of mobilizing resources since 1987-88 when public sector banks were allowed to set up subsidiaries to undertake mutual fund business. At present, this country has four types of mutual funds-Unit Trust of India, MF subsidiaries of pubic sector banks, MF subsidiaries of investment institution like LIC and GIC and private sector mutual funds. Resources mobilised by the MFs (including UTI) under various schemes rose substantially from Rs. 2,310 crore in 1987-88 to Rs.12, 201 crore in 1992-93. In 1994-95, resources mobilised by MFs stood at Rs.11, 243 crore. There was reverse flow of funds from the mutual funds during 1995-96 and 1996-97 in view of sluggishness in the capital market. During 1995-96 and 1996-97, the total funds raised by MFs aggregated a negative amount of Rs.5,883 crore and Rs.2,037 crore respectively, mainly due to high level of repurchases coupled with inability on the part of mutual funds to float new schemes in a downward market. However, in 1997-98 and 1998-99, the mutual funds were able to mobilize Rs. 4,064 crore and Rs.2, 695 crore respectively. In 1999-2000, there was a spectacular increase in resource mobilization by mutual funds. The total resources raised by mutual funds under various schemes amounted to Rs. 22,113 crore. However, this amount fell to Rs.10, 121 crore in 2001-02 and to Rs.4,583 crore in 2002-03. Conditions improved for this industry in the subsequent years as several tax concessions were announced for mutual funds investors. In 2005-06, total resources mobilised by the mutual funds amounted to Rs.50, 674 crore largely due to spectacular mobilization of Rs.40811 crore by private sector mutual funds. in the Union Budget 1999-2000. Due to bullish trends in the secondary market, private sector mutual funds accounted for more than two-thirds of the total resource mobilization. (SEBI Annual Report, 2007 and RBI various Issues).

3.7.8 Proportion of various issues in the total capital raised by Non-Government Public limited Company

Table 3-6 reveals that equity issue gains popularity after the initiation of reforms. The abolition of the CCI and free pricing has given a tremendous boost to the equity market since 1992-93. The amount of preference shares issues in the total issue was negligible during the year.

Table 3-6 Proportion of Equity, Preference and Debenture issues in the total Capital issued by Non-government Public Limited Company

Year	Equity(%)	Preference(%)	Debentures(%)
1995-96	74.24053	0.937617	24.8156
1996-97	58.60711	0.720461	40.66282
1997-98	37.02996	0.12747	62.84257
1998-99	51.12707	1.196888	47.69599
1999-2000	53.42519	0	46.59422
2000-01	44.8264	2.440701	52.7329
2001-02	15.10892	0	84.89108
2002-03	24.49414	0	75.50586
2003-04	66.38904	0	33.61096
2004-05	87.56021	0	12.43979
2005-06	98.79455	0.047272	1.158173

Source: RBI Annual Report, various issues

Table 3-6 suggests that the total amount of funds raised by equity registered rise during the recent past whereas the funds mobilised through preference and debentures showed a decline. Debenture issues were prominent till 1997-98. Their prominence declined in the free pricing era wherein private sector preferred to issue equity shares. The year 1997-98 and 2001-02 were exceptions as debenture issues gained prominence over equity issues with large companies in the financial sector relying on debt issues.

3.7.9 Stock Market Indicators

Market capitalization to GDP ratio is a good indicator of the health of stock market of an economy. Leading economies of the world have market capitalization far in excess of their gross domestic product. This indicates not only the investor confidence but also the strength of the economies. The market capitalization to GDP ratio of Indian stock market has increased over the last four years. It roses from 23.2 percent of GDP in 2002-03 to 85.9 percent of GDP in 2006-07(SEBI Annual report various issues).

Liquidity of stock market indicates the ease with which stocks can be traded. One way to gauge the liquidity is to look at the ratio of value of shares traded to GDP at current market prices. This ratio increased from 67 percent in 2005-06 to 70.4 percent in 2006-07(SEBI Annual report, 2006-07). Another important indicator is price/earnings (P/E) ratios of Indian indices. The ratios of BSE and NSE were at sixth and ninth positions among the emerging markets. The highest P/E ratio was for Shanghai Composite Index of China followed by Nikkei index of Japan and NASDAQ composite of USA (SEBI Annual Report, 2006-07).

The stock markets of emerging economies were more volatile as compared to developed markets during the financial year 2006-07. Among the emerging markets, Colombia displayed the highest volatility (37.9 percent) followed by Russia (35.9 percent) and India (27.6 percent). Volatility of the international markets was higher in 2006-07. Japan was the most volatile (18 percent) among developed markets followed by South Korea(17 per cent), Hong Kong and Singapore (16.5 percent) (SEBI Annual Report, 2006-07).

3.7.10 Resource Mobilization from the international Capital Markets

After the reforms were initiated in 1991, Increasing numbers of Indian companies have been raising resources by way of equity issues in the international capital markets through American Depository Receipt (ADR), Global Depository Receipt (GDR), Euro issue and External commercial borrowings (ECBs). In 1993-94 and 1994-95, a record number of euro issues were issued. Indian companies raised Rs.14, 500 crore through euro issues in these two years. India became the only country to have the unusual distinction of the largest number of GDR issues. Indian companies prefer ADR/GDR to raise capital from international markets. A considerable amount of resources has been raised from the international capital market through ADR/GDRs. Good companies through good governance practices have been successful in getting themselves listed on London Stock Exchange (LSE), NASDAQ and New York Stock Exchange (NYSE). Total resource mobilised through ADR/GDR has increased from Rs.240 crore in the year 1992-93 to Rs.2552 crore in the year 2005-06.

3.8 Reforms in Capital Market

The Indian capital market has a long history spanning over more than 100 years. The government of India has initiated a number of steps to strengthen the capital market. Various regulatory bodies like SEBI have been trying to ensure orderly development in Indian capital market with various regulatory measures and reforms. A brief discussion of important measures is as follows:

(1) The Securities and Exchange Board of India (SEBI), was given statutory powers in January 1992 through an enactment of the SEBI Act, 1992 for regulating the securities markets with main objectives to protect interest of investors and ensure orderly development of the capital market.

(2) The most significant development in the primary capital market has been the introduction of free pricing. The Capital Issue (Control) Act, 1947 was cancelled in May, 1992. The issuer of securities can float an issue or decide its pricing without prior permission from an authority. However, the new issue of capital has now been brought under SEBI's purview and issuers are required to meet the SEBI guidelines for disclosure and investor protection.

(3) Depositories Act, 1996 passed to provide a legal framework for the establishment of depositories and to facilitate dematerialization of securities. The Depositories Related Laws (Amendment), 1997 issued through ordinance now allows banks, mutual funds and IDBI to dematerialize their scrips.

(4) The infrastructure of the primary capital market has been fairly diversified over the years with setting up of large number of merchant bankers, investment and consulting agencies, registrars to the issue. The requirement to issue share at a par value of Rs.10 and Rs.100 was withdrawn. This gave companies the freedom to determine a fixed value per share. This facility is available to companies which have dematerialized their shares. Greater transparency are encouraged in terms of disclosure all material facts and risk factors associated with their projects while launching public issues and give justification for pricing on their prospectus.(SEBI Guidelines).

(5) Foreign institutional investors such as mutual funds, pension funds are allowed to function in the Indian market. It is considered to be one of the significant steps towards integrating the Indian Capital market with the international capital market. Foreign Institutional Investors were initially allowed to invest only in equity shares, later they were allowed to invest in the debt market, including government securities and treasury bills. The upper limit for investment by foreign institutional investors was increased from 40 per cent to 49 per cent in 2000-01.

(6) Indian companies can raise capital from international capital markets through issues of Global Depository Receipts, American Depository Receipts, Foreign Currency Convertible Bond and External Commercial Borrowings. Companies were permitted to invest abroad in all ADR/GDR proceeds.

(7) Corporates with infrastructure projects and municipal corporations are exempted from the requirements of rule 19(2)(b) of the Securities Contracts (Regulation) Act, 1956 to facilitate the public offer and listing of its pure debt instruments as well as debt instruments fully or partly convertible into equity without requirement of prior listing subject to conditions such as investment grade rating. The freedom to issue debt security without listing security granted to infrastructure companies and municipal corporations has been extended to all companies subject to certain conditions like issues below Rs.100 crore shall carry an investment grade credit rating, issues above Rs.100 crore shall carry an

investment grade credit rating from two credit rating agencies and promoters should bring the equity contribution of 20 percent and lock in period of three years(SEBI, 1997).

(8) SEBI has expanded its net by bringing under its purview various the activities of various financial intermediaries such as mutual funds, portfolio managers, registrar to the issue, share transfer agents, underwriters, debenture trustees, bankers to an issue, custodian of securities, venture capital funds and issues.

(9) SEBI has approved the use of book building process in pricing of issues with effect from November, 1995. In April, 2000 SEBI modified the guidelines for the 100 per cent one-stage book building process and 75 percent book building process. Book building is a method of marketing the shares of a company whereby the quantum and the price of the securities to be issued will be decided on the basis of the 'bids' received from the prospective shareholders by the lead merchant bankers. According to this method, share prices are determined on the basis of real demand for the shares at various price levels in the market. In 100 percent book building method, 100 percent of the net offer is made to the public through book building process. It is available to the companies whose issue amount is Rs. 25 crore and above. In 75 percent book building process, 75 percent of net offer is made through book building process and remaining 25 percent of the net offer to the public can be offered at a price determined through book building. Under the new guidelines, a maximum of 60 percent of the issue was allowed to be allotted to the institutional investors and at least 15 per cent to non-institutional investors who had applied for more than 1000 shares. Non-institutional investors include companies, overseas corporate bodies, non-resident Indians, high net worth individuals, Hindu Undivided families, societies and trusts. The remaining 25 per cent could be allotted to small investors on a pro-rata basis. (SEBI Guidelines, 2000).

(10) Disclosure and Investment Protection (DIP) guidelines have been modified. According to the new guidelines, company which has a record of profitability and a net worth of Rs.1 crore in three out of the past 15 years, is allowed to float IPOs with five times the size of the pre-issue net worth. Companies without such track record or a issue size beyond five times the pre-issue net worth are allowed to make IPOs only through the book building rout, with 60 per cent of the issue to be allotted to qualified institutional borrowers (QIBs). For shares issued on a preferential basis to any person by listing companies, a lock-in-period of one year has been stipulated. Infrastructure companies are exempt from the requirement of eligibility norms if the project has been appraised by a public financial institution and not less than 5 per cent of the project cost is being financed by any of the institutions jointly by way of loan or subscription to equity. Permission has been granted to Foreign Venture Capital Investors (FVCIs) registered with SEBI and State Industrial Development Corporations (SIDCs)

to participate in public issues through book building route as Qualified Institutional Buyers (QIBs). There is no lock-in requirements for the pre-issue capital of an unlisted company held by Venture Capital Funds (VCFs) and FVCIs. Exemptions from the public offer requirement in view of a reduction in quantum from 25 per cent and restriction of a minimum public issue size of Rs.25 crore in respect of an IPO through the book-building issue have been removed. (SEBI DIP Guidelines, 2000).

(11) Companies in the Information Technology, telecom, media and entertainment sectors are allowed to tap the market with a minimum offering of 10 per cent of their equity. All public issues through this route have to satisfy the criteria on of a minimum Rs.100 crore issue size, follow book-building route with allocation of 60 percent to QIBs and maintain minimum floating post-listing stock on a continuous basis.

(12) The issuer can make a public or rights offer of shares in demat form only. Investors have the option of subscribing to securities in either the physical or the dematerialized form. Companies making their first public issue are eligible to do so only if they have three years of dividend paying track record preceding an issue. Those not meeting this requirement can still make an issue if their projects are appraised by banks or Financial Institutions with minimum 10 per cent participation in the equity capital of the issuer, or their securities are listed n the Over the Counter Stock Exchange of India (OTCEI).

3.9 Summary

A financial system plays an important role in economic growth of the country. Some empirical studies reveal that there is a close relationship between the effectiveness of the financial system and economic growth. Stock markets and banks are likely to play an important role in channeling funds from savings to investments. The Indian stock markets have a history of more than 125 years. They have undergone sea of change in the last decade. Technology has changed the face of the stock markets. New trading systems, new stock exchanges, new players, new instruments have come into existence. Today, Indian equity market is one of the most technologically developed in the world and is on par with other developed markets abroad. Strong macro-economic fundamentals and favourable investment climate followed by upbeat secondary market performance encouraged a number of companies to raise capital from Indian stock markets.

The review of studies examining the stock market volatility and its relationship with other factors, econometric modeling of volatility and transmission mechanism of return and volatility is provided in the next chapter.

* * *

CHAPTER 4 Review of Literature

Chapter two presents conceptual and analytical frameworks on risk, return and stock market volatility. It explains various factors affecting volatility. It further offers discussions on various time varying volatility models useful in modeling stock market volatility and examining its interactions effects. The chapter also explains Multivariate GARCH model to capture return and volatility spillover effects.

Chapter three provides overview of Indian capital markets. It focuses on functioning of Indian capital markets. It discusses recent trends in the stock markets. The chapter also presents various reforms initiated in Indian capital market.

Volatility can be defined as variability or randomness of asset prices. Considerable attention has been paid to estimate and predict stock market volatility over the past decades. It has been observed that many financial time series in developed and developing countries exhibit volatility clustering which refers to a situation where tranquil period of small returns are interspersed with volatile periods of large returns. In finance literature, this is called time varying conditional volatility. Conditional volatility plays a key role in various financial activities.

Beginning with the mean variance analysis of portfolio and asset returns, volatility has become central in much of modern finance theory. In recent time empirical work involving high frequency time series data has focused on volatility of asset returns which calls for careful attention. It has been observed that the asset returns exhibits changes, which are not independent over time.

The chapter presents review of empirical studies that have been taken place on the subject of stock market volatility. It is organized into four sections on the basis of theme and issues of volatility. Section 4.1 examines the literature on extent of volatility and factors affecting volatility. Section 4.2 reviews studies on econometric modeling of volatility while Section 4.3 deals with studies on transmission of return and volatility among different stock markets of the world.

There have been very few studies on stock price behavior in India. Most of the studies on volatility have been done outside India. These studies cover a range of issues which include extent of volatility and its determinants like the arrival of information, traded volume, trading mechanism, day of the week effect etc. Some of the studies have focused on the effect of regulatory interventions like price limit, margin requirements etc. on the stock market volatility. Some studies focus on econometric modeling of volatility and transmission mechanism of return and volatility across different stock markets of the world.

Broadly, the studies on stock market volatility fall into three categories:

1. Studies focusing on the extent of volatility and its relationship with various factors.
2. Studies on econometric modeling of the time series behavior of return and volatility.
3. Transmission of return and volatility among different stock markets of the world

In the ensuing sections, review of studies concerning major area of research on the issue of volatility is presented.

4.1 Studies Focusing on Extent of Volatility and its Relationship with Various Factors

These studies focus on with the level of volatility prevalent in a given stock market and its comparison with other stock markets. The studies consider various factors like volume, trading mechanism, dividend payout, debt-equity ratio etc. and regulatory measures like price limit, introduction of derivatives, margin limit, introduction of computerized trading, banning of insider trading etc. which affect stock market volatility.

Heins and Allison (1966) measured the effects of several factors like average price of the stock, earning variability, price earning ration of stock, activity or turnover of the stock and principal exchange on which stock was listed on relative price variability of A rated and B rated stocks. The authors selected the stocks rated A and B by Standard and Poor's Corporation. The samples for the A and B rated groups contain forty-eight and sixty-two observation, respectively and represent one-fourth of the stocks in each group which were listed on either the New York or American Stock Exchange. The data was obtained from the Security Owner's Stock Guide by Standard and Poor's Corporation for the year 1959. The study used multiple regression analysis. The relative price variability was measured by the difference between the high and low annual earnings per share for the previous four years as a percentage of the average annual earnings for the 4 year period. The choice of four year period was due to the fact that it provided an adequate indication of degree of earnings variability and yet was recent enough to provide a reasonable indication of future variability. The price earnings ratio of the stocks was measured by the average price divided by the latest annual earnings per share. Activity or turnover in the stock was measured by the total shares traded during the year as a percentage of the number of shares of the stock outstanding during the year. Principal exchange on which the stock was listed was measured by the dummy-variable techniques. It was considered that the nature of the exchange itself might lead to more or less price variability. The study considered value of dummy variable as zero if the principal exchange was New York Stock Exchange and it took value one if stock was listed on American stock exchange. Using the data, the study found that the variability of stock prices A and B rated stocks were not significantly related to their average price. However, the effects of price earnings ratio and turnover of A rated stock on its stock return variability are positive and statistically significant. The results of multiple regression analysis suggested that earning variability and turnover of B rated stock positively affected its price variability. The results of the regression on B stocks showed that the exchange listing of the stock on New York or American had no significant effect on price variability. The study found that the coefficients of multiple correlations for A and B rated stocks were moderate. Their values are 0.44 and 0.51 for A and B rated stocks respectively. The unexplained variances (1-R2)[3] were high. Their values were equal to 0.81 and 0.74 for A and B rated stocks respectively which suggest that more reasons needed to be explored to understand the causes of stock price fluctuations.

French and Roll (1986) analyzed the volatility of equity returns during exchange trading and non-trading hours in New York and American Stock Exchange for 20 years period from 1963 to 1982. Using daily return data, they calculated return variances for weekdays, weekends, holidays and holiday weekends. They found that equity returns were more volatile during exchange trading hours then non-trading hours. Their study suggested that among non-trading hours, weekends had lower volatility than normal holidays while holiday weekends had the lowest volatility.

Amihud and Mendelson (1987) examined the effects of the two prevalent trading mechanisms-the periodic clearing house[4] and the continuous dealership market[5]-on the behavior of stock returns. The empirical investigation employed daily price data from

---

[3] R2 is a measure of goodness of fit for a regression model. It suggests the variance of dependent variable explained by independent variables. 1-R2 is known as unexplained variance which is not captured by the estimated regression model. In a multiple regression model, the strength of relationship among the variables is measured by R2 or its square root R which is known as coefficient of multiple correlations.

[4] Here, traders submit two types of orders to buy or sell specified quantities of the traded security: limit orders, which state the order quantity and the minimum sale price or the maximum purchase price at which the order is to be executed; and market orders, which specify only the quantity to be sold or bought with no price limits. Orders accumulate and remain sealed until clearing time. Then, all sell orders are sorted according to the type of order (market or limit; market orders are sorted first) and limit orders are further sorted by increasing price sequence. Buy orders are sorted by type of order (market orders first) and by decreasing price sequence. This gives rise to supply and demand schedules constructed from the orders submitted to the market. These schedules are then intersected at a single price which clears the market and applies to all executed orders.

[5] In the dealership market, trading is carried out continuously through market-makers who quote bid and ask prices at which they are willing to buy or sell (respectively).

the opening and closing transactions in active New York Stock Exchange (NYSE) stocks during the period February 8, 1982 through February 18, 1983. The clearing house mechanism was represented by the opening transaction, whereas the closing transaction represented the dealership market. The results showed that the trading mechanism had a significant effect on a number of characteristics of stock returns. First, the distribution of open-to-open returns had greater variance than that of close-to-close returns. While both show deviations from normality, the opening return distribution exhibited greater peakedness and fatter tails than that of the closing returns. Second, the serial correlation patterns of both the trading mechanisms were quite different in the two return series. The pattern of first-order serial correlation was generally negative in the opening and positive in the closing. Further, employing an ARMA[6] (1, 1) model, they found that in the opening, returns exhibited stronger dependence on past returns, reflecting stronger deviations from the random-walk form of the market efficiency hypothesis[7]. Finally, study analyzed the effects of the bid-ask spread[8] on variance of stock returns with the help of regression analysis by taking bid-ask spread as an independent variable and variance of stock return as dependent variable. The result suggested that the greater the bid-ask spread, the greater the close-to-close return variance. The evidence suggested that trading at the opening exposed traders to a greater variance than in the close, reflecting the differences between the trading mechanisms.

Schwert (1989) analyzed the relations of stock volatility with bond returns, short term interest rates, inflation rates, money growth, economic activity, financial leverage, and stock trading activity. The study used monthly data of Standard and Poor's Composite Portfolio and the economic series from 1857 to 1987. The data for bond returns, short term interest rates, inflation rates, money growth, financial leverage and stock trading activity were obtained from Moody, Centre for Research in Security Prices (CRSP), Warren and Pearson Index, National Bureau of Economic Research, National Account and trading volume reports of Standard and Poor respectively. The main findings of the study were as follows:

(1) The stock market volatility was related to the level of economic activity. The bond returns, short-term interest rates and money growth rates did not have higher volatility during recessions.

---

[6] It is an acronym for Autoregressive Moving Average. It is defined as a process that combined Autoregressive (AR) and Moving Average (MA) terms. An ARMA(1,1) process is a combination of AR(1) and MA(1). AR(1) is a process where the present observation depends only on the most recent past observation. MA(1) process is a weighted average of the present and the most recent past observations of a white noise process with a constant mean and a variance.

[7] Fama (1976) suggested that "if the market is efficient, there is no way to use any information available at time t - 1 as the basis for a correct assessment of an expected value of Rt and prices are said to follow random walk which makes the prediction using past information difficult.

[8] The amount by which the ask price exceeds the bid. This is essentially the difference in price between the highest price that a buyer is willing to pay for an asset and the lowest price for which a seller is willing to sell it. An Ask price is the price a seller is willing to accept for a security, also known as the offer price. A Bid price a buyer is willing to pay for a security.

(2) Stock market volatility and volatility of industrial production as measured by the standard deviation was high during 1929 to 1939 (recessionary period-Great Depression) for economic series including inflation, money growth, industrial production.

(3) Using 12thorder Vector Autoregression analysis[9], it was found that macro-economic volatility as measured by growth rate of industrial production and money supply growth rate did not influence stock and bond return volatility.

(4) The relationship between stock volatility and several measures of corporate profitability like dividend and earnings yield were also examined with the help of multiple regression analysis. The results revealed that that there was no relation between earnings, dividend policy and stock volatility.

(5) Using simple linear regression analysis, the study found that the stock market volatility increased with financial leverage. Results revealed that the interest rate and corporate bond return volatility are correlated with stock return volatility.

(6) There seemed to be a positive relation between trading activity and stock volatility. The number of trading days in the month was positively related to stock volatility, especially in 1953-1987. Share trading volume growth was positively related to stock volatility.

Schwert (1990) surveyed the academic evidence on stock market volatility in an attempt to put the current policy debate that the general level of stock market volatility had been rising. He examined stock market volatility of Standard and Poor 500 (S & P 500) using monthly and intraday-15 minute data from 1802 to 1989 period. Volatility was measured by the standard deviation of rate return. The study found that the standard deviations of monthly and every fifteen minutes within a day return were 4 percent per day and 0.75 percent respectively. The estimates of standard deviation showed that the volatility had been stable since mid-19thcentury in United States. It was observed that high level of volatility following Black Monday (October 19, 1987) were short-lived. The growth in stock index futures and options trading had not been associated with an upward trend in stock volatility. The evidence suggested that future returns were more volatile than the stock index returns when there were big price movements. There was no evidence that computerized trading increased volatility. The evidence was inconclusive as to whether the trading halts or circuit breakers could reduce volatility in a beneficial way. He argued that several economic factors like financial leverage, operating leverage, personal leverage and the condition of the economy caused slow changes in stock market volatility-that is changes that become noticeable over many months or years while trading volume, trading in futures and options caused short term volatility of stock return.

[9] A univariate autoregression involves one variable. In a univariate autoregression of order p, we regress a variable on p lags itself. In contrast, a multivariate autoregression known as Vector autoregression or VAR involves N variables. In an N-variable vector autoregression of order p, each endogenous or dependent variable is explained b its lagged or past values and the lagged values of all other endogenous variables in the model. Usually, there are no exogenous or independent variables in the model.

Hsieh and Miller (1990) examined the effect of margin requirement on stock market volatility of S&P 500 of USA. The study analyzed the long run and short term relationships between volatility and margin requirement using monthly and daily data covering the period October 1934 to December 1987. Major findings of the study were as follows:

(1) The study found no effect of margin requirement on volatility at various changes of margin limit on several time periods using modified Levene's[10] test. The test was used to check whether the standard deviation of stock returns in the 25 days preceding margin changes was the same as that in the succeeding 25 days. The study chose 25 days because 25 days was half the smallest number of trading days between two margin changes.

(2) Bivariate regression of volatility on margin requirement found no effect of margin on volatility.

(3) Multiple regression of volatility on margin requirement, return, margin credit and other economic variables like industrial productions, volatility of industrial production and Consumer Price inflation rate revealed weak influence of the margin credit on the volatility while the rest of the variables did not have any effect on volatility.

(4) The results of Granger causality test[11] between margin and volatility indicated that margins did not cause volatility but volatility caused margins.

Lockwood and Linn (1990) examined the stability of the variance of hourly market returns on the Dow Jones Industrial Average for the period 1964-1989. Test of stability on ordering of market volatility were performed using data (a) across intraday hours, (b) between trading and non-trading periods, and (c) between open-to-open and close-to-close periods. Market volatility was also examined between the dates of important structural changes in financial markets such as the introduction of NASDAQ in the year 1971, standardized stock options in 1973, negotiable commissions introduced in1975, stock index futures in 1982 and increased margin requirements for trading in stock index future in the year 1988. Levene's test for equality of variance tests was performed across hourly intraday returns, between close-to-open and open-to- close returns, and between open-to-open and close-to-close returns. The results of the test indicated that hourly intraday return variances were falling from the opening hour until the early afternoon and rising thereafter. Results also suggested that market volatility was significantly higher

---

[10] Modified Levene's test is an inferential statistic used to assess the equality of variance in different samples. It tests the null hypothesis that the population variances are equal. If the resulting p-value of Levene's test is less than some critical value (typically .05), the null hypothesis of equal variances is rejected.

[11] Granger causality is a technique for determining whether one time series is useful in forecasting another. A time series X is said to Granger-cause Y if it can be shown, usually through a series of F-tests on lagged values of X (and with lagged values of Y also known), that those X values provide statistically significant information about future values of Y.

during intraday than overnight periods. Levene's test for equality of variance found that the variance was not constant across the intraday period and it was larger when the stock market opened than when it is closed. The Levene's test results also indicated that Market return variance was shown to be significantly higher for open-to-open versus close-to-close periods during the pre-NASDAQ, Options and Commissions periods but it was significantly lower for open-to-open versus close-to-close periods during the Futures period. The test results further pointed out that the market return Variance was rising after NASDAQ began in 1971, rising after trading in standardized options began in 1973, falling after commissions became negotiable in 1975, rising after trading in stock index futures began in 1982, and falling after margin requirements for trading in stock index futures became larger in 1988. Levene's test for equality of variance for the hourly intraday return following the holidays suggested that the hourly intraday variances were unequal and higher during intraday than overnight. Test of equality of variance was also performed between trading days following holidays and all trading days excluding days following the holidays. The results showed that the variance of open-to-open returns was significantly less for trading days that follow holidays versus trading days that did not follow holidays.

Waghmare (1998) analyzed the effect of short sale[12] and badla[13] restrictions on the behavior of the stock price volatility using daily values of the return of Bombay Stock Exchange during the period December 1, 1992 to September 13, 1996. The major findings of the study are summarized as follows:

(1) The variance test[14] results showed that banning badla reduced the overall volatility while banning short sales did not have any effect on the volatility.

(2) The results of Schewert's two step methodology[15] indicate that banning badla did not help in reducing volatility while banning short sales resulted in curbing the volatility.

---

12 Short selling or "Shorting" is the practice of selling securities the seller does not own, in the hope of repurchasing them later at a lower price. An Investor borrows a share of stock from a broker and sells it. Latter, the short seller must purchase a share of the same stock in the market in order to replace the share that borrowed.

13 Badla trading involved buying stocks with borrowed money with the stock exchange acting as an intermediary at an interest rate determined by the demand for the underlying stock and a maturity not greater than 70 days. Badla were banned by the Securities and Exchange Board of India or SEBI in 1993

14 The studies has employed F test to test and estimate a ratio of the two variances with null hypothesis will always be expressed as the ratio of variances of no short sales to short sales and ratio of no short sales to restricted short sale variances to be one.

15 First step includes regressing time series of return on day of the week dummies created for Tuesday, Wednesday, Thursday, Friday, holiday dummies excluding weekends between successive trading days and dummies for badla in operation during December 1, 1992 to December 12, 1993, banned badla during March 15, 1994 to March 1, 1995 and dummies for modified badla during August 1, 1995 to September 13, 1996 and on the lagged values of return for four consecutive days. In second step, the residual obtains from first step is regressed on dummies for days of the week and lagged values of residuals for four days.

(3) Analyzing the effects of banning badla using a GARCH model, results suggested that the banning of badla did not result in a reduction in volatility in majority of the stocks. The volatility was decreased in 18 out of 26 stocks after the modified system of badla was reintroduced. The variance test results were different from the other two tests since the variance test did not account for volatility clustering; an effect commonly found in stock returns and impact of past news on volatility.

(4) The GARCH model results show presence of asymmetry effect in stock price which indicated different response to positive and negative news by stock price.

Roy and Karmakar (1995) focused on the following two questions: (a) what was the average level of volatility and whether it had decreased during the period January, 1935 to December, 1965. (2) Whether the trend of share price movement retarded the development process of our economy. The study spread over the period of 58 years. The sample data consisted of two sets of index numbers. While first set covered the 'Capital Stock and Share Index', compiled and published by 'Capital' magazine on a monthly basis for a period from January, 1935 to December, 1960. The second set composed of 'The Economic Times' index number of ordinary share prices compiled and published by The Economic Times on a daily basis for a period May, 1961 to December, 1992. The volatility for the period 1935-92 had been measured as a standard deviation of the monthly returns within each year. They calculated the 'spike volatility' to account for unusual days when extreme variations in volatility occur. Spike was defined as only those price variations which lie outside the plus or minus three standard deviation limits. The major findings of the study were listed below

(1) Unexpected changes in share prices cluster around the boom of the 40s and share mania of the 80s that continued upto 1992. The formation and eventual burst of Second World War bubbles during the 40s was a period of extreme volatility of the Indian stock market.

(2) Unexpected fluctuation of 40s was followed by a tranquil period of more than three decades. During this period mean fluctuations in return were modest with an average standard deviation of 3.25%.

(3) Volatility touched a new high of 13.5% in the year 1992. The year 1992 witnessed 40 spike days where changes in daily price were in excess of plus or minus three standard deviation (2.34134) which suggested that the year 1992 was the most volatile period in the history of the Indian stock market.

(4) The study found that the volatility had increased during the current period after the year 1990.

(5) The study favored suitable steps like reduction in anomalies of interest rate structure between formal and informal money market, pursuance of basic principle of investment-buy low and sell high by institutional investors and introduction of short term capital gain to curb the volatility.

Allen and Rachim (1996) examined the relationship between dividend policy and risk in an Australian context using monthly data from Australian Stock Exchange Journal covering the period from 1972 to 1985 consisting of a total sample of 173 companies grouped into five industries namely resources, developers, wholesalers, Industrials and services. Multiple regression analysis was used to analyze the impact of dividend yield, earning volatility, payout ratio, logarithm of market value (size), long term debt and growth in asset on stock market volatility. The results suggested that there was a statistically significant negative relationship between the payout ratio and price volatility and positive correlation between the stock price volatility and earnings volatility and debt. It was also discovered that a statistically significant positive correlation existed between size and stock price volatility. However, the major determinants of price volatility were pay-out ratio, the size of the firm, level of debt and earning volatility. Evidence revealed that dividend yield was not related with price volatility. The variable - dividend yield was dropped from the analysis to overcome the potential problem of multicollinearity. Therefore, the effect of dividend yield on stock market volatility could not be examined.

Chowdhary(1997) examined the effect of margin requirement on stock market volatility of Thailand. Using data for the sample period from May, 1975 to December, 1995, he found that the margin requirements had an important impact on stock prices in Thailand. The study calculated the geometric return of Stock Exchange of Thailand before and after 15 days of the introduction of the margin limit. The study showed that the increase (decrease) in margin requirement usually led to a downward (upward) trend in stock prices suggesting the asymmetric nature of the response of stock prices to changes in margin requirements.

Colm and Kevin (1998) examined the causes of volatility in Australian stock market. The dataset for the study consisted of monthly observations on the Australian stock market and business cycle variables like including the interest rate on 3-month bank accepted bills, the Australian US dollar exchange rate, the rate of inflation of the wholesale price index, the current account deficit and the level of industrial production over the period July 1970 to January 1994. The study employed ARCH model to study the impact of conditional volatility of business cycle variables on conditional volatility of stock market return. Among the most important determinants of the conditional volatility of the Australian stock market were found to be the conditional volatilities of inflation, interest rates and inflation and current accounts deficit. Statistically significant relationship between the conditional volatility of the foreign exchange rate and the conditional volatility of the stock market in Australia was not found.

Kim, Kim and Kim (2004) examined the relationship between the trading activities of Korea Stock Price Index (KOSPI 200)'s derivatives[16] contracts and the stock market

[16] A security whose price is dependent upon or derived from one or more underlying assets namely stocks, bonds, commodity, currencies etc. The derivative itself is merely a contract between two or more parties. Its value is determined by fluctuations in the underlying asset.

volatility using data of futures and options from 3rd May, 1996 to 7th July, 2002. Employing Exponential Generalized Autoregressive Conditional Heteroscedasticity (EGARCH), the study found positive relationship between the stock market volatility and the volume for both futures[17] and options[18] contracts. The results suggested that the derivatives volume tend to increase the underlying stock market volatility. Using Granger causality test, it was found that the lagged futures (options) volume caused the current stock market volatility, and that the lagged cash volatility also caused the current volume. The causality test requires that the variables must be stationary. The study had not performed unit root test to check for stationarity of variables used in the Granger causality test which makes the results less reliable.

Sioud and Hmaied (2003) examined the effects of stock exchange automation on the liquidity, volatility, returns and efficiency of shares traded on the Tunisian stock exchange (TSE). It used the daily closing price data provided by TSE for the period January 2, 1995 to December 31, 1998. The sample consisted of 20 stocks transferred for automation. The effect of automation on liquidity was studied by examining the volumes of trades before and after the introduction of stock exchange automation in the year 1996. The study found a substantial increase in trading volume followed the trading automation. The mean trading volume was 0.58 before the transfer, compared to 0.72 under the automated trading, reflecting an enhanced liquidity of stocks after automation. he study Estimated market model[19] to examine the impact of automation on returns of stocks. An event study analysis[20]was undertaken to analyze abnormal return for ten weeks before and after the introduction of automation. The study revealed that the automation led to reduction in return. The volatility of stock prices was estimated by the variance or the standard deviation of stock returns. If the change in the trading mechanism had no effect on stocks' volatility, the variance would be the same for the two return series (before and after the transfer). Variances were calculated on weekly returns: 35 weeks before and 35 weeks after the event window for each stock. The results of F-ratio[21] suggested that variances of returns were increased for 12 stock, decreased for 2 stocks and no impact on rest of the stocks after automation. Thus, it suggested that the

---

17 A future contract calls for delivery of an asset at a specified delivery or maturity date for an agreed upon price, called future price to be paid at contract maturity.

18 A financial derivative that represents a contract sold by one party (option writer) to another party (option holder). The contract offers the buyer the right, but not the obligation, to buy (call) or sell (put) a security or other financial asset at an agreed-upon price (the strike price) during a certain period of time or on a specific date (excercise date).

19 The market model is a statistical model which relates the return of any given security to the return of market portfolio. Here, security return is regressed on market return to find an abnormal return. Abnormal return is defined as the actual return minus the expected return. Positive abnormal return is the indication of an improvement.

20 It is the test of the efficient market hypothesis that look at the prices of a stock both before and after a news announcement about that stock known as event window.

21 The F-ratio is the ratio of two sample variances with the larger variance in the numerator.

transfer to electronic trading did not have the same effects on volatility for all securities. Market efficiency was analyzed by examining variance of the residuals of the market models before and after automation. The results showed that the variance of the residuals after automation was not decreased indicating no improvement in market efficiency. The market model used by the study only considered market return as proxy for risk to study abnormal return. The behaviour of the abnormal return could be explained better by considering other risk factors like inflation, investments by foreign institutional investment, growth rate of economy etc .

Singh and Bhatia (2006) examined the effect of the introduction of derivatives and future trading on the spot market volatility in India. It also tried to find out the spot market volatility on the day when future contracts expire. Applying GARCH (1, 1) model in daily closing prices of S&P CNX Nifty and Nifty Junior for the period October 4, 1995 to March 31, 2005, the study showed that the conditional volatility of daily spot market in India had declined after the introduction of futures in June 12, 2000 in India. The sum of coefficients of GARCH was 0.97 and 0.71 before and after introduction of futures respectively, suggested that the spot market was absorbing information faster in the post derivative period and the level of persistence of volatility had declined. Introducing dummy variable into conditional volatility equation of GARCH, the study found that the spot market volatility declined on the expiration date of future contracts as the value of dummy was negative and statistically significant. The study had not studied the impact of introduction of derivatives on asymmetric volatility using EGARCH and TARCH models. The study used closing prices which do not capture the volatility behaviour during intraday periods.

Sen and Ghosh (2006) examined the relationship between stock market liquidity and volatility of CNX Nifty index of India. The study used daily closing price value for the period from January 2001 to June 2005. Volatility had been measured by standard deviation of return and liquidity has been measured by impact cost[22]. Using multiple regression analysis, the study found the impact of volatility and turnover on liquidity. The study found negative impact (-0.107) of volatility on liquidity while no relationship between liquidity and turnover was observed. The study did not address the issues of autocorrelations[23] in residuals and multicollinearity[24] of independent variables used in the results which might make the estimates biased and inefficient.

---

22 Impact cost represents the cost of executing a transaction in a given stock, for a specific predefined order size, at any given point of time.

23 It is defined as the correlation between members of series of observations ordered in time. The classical linear regression model assumes that such autocorrelations does not exist in the disturbance term or residuals. The consequence of ignoring autocorrelation is that the standard error of the estimates could be wrong.

24 An implicit assumption that is made when using OLS estimation method is that the explanatory variables are not correlated with each other. When the explanatory variables are correlated with each other, there is a problem of multicollinearity. It leads to high value of standard errors making individual variables not significant. As a consequence, it is a difficulty in observing the individual contribution of each variable to the overall fit of the regression.

4.2 Studies on Econometric Modeling of Return and Volatility

The focus of the studies in this category is on the modelling time series behavior of stock return volatility. The studies reviewed here attempt to construct a market model from past stock return data to study nature and characteristic of volatility. Most of the studies have endeavored to use ARCH/GARCH class of models to high frequency stock return data.

Moving averages[25] have been used in past to model financial data. For example, in technical analysis of stock markets, the relationship between moving averages of different lengths can be used as a signal to trade. Simple moving averages have also been used to estimate and forecast unconditional volatility and correlation. The terms volatility and correlation are applied to the statistical forecasts that are based on equally weighted moving averages. The models were used in past to study and predict volatility. The equally weighted average is calculated on a fixed size data window that is rolled through time, each day adding the new return and taking off the oldest return. Another common form of weighted average measure for volatility and correlation is an exponential weighted average. An exponential moving average (EWMA) puts more weight on the more recent observations and thus takes some account of the dynamic ordering system. The moving average models assume that asset returns are independent and identically distributed. There is no time varying volatility assumption in any weighted moving average method. They only provide the estimate of unconditional volatility, assumed to be constant, and current estimate is taken as forecast. The volatility estimates do change over time. There is nothing else in the model that allows for variation in volatility (Alexander, 2004).

Returns in many financial markets are not well modeled by an independent and identically distributed process. At very high frequencies, returns may show sign of autocorrelation, so they are not independent. Lower frequency returns may not be autocorrelated, but there is often a strong autocorrelation in squared returns and so again returns are not independent (Tsay, 2005).

Positive autocorrelation in squared returns indicates that financial market volatility comes in 'clusters' where tranquil periods of small returns are interspersed with volatile periods of large returns. The technical term given to this is autoregressive conditional heteroscedasticity. This phenomenon has been documented for a very long time. As long ago as 1963, Benoit Mandlebrot observed that financial returns time series exhibit periods of high volatility interspersed with tranquility, where 'Large returns follow large returns, of either sign'. However, it is only relatively recently that useful models of volatility clustering have been developed.

---

25 Moving averages method is a simple device of reducing fluctuations and obtaining the trend values. In this method, the average value of a number of years (month, weeks or days) is taken as the trend value for the middle point of the period of moving average.

Engle (1982) introduced the Autoregressive Conditional Heteroscedasticity (ARCH) model. The model is used to estimate the means and variances of inflation in the U.K. using quarterly data for the period 1958-II to 1977-II. The results indicated that the ARCH effect was significant in the inflation series and the estimated variances increased substantially during the chaotic seventies having severe inflation. He suggested that the ARCH model was useful in obtaining more realistic forecast variances.

Bollerslev (1986) introduced model Generalized Autoregressive Conditional Heteroscedasticity (GARCH). The GARCH model allows the conditional variance to be dependent upon its own lags. He estimated GARCH (1, 1) model on the quarterly data set of U.S. inflation for the period 1948-II to 1983-IV. The results suggested the presence of GARCH effect in the inflation data. It indicated that the volatility of inflation was persistent. He presented the several limitations of ARCH models which are as follows:

(1) Determination of the number of lags of squared residual in the model is difficult

(2) The number of lags of squared error that are required to capture all of the dependence in the conditional variance might be very large. This would result in a large conditional variance model that was not parsimonious.

(3) The inclusion of more parameters in conditional variance equation leads to violation of assumption of non-negativity constraint. He argued that a simple GARCH model provides a marginally better fit and a more plausible learning mechanism than the ARCH model.

Akgiray (1989) studied time series behavior of the stock prices using GARCH models. The data were obtained from the Centre for Research in Security Prices (CRSP), Chicago and they contained 6030 daily returns on CRSP index covering the period from January 1963 to December 1986. This sample was divided into four different periods of 6 years each and each period was analyzed separately. The findings suggested the following:

(1) The daily returns were leptokurtic and not identical and independently distributed (I.I.D.)[26].

(2) GARCH (1,1) process fitted to the data very satisfactory. High order ARCH and GARCH model were tried but there were no significant improvements in goodness-of-fit based on likelihood-ratio tests.

(3) Various out-of-sample forecasts of monthly return variances were generated using historical estimate, exponential weighted moving average, ARCH and GARCH and compared through a number of statistics like Mean Error (ME)[27],

---

26 A sequence of random variables is i.i.d. if the random variables are mutually independent and they have the same probability distribution. An i.i.d. sequence from a probability distribution is called a random sample from that distribution.

27 It is the mean or average of the sum of all of the percentage error for a given data set .

Root Mean Square Error (RMSE)[28], Mean Absolute Error (MAE)[29] and Mean Absolute Percent Error (MAPE)[30]. Based on the relative values of these statistics, it was found that GARCH (1,1) model was superior to other models.

Using daily returns from CRSP for July 1962-December 1987, Nelson(1991) presented a new class of ARCH models called E-GARCH model that do not suffer from some of the drawbacks of GARCH models. He found that GARCH models have at least three major drawbacks in asset pricing applications which are as follows:

(1) Researchers beginning with Black (1976) found a negative correlation between current returns and future returns volatility. GARCH models do not rule out the assumption of the symmetric response of shocks to positive and negative return.

(2) GARCH models put restrictions on parameters that are often violated by estimated coefficient and that may unduly restrict the dynamics of the conditional variance process.

(3) GARCH models assume that the only the magnitude and not the positivity or negativity of unanticipated excess returns determines conditional variance. The new form of ARCH model proposed by him was used to estimate a model of the risk premium on the CRSP index. He found that the new model successfully captured the asymmetric effect and overcome the above drawbacks associated with GARCH models.

Using monthly data of Centre for Research in Security Prices of US for the period April, 1951 to Decedmber, 1989, Glosten, Jagannathan and Runkle (GJR) (1993) showed how the effects of good and bad news have different effects on volatility. They developed GARCH model taking into account asymmetric effect by incorporating an additional term to account for asymmetries. The additional term was a dummy variable in conditional variance equation which took on value one when residual obtained from the mean equation was positive (good news) otherwise its value was zero (bad news). Applying the model in the data set, they found that the positive unanticipated returns decreased volatility whereas negative unanticipated returns caused higher volatility implying existence of leverage effect in the stock market.

Engle and Ng (1993) recommended the news impact curve as a standard measure of how news was incorporated into volatility estimates. Various new and existing ARCH models like GARCH (1,1), EGARCH(1,1), GJR-GARCH(1,1) were fitted to the daily data of Japanese Tokyo Price Index (TOPIX) index from January 1, 1980 to December 31,

---

28 It is a measure of accuracy computed by squaring the individual error for each item in a data set and then taking the square root after finding the average or mean value of the sum of those squares.

29 It is the mean or average of the sum of all of the percentage error for a given data set taken without regard to sign.

30 It is sum of ratio of error to variance of the return.

1988. EGARCH(1,1) and GJR-GARCH(1,1) model found that negative shocks introduced more volatility than positive shocks. ARCH-LM[31] test of model adequacy suggested that the model proposed by Glosten, Jagannathan and Runkle (GJR) was the best model to capture asymmetric effect.

Zakoian (1994) introduced the Threshold ARCH (TARCH) model. His motivation to develop the model was driven by the work of Davidian and Carrol(1987) who suggested that the absolute value of residuals gave more accurate variance estimates than the squared residuals. Therefore, he presented the model to capture asymmetry by specifying the conditional standard deviation and absolute value of residuals in variance equation instead of the squared residuals and conditional variance in the variance equation. He compared Threshold ARCH approach with the classical and exponential GARCH models using daily stock-index data of French Cotation Assistée en Continu (Continuous Assisted Quotation) CAC stock index. It consisted of 3606 observations covering the period from January 1976 to July 1990. The whole period was partitioned in three sub periods of about five years each. Four models like classical GARCH, the Threshold GARCH, the Exponential GARCH and the GARCH with absolute values of residuals instead of squared values were estimated. The results stated that the volatility of stock reacted differently to increases and decreases of stock price. He found that Threshold ARCH led to a more subtle analysis of leverage effect than other models.

Corhay and Taurani (1994) investigated whether the class of ARCH models and its generalized versions (GARCH) could adequately described daily stock price behavior in European capital markets namely France, Germany, Italy, Netherlands and the United States for the period 1 Janurary, 1980 to 30 September, 1990. The findings indicated that the daily stock returns were not normally distributed and were leptokurtic and skewed. The result clearly pointed out that conditional heteroscedasticity was a prime feature of daily returns behavior of five European equity indices. They exhibited non-linear dependence that could not be captured by ordinary least square method of regression analysis. The evidence revealed that the GARCH (1,1) model was appropriate in modeling volatility. Each country's return volatility depended on last period's squared error and its own past conditional variance.

Li and Lim (1995) demonstrated that the return series had a conditional mean structure which depended on the rise and fall of the market on previous day. Using daily return series of Hong Kong Hang Seng index from 1970 to 1991, he found that the threshold model with conditional heteroscedasticity was a useful tool in describing non-linear behavior in financial time series of Hang Seng.

---

[31] ARCH LM test is Lagrange multiplier (LM) test is for autoregressive conditional heteroskedasticity (ARCH) in the residuals ARCH LM test statistics is computed from an auxiliary regression to test the null hypothesis of no ARCH effect. The auxiliary regression is a regression of the squared residuals on a constant and lagged squared residuals. Lagrange Multiplier (LM) test statistic is equal to T times R-squared from the regression. LM statistics follow a chi-squared distribution.

Nicholls and Tonuri (1995) presented an overview of the GARCH family of variance models and examined the behavior of aggregate stock market volatility of Australia over the period 1988-91 using the GARCH framework. The study considered daily returns on the Australian fifty leaders Statex-Actuaries Accumulation Index from 4 January 1988 to 31 December 1991 consisting of 1023 observations. Statistical data analysis had been done on the excess returns-the returns on stocks over and above the return on a riskless instrument. The return series was thus converted to an excess return series by subtracting the daily yield on the 90 day Bank Bills (risk less rate of return). The study found that stock return data was typically negatively skewed, leptokurtic and sharply peaked about mean when compared with the normal distribution. Stock return data showed evidence of autocorrelation in return and squared returns. Because of these empirical observations, it had been stated that the GARCH type of models might be appropriate to describe the evolution of the conditional variance for this set of data. The study attempted three asymmetric GARCH type models-EGARCH, the absolute value GARCH(AGARCH)[32] and the GJR-GARCH. The results suggested that the asymmetric EGARCH(1,1) model was a suitable model for the data set.

Jiangang Xu (1999) explored the Shanghai Stock market daily stock return volatility from May 21, 1992 to July 14, 1995 by comparing the GARCH, EGARCH and GJR-GARCH models. The study found that all the models captured time varying volatility. The study employed Pagan-Sabau test[33] to evaluate the adequacy of models. The test statistics indicated that the value of the coefficient of determination R2 form Pagan and Sabau's regression was highest (7.92%) for GARCH model implying that it was superior to the EGARCH and GJR-GARCH models of the same order. The study did not use model selection criteria like AIC and SBC to choose from competing model to get accurate results.

Prabir Mohanty and B Kamaiah(2000) modeled volatility and its persistence of 30 blue-chip securities traded in Bombay Stock Exchange using daily closing price from period 1992-1996. They estimated ARCH(5), GARCH(1,1) and GARCH(1,1)-M models for the thirty securities' return. The findings suggested the presence of ARCH effects in 24 out of 30 scrips. The results of ARCH(5) model suggested that the time varying volatility was persistence. However, the coefficient of GARCH(1,1) model show that volatility was changing slowly over time. The implications of GARCH(1,1)-M model showed that the returns on security was not significantly affected by volatility changes. The study suffered from several limitations. First, it has assumed that the security return follows AR(1) process which could have been modeled by Box-Jenkins methodology to get more reliable results on nature and characteristic of the mean return of the securities and index. The study has not performed the diagnostic checking using ARCH-LM test after estimating ARCH(5), GARCH(1,1) and GARCH(1,1)-M models. This may make the results less reliable. They did not examine the leverage effect using asymmetric GARCH models like EGARCH and TARCH models in the selected thirty companies and BSE Index.

---

32 AGARCH is similar to GARCH but it considers the evolution of standard deviation than variance in volatility equation.

33 It is used to evaluate the adequacy of models. Here, squared residuals are regressed on conditional variance. The value of R2 from the regression is used to evaluate the model.

Engle (2001) presented the use of ARCH/GARCH models in applied econometrics. He explained that ARCH/GARCH models treated heteroscedasticity as a variance to be modeled which corrects the deficiencies of least squares. He said that the rolling standard deviation calculated using fixed number of the most recent observations was unattractive to forecast the mean and variance of the return, conditioned on the past information. It was unattractive because it assumed that the variance of tomorrow's return was an equally weighted average of the squared residuals from the last 22 days. The assumption of equal weights seemed unappealing; as one would think that the more recent events would be more relevant and therefore should have higher weights. Furthermore, the assumption of zero weights for observations more than one month old is also unattractive. He said that ARCH and GARCH models allowed the data to determine the best weights to use in the parameters to be estimated. He showed that GARCH (1,1) is the simplest and most robust of the family of volatility models. He suggested that GARCH(1,1) could be generalized to a GARCH(p,q) model of higher order which are often useful when a long time span of data is used, like several decades of daily data or a year of hourly data. He opined that ARCH and GARCH models had been applied to a wide range of time series analysis, but applications in finance have been particularly successful. His discussion opened the door to multivariate modeling where not only the volatilities but also the correlations are to be investigated. He said that the ARCH and GARCH models and their extensions helped in building many theories of asset pricing, portfolio analysis and risk management.

Poshakwale and Murinde(2001) investigated stock market volatility in the East European emerging markets of Hungary and Poland using daily indexes for the period 1 January 1994 to 30 June 1996 for Hungary and 16 April 1994 to 30 June 1996 for Poland. The results suggested the presence of non-linearity in the indices through the BDSL[34] statistic, while the presence of conditional heteroscedasticity was detected through LM tests. The results suggested that the volatility was best specified as a process of the conditional heteroscedasticity in both the markets which is captured well by the GARCH process. Volatility is found to be persistent in both the markets. The result of GARCH-M model implied that the returns on both the markets were not affected by the volatility changes. The well-known day-of-the-week effect, reflected in significantly positive Friday and negative Monday returns, did not seem to be present in these markets. The conditional volatilities in the Polish and Hungarian markets found to decline after June 1995 which may be explained by appreciating Zloty exchange rates against the German Mark and increasing integration with developed markets.

Engle and Patton (2001) characterized a good volatility model by its ability to forecast and capture the stylized facts about conditional volatility like persistence in volatility, its mean reverting behavior, asymmetric impact of negative versus positive return innovations and the possibility that exogenous variables may have a significant influence

---

[34] The BDSL (Brock,Dechert,Scheinkman and LeBaron) test is a nonparametric test with the null hypothesis that a time series is independent and identically distributed. The alternative hypothesis encompasses both deterministic chaos as well as linear and nonlinear stochastic behaviour. The test is based on the correlation integral of a time series, introduced by Grassberger and Procaccia (1983).

on volatility. The study used twelve years of daily data on the Dow Jones Industrial index over the period 23 August, 1998 to 22 August, 2000 to illustrate these stylized facts and ability of models from the GARCH family to capture these characteristics. The findings of the study summarized as follows:

(1) The conditional volatility Dow Jones Industrial Index was found to be quite persistent with a volatility half-life of about 73 days.

(2) Test for non stationarity indicates that the volatility was mean reverting. Estimation of TARCH model indicated the presence of leverage effect in the stock market and a negative lagged return innovation was found to have an impact on conditional variance four times as large as a positive innovations.

(3) 3-month Treasury bill rate was found to be positively correlated with volatility, implying that higher interest rates lead to higher equity return volatility.

(4) GARCH (1,1) successfully captured the volatility characteristics.

Kaur (2002) examined the following issues:

(1) Is there any evidence of time varying volatility in daily return on Sensex and Nifty?

(2) What is the nature and characteristic of the volatility process?

(3) Is there any 'day-of-the-week effect?'

(4) Does any particular month of the year have significant impact on mean return or volatility?

(5) Is there return and volatility spillover across the Indian and the US stock markets?

She used daily stock price data for the period January 1993 through March 2003 for the stock markets of India presented by BSE Sensex and S&P CNX Nifty, Nasdaq and S&P 500 indices to represent the US market to examine the above issues. She estimated GARCH(1,1), EGARCH(1,1) and TARCH(1,1) models to analyze nature and characteristic of volatility of Indian stock markets. The day of the week effect and weekend effects were studied by including dummies for various days of the week one by one in the mean equation of return and then in the conditional variance equation, respectively, of the GARCH model. The study explored the possibility of calendar month effect in the Indian stock markets by creating dummies in the same fashion as done for day of the week effect. The study used asymmetrical GARCH models namely EGARCH and TARCH to study relationship between the US and the domestic stock markets. The daily return series of US stock markets were then introduced as explanatory variables first in the mean equation and then in the variance equation. The major findings of the study were as follows:

(1) The volatility in the Indian stock market exhibited autocorrelation and negative asymmetry in daily returns.

(2) For both the Indian indices, February exhibited highest volatility and corresponding highest return. The month of March exhibited significantly higher volatility but the magnitude was lesser as compared to February. This implied that during these months, the conditional volatility tends to increase.

(3) Month of December gave high positive return without high volatility and therefore offered good opportunity for the investor to make safe returns on Sensex and Nifty.

(4) The 'weekend effect', the 'day-of-the-week effect' and 'calendar month effect' were not present.

(5) Using Log likelihood[35], AIC[36] and SBC[37] criteria of model selection, the study found that the asymmetrical GARCH models outperformed the symmetrical GARCH models. EGARCH model was better fit for Sensex and the TARCH model was better fit for Nifty.

(6) There was mixed evidence of return and volatility spillover between the US and the Indian stock markets. S&P 500 exhibited statistically significant positive correlation with Nifty returns while Nasdaq returns exhibited statistically significant weak positive correlation with Sensex during the period 1999-2003. The picture is different in case of volatility. Negative correlation in volatility was seen between the US indices and the domestic indices during the 1993-1999. No explanations were given for this phenomenon.

Siourounis (2002) employed GARCH models to explore properties of the stock returns for the Athens Stock Exchange. Using daily closing price values of Athens Stock Exchange (ASE) for the period 1st January, 1988 to 30th December, 1998, the study found that the returns were conditionally heteroscedastic and current volatility was positively related to past realizations. The volatility was found to be persistent. GARCH (1, 1) model with dummy variable to capture the effect of political instability on stock market volatility was estimated. The result showed that the political instability induced negative excess return and volatility in ASE. Application of TARCH(1, 1) suggested the presence of asymmetry in the stock market.

The study didn't employ model selection criteria like AIC and SBC to choose order of GARCH and its variants.

35 Log likelihood is the joint density function of the data, viewed as a function of the model parameters. Maximum likelihood estimation is to find the parameter values that maximize the likelihood function. In case of normally distributed regression disturbances, maximizing the likelihood function turns out to be equivalent to minimizing the sum of squared residuals. The value of log likelihood is useful for comparing models.

36 Akaike Information Criterion (AIC) provides a measure of goodness-of-fit of a model which takes into accout the number of terms in the model. It is commonly used with ARIMA models to determine the appropriate model and its order. The AIC is equal to twice the number of parameters in the model minus twice the log of the likelihood function. Good model has a small value of this criterion.

37 Schwarz Bayesian Information Criterion (SBC or BIC) is an order selection criteria for ARIMA model selection. SBC is similar to AIC but compared to AIC, models with a smaller number of parameters tend to be selected by SBC.

Poon and Granger (2003) provided comprehensive review on volatility forecasting. They examined the methodologies and empirical findings of 93 research papers and provided syneptic view of the volatility literature on forecasting. They found that ARCH and GARCH classes of time series models were very useful in measuring and forecasting volatility.

Robert Engle (2003) applied ARCH models in Standard and Poor 500 composite index from 1963 through November 2003. He found that volatility was persistent and explained adequately by GARCH (1, 1) model. Application of TARCH (1, 1) model showed the presence of leverage effect in the stock market.

Padhi (2004) analyzed time varying volatility of individual stocks of fifteen companies and two aggregate indices such as Sensex and Nifty of India. Fifteen companies were selected from various sectors namely Electrical, Electronics, Machinery, Power Plants, Diversified and Non-metallic. Using daily closing price of the companies and indices, the study examined the presence of leverage effect. It found the evidence of ARCH effect in returns of stocks and indices. Estimation of GARCH(1,1) model indicated that the shock to conditional variance takes long time to die out suggesting that the volatility was persistent. The application of EGARCH and GJR-GARCH models revealed that the coefficient of leverage term was negative and statistically significant implying presence of asymmetric effect. The electronics sector had higher volatility persistence. The study had considered only fifteen companies. It would be insightful to extend the study to all the listed companies on the two indices.

Shah Saeed and Iqbal (2005) investigated various features of volatility and its impact on weekly return of Dhaka Stock Exchange (DSE) from January 1989 through November 2001 with the use of ARCH, GARCH, TARCH and ARCH-M models. The study was divided into two periods. First part of the study focused on the entire period. The second period dropped the data from 6th June, 1996 through September, 25, 1997. The analysis for the whole period indicates that DSE returns have high volatility persistence and it tends to diverge from mean return infinitely. They found that the volatility persistence had reduced when the data of few months before and after crash were omitted. Application of TARCH model suggested that there was no leverage effect in Dhaka Stock Market implying that investors do not differentiate between positive and negative shocks to volatility. The results of ARCH-M revealed that the market did not give risk premium to additional risk takers since risk-return relationship was found to be insignificant. The study did not use the daily data to study the return and volatility. High frequency data like daily return would have provided additional insight into the volatility characteristics. It has not used TARCH model to capture leverage effect.

Karmakar (2005) estimated conditional volatility of daily returns of S&P CNX Nifty and BSE India for the period from 2nd January, 1991 to 10th June, 2003 and of fifty individual companies during June 1994 to October 2003. GARCH (1, 1) model had been fitted to both the indices and its forecasting ability had been evaluated using forecast evaluation parameters namely RMSE, MAPE, MAE and MSE. The major findings of the study were as follows:

(1) There were strong evidences of time-varying volatility, volatility clustering and a high persistence and predictability of volatility.

(2) GARCH (1, 1) model provided reasonably good forecast of market volatility.

(3) Results of asymmetric GARCH test[38] and Lagrange Multiplier test suggested that there were leverage effects in NSE and BSE stock indices while only eight out of fifty companies showed significant leverage effects.

The study has not captured the asymmetric effect using EGARCH or TGARCH model.

Kumar and Sumanjeet (2006) estimated time varying volatility and its persistence in Indian stock market during pre(1985-92) and post (1993-2004)liberalization periods using both daily and monthly data on closing price. It investigated whether the volatility can be attributable to stock market reforms. The major findings of the study were as follows:

(1) The coefficient of GARCH(1,1) model in daily return series show that volatility was persistence. The volatility was marginally higher in pre-liberalization period than post-liberalization period. The period of 1991-92 was more volatile in the history of Indian Stock Market. For monthly data, volatility persistence was more during post liberalization period than pre-liberalization. This was just opposite to the finding of daily return series. The authors argued that daily data suffered from 'noise'[39] content which played a big role in volatility persistence causing high volatility. At less frequent observation like monthly data, noise content died away.

(2) EGARCH estimation revealed the presence of leverage effect in daily and monthly return series. Bai-Perron[40] test for structural break indicated that economic reforms in general and some political events led to structural shift in volatility. It showed that there were no break dates corroborate to liberalization events.

---

[38] It is a simple test to compute the first order autocorrelation coefficient between lagged returns and current squared returns. If the value is negative and the corresponding Box-Pierce test is significantly different from zero, then there is an asymmetry in volatility clustering.

[39] Used in the context of equities, it is stock market activity caused by program trading, dividend payments or other phenomena that is not reflective of overall market sentiment. It is also known as "market noise". In general, the shorter the time frame, the more difficult it is to separate the meaningful market movements from the noise.

[40] Bai and Perron (1998, 2003) developed a procedure that can estimate a model with an unknown number of structural breaks that occur at unspecified dates. The key feature of the Bai-Perron procedure is that the number of breaks and their timing are estimated along with the autoregressive coefficients.

(3) There was no structural change which could be related to buying or selling by FIIs indicating that FIIs were not the source of volatility persistence.

(4) When large shocks in stock returns were controlled by adding dummy variables for the structural change in the variance equation of EGARCH mode, there is a significant reduction in ARCH effect indicating that volatility did not react quite intensely to market movements however, the volatility was still persistent. The study had not incorporated the application of Threshold ARCH (TARCH) model to study leverage effect. Threshold GARCH preserves features of classical GARCH models which makes it more reliable to capture asymmetric effect (GJR, 1993 and Zakoian, 1994).

Karmakar (2006) measured the volatility of daily stock return in the Indian Stock market over the period from 1961 to 2005. He analyzed the volatility using the combined data set of the Economic Times Index and the S & P CNX Nifty. Estimation of GARCH (1,1) model suggested that volatility was time varying, highly persistence and predictable. TARCH model was used to test the asymmetric effect in volatility. The findings revealed that the bad news slightly reduced the volatility during pre-1990 period while the bad news increased the volatility substantially for the post 1990 periods and thus it could be said that there was asymmetry in volatility.

Kumar (2006) analyzed the forecasting capabilities of the models like random walk[41], historical mean[42], moving average[43], simple regression[44], exponential weighted moving average (EWMA)[45] and GARCH models in Indian stock and foreign exchange market. The daily stock market data was collected from June 3, 1990 till December 31, 2005 while daily exchange rate data was pertaining to the Indian rupee/US dollar exchange rate over the period January 3, 1994 till December 31, 2005. The study compared the forecasting performance of each model using MAE, RMSE, MAPE and Theil-U error statistics. The results of the study indicate that GARCH (4,1) methods led to better volatility forecasts in the Indian stock market and GARCH(5,1) achieved better volatility forecasts in the forex market. Thus, the study suggested that GARCH models outperform other class of models in forecasting performance.

---

41 It means that future changes in a random walk are uncorrelated with the present and past changes and so future changes are not predictable.

42 It assumes the conditional expectation of volatility constant, this model forecasts volatility as the historical average of the past observed volatilities.

43 In the model, forecast is based on all the available observations and each observation, whether it is very old or immediate, is given equal weight.

44 Regression of actual volatilities on lagged values is run. The estimated values thus obtained are used for forecasting volatility for next period.

45 It is a forecasting method that gives greater weightage to more recent observation so that finite memory of the market presented. This method adjusts the forecasts based on past forecast errors and the forecast is calculated as a weighted average of the immediate past observed volatility and forecasted valued for that same period.

Ane (2006) examined the ability of component-GARCH[46] model to capture the stylized features of volatility namely its short and long term components in 14 stocks traded on the stock exchange of Hong Kong. The study evaluated the forecasting ability of GARCH and Component-GARCH models using daily closing price from January, 1990 to December, 2004 of 14 companies selected in the four sectors representing finance, Utilities, Commerce and Industrial Sectors. The Estimation of GARCH(1,1) model suggested that the volatility was persistent for all the fourteen companies. The estimation results for component-GARCH show that the permanent component of the conditional variance exhibited a high degree of persistence while the transitory component happened to be much weaker. Out of sample forecast performance with mean square error of variance[47] revealed that the traditional GARCH model provided more accurate short run forecast for five days than component GARCH model. Component-GARCH model gave better long term forecast from 10 days to 90 days. The authors obtained the similar finding using weekly returns. The study has not examined applications and forecasting abilities of other classes of asymmetric GARCH models like EGARCH, TARCH or GARCH-M which may give better forecasting results.

Prabir Mohanti (2006) compared asymmetric volatility models with standard symmetric GARCH models in the context of Indian Stock Markets using daily closing price of four stock market indices-namely Sensitivity Index (Sensex) and BSE 100 from Bombay Stock Exchange(BSE) and S&P CNX 500, S&P CNX Nifty from National Stock Exchange(NSE) from April 1, 1995 through March 31, 2005. He examined the forecasting ability of above models using forecasting encompassing test[48]. The significant of parameters of asymmetric GARCH models in the context of Indian stock markets indicated presence of asymmetric effect. Forecast Encompassing test revealed that all the asymmetric models encompassed GARCH's forecast error while GARCH volatility forecast did not encompass the forecast error of EGARCH or GJR models. This clearly indicated the superior forecasting performance of the asymmetric class of models.

Using daily closing price from July 1, 1997 through February 27, 2006 for BSE 30 price index known as SENSEX, Islam (2007) examined the asymmetric volatility behavior by applying family of ARCH models. The results suggested that GARCH (2,1) model described the behavior of volatility. TARCH(1,1) and EGARCH(1,1) showed that news impact was symmetric and there was no existence of leverage effect in stock returns. The study had neither modeled the mean return using Box-Jenkins methodology nor given justification for selection of GARCH(2,1) model over GARCH(1,1). It had not used any

---

46 This models variance as the sum of two or more components. In a two-component model, for example, one component is used to capture short-term and another the long-term effects of shocks. This model therefore has the long memory, slow decay of volatility seen in practice.

47 It is the variance of the error term of the estimated model.

48 Chong and Hendry (1986) forecast encompassing test is based on a set of Ordinary Least Square regressions of the forecast error from one model on the forecast from the other model to obtain the estimated coefficient of forecast error of the other model which is an independent variable. If it is statistically significant, we can say that one model encompasses forecast of the other model.

model selection criteria like Akaike Information Criteria(AIC) and Swarz Baysian Criteria(SBC) to choose between the competing models. The study had not performed any diagnostic testing on ARCH models and their extension to test for the models' adequacy.

Basher, Hassan and Islam (2007) empirically examined the time-varying risk – return relationship within a GARCH-type framework, the persistence of shocks to volatility and the impact of institutional factors such as lock in period[49] and circuit breaker[50] on volatility for the emerging equity market of Bangladesh [namely The Dhaka Stock Exchange (DSE), Bangladesh using daily and weekly stock returns for the period beginning September 1, 1986 to January 30, 2002. The DSE equity returns showed negative skewness and excess kurtosis suggesting deviation from normality. The returns displayed significant serial correlation suggesting stock market inefficiency. For the daily returns, the measure of volatility persistence coefficient was greater than unity and statistically significant for the pre-liberalization samples implying nonstationarity of conditional variance due to the presence of serial correlation in the returns. However, for the post-financial liberalization period (January 1991 to January 2002), the sum of the ARCH and GARCH coefficient turned out to be less than unity and statistically significant at 1% level. In contrast, the sum of ARCH and GARCH coefficient always exceeded unity for weekly returns suggesting higher volatility associated with low frequency of the data. The results indicated that the tendency for a volatility response to shocks displayed a long memory. The impacts of introduction of lock-in and circuit breaker were examined by introducing dummy variables[51] in conditional variance equation. The results suggested that the lock-in did not have any significant impact on stock volatility, while circuit breakers reduced the volatility of both daily and weekly returns for both pre- and post-liberalization samples.

The literature review suggests that GARCH model and its extensions have been widely used to study nature and characteristics of volatility. The models have their application in modeling and forecasting volatility of stock markets. The literature review further suggests that symmetric GARCH model is appropriate to model stylized facts about volatility like volatility persistence and clustering. Asymmetric volatility response where volatility increases more following a market fall than following a rise in prices is

---

49 In order to curb inflation, the government of Bangladesh introduced the system of lock-in for primary securities on February 11, 1995. Under this lock-in provision, foreign investors are not allowed to trade in initial public offering for a year. However, this lock-in system was abolished on July 08, 1996 to encourage foreign investment in the equity market. Under this new rule, foreign investors do not face any lock-in period either for primary or secondary shares. However, the Bangladeshi sponsors face a 3-year lock-in period in sponsor's equity, while foreign investors do not face such a lock-in period.

50 After an index has fallen a certain percentage, the exchange might activate trading halts or restrictions on program trading. In 1996, Security exchange commission introduced circuit breaker system in Bangladesh to protect the interest of investor which controls abnormal and unusual price fluctuations.

51 A variable takes on value zero or one.

simple to capture in the asymmetric GARCH framework. Several alternative asymmetric GARCH specifications like TARCH or EGARCH have been developed which provides the best fit to capture successfully leverage or asymmetric effect in stock market. The review implies that GARCH-M model is useful in explaining risk-return relationship in stock market. GARCH-M is used to investigate whether higher conditional volatility causes higher return.

4.3 Studies on Transmission of return and volatility among different stock markets of the world

The growing international integration of financial markets has prompted several empirical studies to examine the mechanism through which stock market movements are transmitted around the world. These studies evaluate how stock returns in one national stock market influence the returns of other stock markets. These studies further examine their implications for pricing securities, for hedging, other trading strategies and for framing regulatory policies. These issues have been of heightened interests to all the participants in the stock markets in the wake of October 1987 international crash of stock markets that saw large correlated price movements across most of the stock markets of the world. It has lead to introduction of various regulations and institutional rules to dampen the cross-market impact of large stock movements.

The extent of the global linkage of emerging markets improves access to the international capital markets. Strong global linkage reduces the insulation of the emerging stock markets from external shocks, hence limiting the scope for independent monetary policy (Li and Majerowska, 2007). From the perspective of the global investors, weak stock market linkage in the form of less than perfect correlation between their returns offers potential gains from international portfolio diversification, while strong market linkage or co-movement in returns eliminates the potential benefits of diversification.

Although Indian economy is linked to the rest of the world through international trade and foreign direct investment, the question about the extent of global integration of the Indian stock markets still remains. Although stock market integration among developed countries has been widely studied for the developed markets, research on linkage of the emerging stock markets in Asia with developed markets is limited. Moreover, the limited literature on the emerging stock markets in Asia has studied the co-movements between the stock markets using cointegration.

Hilliard (1979) used spectral analysis[52] on daily data generated during the period July 7, 1973 to April 30, 1974 for stock indices in ten countries like Amsterdam, Paris, London, Milan, Frankfurt, New York, Sydney, Tokyo, Toronto, and Zurich to examine the structure and relationship between them. Using VAR analysis, the study suggested that correlations among returns of national stock markets were surprisingly low.

---

[52] The decomposition of time series into a set of sine-waves or cosine-waves with differing amplitudes, frequencies and phase angles is known as spectral analysis.

Eun and Shin (1989) found that national stock markets of USA, UK, Canada, Germany, Australia, France, Japan, Switzerland and Hongkong were interrelated. Using daily closing price data during the period January 1980 through December 1985, the study found that innovations in the U.S. stock market were rapidly transmitted to other markets whereas no single foreign market could significantly explain the U.S. market movements.

Over the past 40 years, stock market prices have been analyzed using different methods and data sets by investors and researchers with an objective to determine the forecastability of price changes. Chung and Ng (1992) have shown that developments in the U.S. market have significant influence on return of Tokyo stock market on the next day, but Tokyo stock market of Japan does not influence the returns of U.S. market. Given the U.S.'s dominant economic and political strength in the world market, this finding does not seem surprising. However, the recent leading role of other stock markets of the world and their interactive participation in the U.S. may possibly signal a reversal of the widely-held notion that the spillover stock market effect is solely from the U.S. to other stock markets.

Although there is no dearth of literature on financial integration, there are only a few studies related to India. Bhattacharya and Samantha (2001) investigated the extent to which news on NASDAQ helped price formation at the beginning and at the end of a trading day at the Indian bourses using daily data of stock price indices from January 3, 2000 to October 31, 2000. They analyzed the impact of NASDAQ on SENSEX through Ordinary Least Square (OLS) equations under cointegration and error correction framework[53]. The study showed that the news on NASDAQ had played an important role in price formation at the beginning of the new trading day at the Indian bourses. Thus, the study suggested the integration of the Indian capital market with the US market.

Wong, Agrawal and Du (2004) investigated the long-run equilibrium relationship and short-run dynamic linkage between the Indian stock market and the stock markets in major developed countries (United States, United Kingdom and Japan) after 1990 using the Granger causality and cointegration method. Using weekly closing prices data from January 1, 1991 to December 31, 2003, they found that Indian stock market was integrated with mature markets.

Compared to other emerging stock markets in Asia, the Indian stock market has been recognized as relatively less sensitive to changes of Asian and other developed markets of the world. Therefore, in spite of the fact that Indian stock market has largest number of listed companies, it has received little attention while undertaking studies on interconnectedness of world stock markets. Researchers have rarely included the Indian

---

[51] In Cointegration, a linear combination of two series, each of which is integrated of order one, is cointegrated of order zero. Error Correction Model is a time series model in first differences that contains an error correction term which works to bring two I(1)(the series that can be transformed into statationary by taking first difference) series back into long-run equilibrium.

Stock Market while studying the influence of the U.S. markets on Asian markets and interdependence among Asian stock markets (Ng, 2002). These researches are evidences that Indian stock market has not only received relatively less attention of scholars and researchers in the field of international finance but also the market is considered to be somewhat isolated from international markets.

Although there is a voluminous literature on equity market integration internationally, little research has been undertaken to study the interdependence structure of the Indian Capital Markets with the Asian stock markets and other stock markets of the world.

Ahmad, Ashraf and Ahmed (2005) examined the interlinkages and causal relationship between the Nasdaq composite index in the US, the Nikkei in Japan with that of NSE Nifty and BSE Sensex in India using daily closing data from January 1999 to August 2004. The study used Granger Causality and Johansen cointegration[54] methods to examine short run and long term relationship among the stock markets respectively. The results of Co-integration test revealed that there was no long-term relationship of the Indian equity market with that of the US and Japanese equity markets. Granger causality test suggested that there was a unidirectional relationship from Nasdaq and Nikkei to Indian stock markets.

Hoque (2007) explored the dynamics of stock price movements of an emerging market such as Bangladesh with that of USA, Japan and India using daily closing price data starting from January 1, 1990 to December 31, 2000. The indices used for Bangladesh, India, Japan and USA were Dhaka Stock Exchange(DSE) All Share Price Index, BSE30, Nikkei 225 and S&P500 respectively. They analyzed the long term relationships among the markets using the Johansen multivariate cointegration approach and short-term dynamics were captured through vector error correction models. Vector Auto Regression[55] was used to study the impact of shocks of these markets on own markets and other markets. The analysis showed that there was evidence of long term cointegration among the markets suggesting that stock prices in the countries share a common stochastic trend. Impulse response analysis shows that shocks to US market do have an impact on Bangladesh stock market. The response of Bangladesh stock market to shocks Indian stock market is weak. Shocks to Japanese stock market do not generate a response in the Bangladesh stock market.

Tan III (1998) examined the nature and extent of interactions between the set of Asian emerging markets consists of Indonesia, Malaysia, Philippines, Singapore, Thailand, Hong Kong, Korea and Taiwan using monthly stock price indices in US dollars from January 1991 to February 1978 obtained from Morgan Stanley Capital Integration Index.

---

54 It is applied when series are non stationary and integrated of the same order. The purpose of the test is to determine whether a group of non-stationary series is co-integrated or not.

55 A model for two or more time series where each variable is modeled as a linear function of past values of all variables plus disturbances that have zero means given all past values of the observed variables.

Johansen cointegration test revealed the existence of long term relationship between the stock markets. Using vector autoregression, the study found the presence of interactions among the stock markets.

Gilmore and McManus (2002) used the concept of Johansen cointegration to search for long term relationship between any pair of the three Central and Eastern European emerging markets such as Czech Republic, Hungary and Poland and the US market by using weekly data from 1995 to 2001. There was no evidence of long term relationship between the emerging markets and the US market as per the study.

Voronkova (2004) implemented Gregory and Hansen residual based co-integration test which allows for structural break in cointegration series. The model was applied to data set comprising three emerging Central European stock markets (CE) namely Czech Republic, Poland and Hungary, three developed European stock markets (Britain, France, and Germany), and the United States during the period September 1993–April 2002. The study found long term equilibrium relationship between the emerging CE markets and matured markets of Europe and USA. Furthermore, the results showed that long-run relations did not cease after a structural change has occurred. Voronkova found that the emerging markets had become increasingly integrated with the world stock markets. The use of different technique to account for structural change may yield results different from the findings of Gilmore and Mcmanus(2002).

Cheeley and Steeley (2005) applied Vector autoregression to four Eastern European stock markets namely Hungary, Poland, the Czech Republic and Russia and five mature markets of the world such as Germany, France, Japan, UK and US using daily closing price value during the period July 1994 until December 1999. The results suggested interactions between the four emerging European stock markets and five developed stock markets. The study modeled a system of bivariate equity market correlations as a smooth transition logistic trend model[56] in order to establish how rapidly the countries of Eastern Europe were integrated with developed stock markets. The results indicated that Hungary was the most quickly integrated with the other stock markets.

Yang and Wang (2006) used Johansen cointegration analysis and Vector Autoregression to estimate the linkages across the stock markets in the US, Germany and four Eastern European countries (Russia, Poland, Hungary and the Czech Republic) using daily closing price during January 2, 1995 to June 28, 2002 – a total of 1955 daily

---

56 Smooth transition analysis is an approach to modeling deterministic structural change in a time series regression. These models aim to identify any change as a single structural break, denoting it as a smooth transition between regimes over time. It can be applied to a system of bivariate monthly return correlations to identify the speed of market integration in each country. The advantage of logistic trend models is that they can indicate the speed at which a market is becoming integrated, information which cannot be reliably attained from more conventional tests of market integration such as correlation analysis or variance decomposition analysis. An assumption of the smooth transition trend function is that it assumes market integration takes place as a gradual process

observations for each series. The sample period was divided into the pre- and post-crisis periods to address the potential impact of the 1998 Russian financial crisis on Eastern European stock market integration. They found that the linkages were strengthened in the period of 1999-2002 compared with the period before the Russian crisis. VAR analysis found the noticeable influence of USA stock market on all the stock markets only after the crisis but not before the crisis. The results showed that USA also responded significantly to the shocks from Russia only after the Russian crisis.

The above studies do not take into account the interactions in terms of volatility among the markets. It is believed that if markets are integrated, an unanticipated event in one market will influence not only returns but also variance in the other market. The analysis of volatility is particularly important because it can proxy for the risk of assets. Scheicher(2001) studied the regional and global integration of stock markets in terms of return and volatility shocks in Hungary, Poland and Czech Republic and Financial Times/ S&P's world actuaries index by using MGARCH(Multivariate Generalized Auto regressive conditional heteroscedasticity) with a constant conditional correlation and Vector autoregression framework. Using daily closing price values of the stock markets from January 1, 1995 to October 7, 1997, results revealed that the emerging stock exchanges were integrated with the global market, proxied by Financial Times/S&P's actuaries' world index only in terms of return. MGARCH results showed that the regional influences were the major cause of volatility of the markets. International volatility had no impact on the markets. The Czech market volatility spilt over into Poland and Hungary stock market volatility influenced the Czech market volatility. The results of VAR indicated that the shocks in return measured by impulse response analysis persisted for very limited period of time among the stock market i.e. four days. The response to shocks was found to be quite small. Granger causality test was also performed on the returns of the stock markets. The results suggested that Prague (Stock market of Czech Republic) influences Warsaw (Stock market of Poland) of Poland, Budapest stock market of Hungary influenced both Prague and Warsaw while Financial Times/S&P's world actuaries had an impact in all three countries. Here, the study assumed constant conditional correlations of the stock markets. The assumption of constant conditional correlation is unrealistic. Kaplanis(1988) and Longin and Solnik (1995) were of the opinion that changes in the correlation between markets could be explained by changes in the conditional covariance.

Chou, Lin and Wu (1999) examined the price and volatility linkages of Taiwan stock market with United States using close-to-open, open-to-close and close-to-close returns of indices of Taiwan known as Taikex and United states' Standard and Poor's 500 (S&P 500) composite index during January 1, 1991 to December 31, 1994. The study tested the hypothesis of volatility and price changes spilt over from developed markets mainly United States to the emerging domestic Taiwan stock market using two stage estimation method and simultaneous MGARCH model. In two stage estimation method, firstly, the study used GARCH (1, 1)-MA (1) model for both domestic and foreign market. In second step, it further introduced the most recent foreign return in the mean equation of the domestic market return and the most recent foreign square residuals in the variance equation to examine the effect of foreign return and volatility on Taiex return and volatility. The results found that the volatility and return spilt over from US to Taiwan. However, the method suffered from the drawback of the generated regressor problem formalized by Pagan (1987). More specifically, in the second regression, the generated squared residual contained a measurement error and conventional estimate of the standard deviation was understated, which made the t-test invalid. The results of MGARCH indicated some important linkage from the US stock market to the Taiwan stock market. The spillover effects occurred for both the mean and the variance of Taiwan Stock returns. The spillover effect was significant for the model using Taiwan close-to-open returns. It further pointed out that the US induced volatility amounts to about twelve percent of the total daily volatilities of the Taiwan stock market.

Karolyi (1995) examined the short run dynamics of returns and volatilities for stocks traded on the New York Stock Exchange (NYSE) and Toronto stock exchange (TSE) of Canada by applying multivariate GARCH and Vector autoregression models in time series of daily stock market indices at the close of markets in terms of local currency for S&P 500 and TSE 300 during April 1, 1987 to December 29, 1989. Results of MGARCH indicated the return and volatility spillovers from S&P 500 to TSE 300. The effects of shocks of return and volatility from NYSE to TSE measured by MGARCH were smaller and less persistent. The study showed that the effects of S&P 500 returns shocks on Canadian stocks have dissipated over the decade of 1980s. The study found that the impact of S&P 500 stock-return innovations on portfolios of interlisted versus noninterlisted TSE 300 stocks was significantly different. The magnitude and persistence of S&P 500 shocks are greater for returns on non-interlisted stocks. This evidence suggested that investment barriers faced by US traders interested in Canadian stocks-due to differences in disclosure requirements in accounting standards, restrictions on ownership of foreign securities or perhaps the tax considerations may be important for understanding the dynamics of comovements in stock prices around the world.

Harris and Pisedtasalasai (2006) applied constant conditional correlation MGARCH framework to investigate return and volatility spillover effects between the Financial Times Stock Exchange (FTSE)100, FTSE 200 and FTSE small cap equity indices of UK stock market using daily return during January 1, 1986 to December 2002. They employed GJR specifications of MGARCH model to capture asymmetric effect. The study summarized that there were significant spillover effects in both returns and volatility between FTSE 100, FTSE 250 and FTSE small cap indices. These spillover effects were highly asymmetric. There were significant positive spillover effects in returns from the FTSE 100 index to the FTSE 250 and FTSE small cap indices. There was a marginally significant positive return spillover effects from the FTSE 250 index to the FTSE Small Cap index. There were no significant return spillover effects from the portfolios of smaller stock to the portfolios of larger stocks. For conditional volatility, the study found that there were significant spillover effects from the FTSE 100 index to both FTSE 250 index and the FTSE small cap index and from the FTSE 250 index to the FTSE small cap index. The study found that there was evidence of feedback in volatility from smaller stocks to larger stocks with a significant negative spillover between the FTSE 250 index and the FTSE 100 index, implying that an increase in the volatility of the FTSE 250 index was associated with decrease in the volatility of the FTSE 100 index. The findings showed that there was a positive spillover in volatility from the FTSE Small cap index to the FTSE 100 index and a significant positive spillover from the FTSE small cap index to the FTSE 250 index. The assumption of conditional correlation is unrealistic.

Worthington and Higgs (2004) examined the transmission of equity returns and volatility among three developed Asian markets (Hong Kong, Japan and Singapore) and six emerging markets of Asia (Indonesia, Korea, Malaysia, the Philippines, Taiwan and Thailand) using weekly returns from January 15, 1988 to October 6, 2000. They employed BEKK (Baba, Engle, Kraft and Kroner) parameterization of multivariate GARCH model to identify the source and magnitude of volatility spillover. The results indicated that all Asian equity markets were highly integrated. The study found the presence of positive mean and volatility spillovers. The mean return spillovers from the developed markets to the emerging markets were not homogenous across the emerging markets. Korea and Indonesia exhibited significant mean spillovers from Japan and Thailand exhibited spillover from Hong Kong and Singapore. Application of MGARCH suggested that own stock market volatility spillovers were generally higher than cross-volatility spillovers for all markets, especially for emerging stock markets. This would suggest that the changes in volatility in emerging markets from domestic conditions were relatively more important than the effects of volatility of developed markets.

Li (2007) examined the linkages between the two emerging stock exchanges namely Shanghai and Shenzen of China and the established stock markets Heng Seng of Hong Kong and S & P of the US by a multivariate GARCH approach. The study employed four variable MGARCH model in the line of BEKK model. Using the daily share price indices of the stock markets, the study tested for the return and volatility spillover across the markets from January 4, 2000 to August 17, 2005. The results indicated that there was no evidence of spillover effect in terms of return and volatility between the stock exchanges in China and US market. There was an evidence of unidirectional volatility spillover from stock exchange in Hong Kong to those in Shanghai and Shenzhen. The study found that Chinese stock exchanges were integrated with the regional developed stock exchange in Hong Kong but the extent of the linkages between the stock exchange in Hong Kong and China was weak. The results further showed that there was a bidirectional shock spillover between the two Chinese stock exchanges. The study also found that there was an asymmetric response of volatility in all four stock exchanges under study.

4.4 Research Gaps

In the light of the above review of the literatures, the following research gaps in the existing literature are identified.

(1) Studies focusing on factors affecting volatility employ ordinary least square methods of regression analysis to examine the effects of various factors on stock market volatility. The variance of the error term is assumed to be constant i.e. homoscedastic for using OLS. Studies on econometric modeling of stock market return series show that the series is heteroscedastic. In the presence of heteroscedasticity, the regression coefficients for an ordinary least squares regression are still unbiased, but the standard errors and confidence intervals estimated by conventional procedures will be too narrow, giving false sense of precision. Instead of correcting for heteroscedasticity, ARCH and GARCH models treat heteroscedasticity as a variance to be modeled. As a result not only the deficiencies of Ordinary Least Squares are corrected, but a prediction is computed for the variance of each error term (Engle, 2001). It has been also suggested that ARCH and GARCH classes of models capture appropriately the stylized facts about return and volatility like mean reverting and leptokurtic return, volatility clustering and its persistence (Engle, 1982, Bollerslev, 1986, Akgiray, 1989, Nelson, 1991 and Zakoian, 1992).

(2) Although there is a plethora of research concerning stock market volatility, most of the studies have been undertaken in stock markets of the developed world. A few studies on econometric modeling have been carried out on the Indian stock market. Most of the studies conducted in India have dealt only with the benchmark indices like either BSE (Sensex) or NSE (Nifty). BSE index is widely used for study of volatility. With the growing popularity of NSE, due to its transparent trading mechanism and lower trading cost, the Nifty is considered to be an important and broad based market index. The study using the recent data to analyze the volatility of Indian stock markets are not found. No study has undertaken comparative estimation of volatility models in both the stock markets of India. Effort to model volatility in both the stock markets of India can provide an insight into the nature and characteristics of volatility in the stock markets.

(3) ARCH and GARCH classes of models are useful in modeling time varying volatility of stock markets. They have been developed for most of the developed markets. But their application to the Indian stock markets has not been explored fully with the help of various kinds of asymmetric ARCH and GARCH models namely EGARCH and TARCH.

(4) Majority of the studies related to Econometric modeling of volatility in India have not taken into account various asymmetric GARCH models to capture leverage effect.

(5) Some studies on econometric modeling of volatility have not considered model selection criteria like Akaike Information Criteria (AIC) and Schwarz Bayesian Criteria(SBC) to choose between the competing models. Some studies have not applied the criteria to choose the best fitting model. Some of the studies have not performed any diagnostic testing on ARCH models and their extensions to test for model adequacy. Engle (1982), Enders (1995), Brooks(2008) and Tsay(2005) recommended to use these model selection criteria and diagnostics tests namely ARCH LM for model adequacy. The results are likely to be misleading if these aspects are not taken care of.

(6) Although global stock market linkages have been widely studied for developed markets and some emerging markets in Asia and South America, research on linkages of Indian stock exchanges is limited. The literature on the integration of the emerging markets is carried out in the line of co-integration testing for returns of stock markets. The studies do not take into account interactions in terms of volatility. Engle and Kroner (1995) argued that the unanticipated events in one market influence not only return but also variance of the other markets.

(7) Multivariate GARCH model as proposed by Engle and Kroner (1995) is considered to be an appropriate model to study return and volatility spillover effects among the various stock markets. There are three variants of Multivariate GARCH models: (a) constant conditional correlation (b) Diagonal VECH (c) Diagonal BEKK specifications. Few studies used multivariate GARCH with a constant conditional correlation. The assumptions of constant conditional correlations are unrealistic. Longin and Solnik(1995) and Bekaert and Harvey(1995) have found that the correlations are time varying and the changes in the correlations between markets can be explained by changes in the conditional covariance. Thus, the assumptions of constant conditional correlations do not give meaningful results.

Bollerslev et al. (1988) proposed VECH Multivariate GARCH. Few studies employed this form of MGARCH. The problems with this formulation are that the number of parameters to be estimated is large and restrictions on the parameters are needed to ensure that the conditional variance matrix is positive. Engle and Kroner (1995) proposed new parametrization of conditional variance matrix known as BEKK Multivariate GARCH model to overcome the problems associated with VECH Multivariate GARCH.

(8) Some studies on return and volatility spillover suffer from the drawback of the generated regressor problem formalized by Pagan (1984). It indicates that the generalized squared residual contains a measurement error and the conventional estimate of the standard deviation is understated which makes the t-test invalid. The simultaneous equations method of multivariate GARCH-BEKK overcomes the problem by pooling all equations together and applying the maximum-likelihood method to jointly estimate the parameters in the equation. Thus, the

resulting information matrix and covariance matrix of the estimated parameters are consistently estimated. The resulting tests on parameters are valid and the generated regressor problem does not arise here. (Chou, Lin and Wu, 1999).

(9) Very few studies have used Multivariate GARCH model incorporating asymmetric responses of volatility, i.e., stock volatility tends to rise more in response to negative shocks (bad news) than positive shocks (good news).

The present study attempts to fill the voids by:

(1) Investigating nature and characteristics of Volatility.

(2) Modeling volatility of BSE Sensex and S&P CNX Nifty of India using ARCH, GARCH, EGARCH, TARCH and ARCH-M models.

(3) Examining stock return and volatility spillover effects between India and developed and developing stock markets namely S&P500 of USA, Hang Seng of Hong Kong and Shanghai of China using MGARCH-BEKK model.

4.5 Outline of the Study

The principal objective of this study is to model the volatility of Indian stock markets. The study also attempts to examine the interactions of Indian stock markets with world stock markets and analyze the return and volatility spillover effects across different stock markets of the world.

4.6 Objectives

The study aims at examining following:

(1) To investigate the nature and pattern of volatility of Indian stock markets namely S&P CNX nifty of NSE and BSE Sensex.

(2) To model the volatility of Indian Stock markets with ARCH, GARCH, EGARCH, TARCH and ARCH-M models.

(3) To examine the interactions of Indian Stock markets with world stock markets using Vector Autoregression.

(4) To analyze the return and volatility spillover effects among the stock markets of the world with MGARCH-BEKK model.

4.7 Period of study

The study uses data on daily closing price of BSE and S&P CNX Nifty indices of India, Shanghai Stock exchange of China, Hang Seng of Hong Kong and Standard and Poor (S&P) 500 of United States from 1st January 2000 to 3rd July, 2008. We drop the data when any series has a missing value due to no trading. Thus all data are collected on the same dates across the stock exchanges and there are 2112 observations for each series. The period is most recent and many changes took place during the period like introduction of rolling settlement, transactions in futures and options, the bull run and the highs in the indices, increased FII inflows across the world stock markets, gradual lifting of restrictions on capital flows and relaxation of exchange controls in many countries etc. These changes might have influenced the pattern of returns and volatilities of stock markets under study. It will be instructive to study volatility during this period.

4.8 The Sample

The indices used in this study are widely accepted bench mark indices for four stock markets. The Indian Stock Market is represented by the two most popular indices namely, Bombay Stock Exchange (BSE)'s Sensex and National Stock Exchange (NSE)'s S & P CNX Nifty. The first index launched by BSE was the BSE sensitivity Index (Sensex) in 1986. The BSE Sensex of equity share prices was launched with the base year of 1978-79 with a base value of 100. It comprises of 30 companies from "Specified" and "Non-specified"[57] groups. The companies have been selected so as to represent all major sectors of the economy. They are selected on the basis of market capitalization, volume of turnover and strength of the companies' fundamentals. Since then, in the last 15 years, it has offered 21 indices including 12 sectoral indices. The other popular index is Nifty of National Stock Exchange (NSE). The NSE was incorporated in November 1992. The Nifty was launched on 3rd November, 1995 with a base value of 1000. It consists of 50 stocks listed on two criteria namely market capitalization and liquidity. NSE has 23 indices.

The Shanghai composite index captures the price movement of all the shares listed on the Shanghai Stock Exchange (SSE). It is the largest in mainland China and fifth largest stock exchange in the world with more than 900 stocks listed on it. It is included in the study because China is fastest developing economy in Asia followed by India. It is insightful to study the interactions of the stock markets. For stock exchange of Hong Kong, we use Hang Seng index which includes the 33 largest firms in Hong Kong and represents about 75% of the total equity capitalization for all the Stock Exchanges of

---

57 Specified group companies typically have a large capital base with widespread shareholding, a steady dividend, good growth record and a large volume of business in the secondary market. "A group" or "specified" securities have weekly settlement and "carry forward" is allowed in their case. Contracts in this group are allowed to be carried over to subsequent settlements upto a maximum permissible period of 75 days. Non-specified group has been split into B1 group and B2 group securities. B1 group has weekly settlement but the carry-forward is not allowed in its case; it includes actively traded securities. B2 group is subject to settlement procedure.

Hong Kong. The inclusion of Hong Kong is due to the fact that Hong Kong is regarded as one of the mature financial centres in Asia and plays an important role in the regional economy of the southeastern Asia. BSE and NSE of India, SSE of China and Hong Kong stock exchanges of Asia are among the twenty major stock exchanges of the world (World Federation of Exchanges, 2008). The S&P 500 index tracks 500 companies in leading industries and services and is considered to be the most accurate reflection of the US stock market today. The S&P index is included to represent the global financial centre. The inclusion of the Hang Seng, SSE and S&P 500 indices, therefore, helps to investigate the integration of the Indian stock markets with developed and developing regional and global stock markets.

4.9 Sources of Data

The study uses secondary data. Secondary data are usually available in published form-printed or electronic (CD or Internet). These data are already collected by some agency or research organization. The stock price data used in the study have been collected from www.bseindia.com, www.nseindia.com, http://finance.yahoo.com/intlindices and CMIE prowess online data base.

4.10 Methodology

Daily returns are identified as the first difference in the natural logarithm of the closing index value for the two consecutive trading days for the five indices. It can be represented as:

$$R_t = \log (P_t/P_{t-1}) \text{ or } R_t = \log (P_t)-\log(P_{t-1})$$

Equation 4-1

Where Rt is logarithmic daily return at time t. Pt-1 and Pt are daily prices of an asset at two successive days, t-1 and t respectively.

Volatility is defined as;

$$\sigma = \sqrt{\frac{1}{n-1}\sum_{t=1}^{n}(R_t - \overline{R})^2}$$

Equation 4-2

where $\bar{R}$ = Average return in the sample.

In order to do time series analysis, transformation of original series is required depending upon the type of series when the data is in the level form. We have transformed the series of return by taking natural logarithm of the series. Some scholars (Bollerslev, 1986; Schewert, 1989; Engle and Patton, 2001; Harvinder Kaur, 2002; M.Karmakar, 2005) have pointed out two advantages of this kind of transformation of the series. First, it eliminates the possible dependence of changes in stock price index on the price level of the index. Second, the change in the log of the stock price index yields continuously compounded series.

The study models volatility using ARCH classes of models. The theoretical discussions about the models have been provided in section 2.4 of chapter 2. The chapter has also covered discussion on Multivariate GARCH which is used to examine return and volatility spillover effects. The interactions between the world stock markets can be studied with the help of Vector Autoregression (VAR) model. The VAR model requires variables to be examined should be stationary. VAR model is discussed in the ensuing section followed by the discussion on unit root test.

4.10.1 Vector Auto-Regression (VAR) Model

In order to examine the dynamic interrelationships among world stock indices, the present study estimates five-market Vector-Autoregressive (VAR) system using daily rate of return on the stock market indices from the period January 3, 2000 to July 3, 2008 consisting of 2112 observations. The VAR model contains simultaneous equations in which all the variables are considered to be endogenous. However, each endogenous variable is explained by its lagged or past values and the lagged values of the other endogenous variables included in the system. The VAR model estimated in the presented study is as follows:

$$R_t = C + \sum_{s=1}^{P} {}_{s}R_{t-5} + \varepsilon_t$$

Equation 4-3

Where R_t is the mX1 (m=5) column vector of the jointly determined rates of return of the five stock markets, and C is an mx1 vector of constants; φ_s are mxm coefficients matrices of returns of the stock markets and P is the lag length, and ε_t is n×1 column vector of forecast errors of of R_t using all past R_{t-s}. By construction ε_t is serially uncorrelated, however the components of ε_t may be contemporaneously correlated.

That is, E(ε_t)=0, E($\varepsilon_t\varepsilon_{t-s}'$)=0 for all s#0 and E($\varepsilon_t\varepsilon_t'$)=$\Omega$ for all t, where Ω={ $\sigma_{ij}, i, j = 1,2,....,m$ } is an mxm positive definite matrix. The i, jth component of φ_s measures the direct effect that a change in the return to the jth market would have on the ith market in s periods.

Autoregressive system such as Equation (4.3), especially the coefficients of the regression equations containing complicated cross-equation feedbacks are difficult to describe intuitively. As shown by Sims (1980), it is better to analyze system's reaction to random shock by tracing out system's moving average representation. By successive substituting on the right-hand side of Equation (4.3), we can obtain a moving average representation as follows:

$$R_t = \mu + \sum_{s=0}^{\infty} A_s \varepsilon_{t-s}$$

Equation 4-4

It represents R_t as a linear combination of current and past one-step-ahead forecast errors or "innovations." The i, jth components of A_s shows the response of the ith market in s periods after a unit random shock in the jth market and none in other markets.

As impulse response function measures the time profile of the effect of shock at t on the expected future values of the variables in a dynamic system. Since the component of ε_t is contemporaneously correlated, it is necessary to transform ε_t for the purpose of observing distinct response patterns. The traditional approach (Sim, 1980) uses the Cholesky decomposition of Ω. To achieve this, we choose V be mxm lower triangular matrix, VV'= Ω then equation 5.4 can be rewritten as:

$$R_t = \mu + \sum_{s=0}^{\infty} B_s \varepsilon_{t-s}$$

Equation 4-5

Where $B_s = A_s$ V. Then the i, jth component of the A_s represents the impulse response of the ith market in s periods to a shock of one standard error in the jth market. $\xi_{t-5} = V^{-1}\varepsilon_{t-5}$ is an orthogonalized innovation and the transformed innovations has identity matrix. The advantage of using orthogonalized innovation is that we can also allocate the variance of each element in R to sources in elements of ξ, since ξ is serially and contemporaneously uncorrelated. The orthogonalization provides the quantity which is the component of the forecast error variance in the T+1 step ahead forecast of R_i, $\sum_{s-0}^{T} B_1^2(s)$ which is accounted for innovations in R_j. This decomposition of forecast variance provides a measure of the overall relative importance of the markets in generating the fluctuations in stock returns in their own and other markets.

The VAR model involves certain steps for estimation. The first step is to choose a proper ordering of the variables in the model. Scheicher (2001), Wirthington and Higgs (2004) and Li and Majerowska(2007) suggested ordering of variables on the basis of closing time of the stock exchanges. They further pointed out to use market capitalization to decide the order when closing hours of stock exchanges are same. Since we analyze the close-to-close changes in the market indices, we analyze the markets ordered by their respective closing times. The market which closes earliest is ordered first in the VAR equation. When closing hours are same, market capitalization serves the basis for the ordering in the VAR of the mean equation. The closing time of NSE and BSE are same. We, therefore, consider market capitalization of the two stock exchanges to decide their ordering. The market capitalization of BSE and NSE are Rs. 35,45,041crore and Rs. 33,67,350 crore respectively (Annual Report, SEBI, 20006-07). The market capitalization of BSE is higher than NSE. We, therefore, place BSE before NSE in ordering of the variables in VAR. The study chooses the order of the variables as S&P500, China, Hong Kong, and India. The second step is to verify the stationarity of variables. The VAR model assumes that all variables should be stationary. In this context, the present study uses Augmented Dickey Fuller (ADF) unit root test to verify whether the variables possess unit root or not. The third step is to fix the lag-length of variables in the system through Akaike Information Criteria (AIC) and Schwarz Bayesian Criteria (SBC). It is then further tested for residual autocorrelations using Portmanteau test to judge the adequacy of the selected model. It is imperative to note that the coefficients obtained from the VAR regression cannot be interpreted directly. Hence, the present study uses Innovation Accounting Techniques, which contains both impulse response functions and variance decomposition. The impulse response functions trace out the dynamic responses of the endogenous variables to one standard deviation innovation in each of the variables in the system. On the other hand, variance decomposition shows the extent to which a variable is explained by the innovations or shocks in all the variables in the system.

4.10.2 Unit root Test

A unit root test is a statistical test for the proposition that in a autoregressive statistical model of a time series, the autoregressive parameter is one. It is a test for detecting the presence of stationarity in the series. The early and pioneering work on testing for a unit root in time series was done by Dickey and Fuller (Dickey and Fuller, 1979 & 1981). If the variables in the regression model are not stationary, then it can be shown that the standard assumptions for asymptotic analysis will not be valid. In other words, the usual "t-ratios" will not follow a t-distribution; hence they are inappropriate to undertake hypothesis tests about the regression parameters.

Stationarity time series is one whose mean, variance and covariance are unchanged by time shift. Nonstationary time series have time varying mean or variance or both. If a time series is nonstationary, we can study its behaviour only for a time period under consideration. It is not possible to generalize it to other time periods. It is, therefore, not useful for forecasting purpose.

The presence of unit root in a time series is tested with the help of Augmented Dickey-Fuller Test. It tests for a unit root in the univariate representation of time series. For a return series R_t, the ADF test consists of a regression of the first difference of the series against the series lagged k times as follows:

$$\Delta_{r_t} = \alpha + \delta_{r_{t-1}} + \sum_{i=1}^{p} \beta_i \Delta r_{t-1} + \varepsilon_t$$

Equation 4-6

$$\Delta r_t = r_t - r_{t-1}; r_t = \ln(R_t)$$

The null hypothesis is H0: $\delta = 0$ and H1: $\delta < 1$. The acceptance of null hypothesis implies nonstationarity.

We can transform the nonstationary time series to stationary time series either by differencing or by detrending. The transformation depends upon whether the series are difference stationary or trend stationary.

4.11 Summary

The study aims at modeling volatility of Indian stock market, its integration and spillover effects among world stock markets. It uses secondary data to analyze the volatility of the stock markets. It uses widely accepted bench mark indices for four stock markets of India, China, Hong Kong and USA. The time series of the daily stock return has been estimated by using ARCH (Autoregressive Conditional Heteroscedasticity) and Generalized ARCH (GARCH) class of models. Vector Autoregression (VAR) model has been used to examine the interrelationships between the stock markets. Multivariate GARCH (MGARCH) model has been employed to analyze the return and volatility spillover effects between the stock markets.

***

5 CHAPTER

Stock Market Volatility: Empirical Investigations

Volatility is one of the important aspects of financial asset return. It represents underlying variability of the financial asset return that investors are interested in measuring for investment risk. Since risk and return have a crucial role in financial economics, volatility of return has been increasingly studied with theoretical and practical implications.

Variability of asset returns that exhibits a serial dependence is referred to as a volatility clustering, which is one of the striking phenomena in financial market. Volatility clustering phenomenon is first documented by Mandlebrot (1963) and implies that large price (or return) changes are followed by other large changes in either signs and small change are followed by other small changes. This tendency in price (or return) creates temporal dependence in variability of asset returns, hence time varying volatility. The observation of volatility clustering in financial markets has necessitated the development of new econometrics time series techniques that allow for the modeling of time varying variability of asset returns.

The study proposes the ARCH and GARCH classes of model in Indian stock markets. It also studies the interactions between the stock market of the world. It tries to examine the return and volatility spillover effects among the stock markets.

The chapter is divided into three parts. The first part (section 5.1) investigates nature and characteristics of volatility of Indian stock markets. It also tries to estimate and model the volatility of Indian stock markets using ARCH and GARCH classes of models. The second part (section 5.2) analyses interaction between some of the world stock markets using Vector Autoregression (VAR) model. The third part (section 5.3) discusses return and volatility spillover effects between the stock markets.

5.1 Modeling Volatility of Indian Stock Markets

This section discusses the results of modeling volatility of Indian stock markets. Section 5.1.1 presents statistical analysis, diagnostic tests and descriptive statistics of the stock markets. Section 5.1.2 discusses the results of unit root test. Section 5.1.3 estimates model for stock return and volatility. Section 5.1.4 discusses the results of empirical investigations. Section 5.1.5 summarizes.

5.1.1 Statistical Analysis, Diagnostic tests and Descriptive Statistics

The econometric package EViews 6 is used to test various statistical properties of stock return and volatility and to estimate various ARCH and GARCH class of models.

Figure 5-1 Daily Returns on BSE Sensex (January 2000-July, 2008)

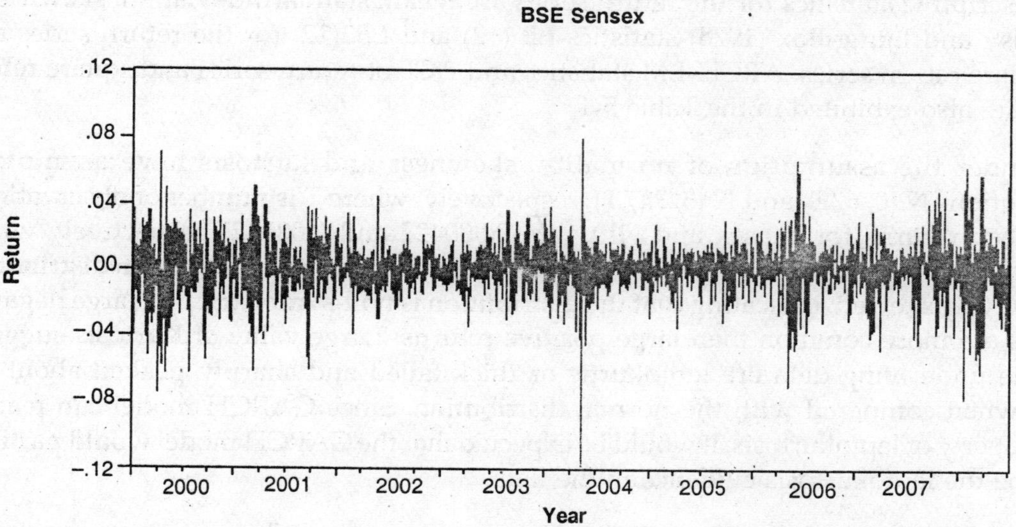

Figure 5 -2 Daily Returns on S&P CNX Nifty (January 2000-July, 2008)

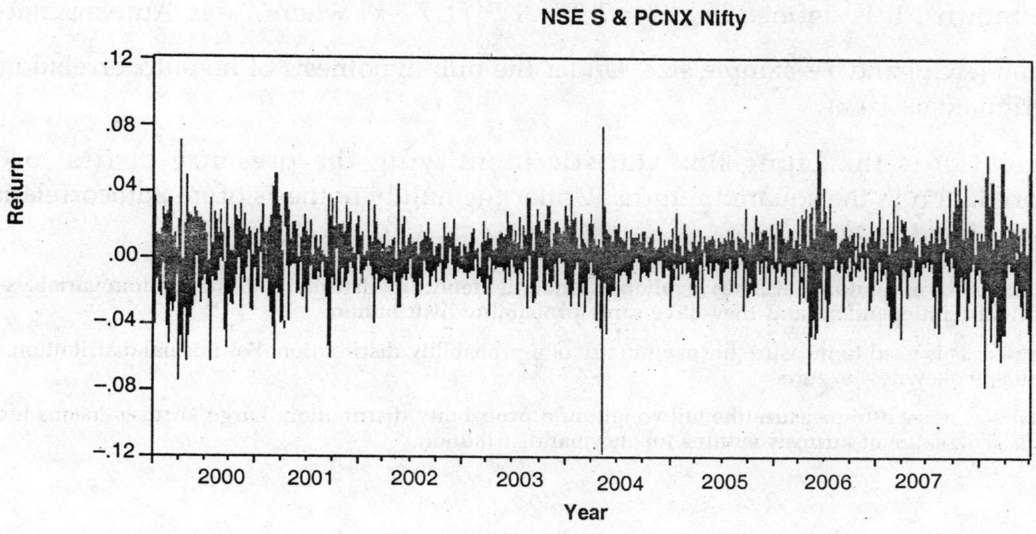

For diagnostics checking, visual inspection of the plots of daily return series of Sensex and Nifty shown in Figure 5-1 and Figure 5-2 respectively will be very useful. It can be seen from Figure 5-1 and 5-2 that returns fluctuate around mean value that is close to zero. Volatility is high for certain time periods and low for other periods. The movements are in the positive and negative territory and larger fluctuations tends to cluster together separated by periods of relative calm. Thus, the above graphs exhibit volatility clustering where large returns tend to be followed by large returns and small returns tend to be followed by small returns leading to contiguous periods of volatility and stability. Statistically, volatility clustering implies a strong autocorrelation in squared returns.

Descriptive statistics on BSE Sensex and S & P CNX Nifty are presented in Table 5-1. It contains the number of return observations for the stock index and statistics, testing the null hypothesis of independence and identically distributed[58] normal variates. The descriptive statistics for the return series are mean, standard deviation, skewness[59], kurtosis[60] and Ljung-Box (1978) statistics-LB (12) and LB2(12) for the return series and the square return series. ARCH-LM statistics and ACF of return series and square return series are also exhibited in the Table 5-1.

Under the assumption of normality, skewness and kurtosis have asymptotic distributions N (0, 6/T) and N (3, 24/T), respectively, where T is number of observations. The mean returns for Sensex and Nifty are 0.000422 and 0.000427 respectively which are very close to zero indicating that the series are mean reverting. The return distribution is negatively skewed, indicating that the distribution is non-symmetric and large negative returns are more common than large positive returns. Large value of Kurtosis suggests that the underlying data are leptokurtic or thick tailed and sharply peaked about the mean when compared with the normal distribution. Since GARCH model can feature this property of leptokurtosis, it would be expected that the GARCH model would partially describe the leptokurtosis evidence in the data.

a. Q(k) is the Ljung Box statistic identifying the presence of first order autocorrelation in the returns. It is defined as, $LB = T(T+2)\sum_{k-1}^{k}\left(\hat{p}_k^2/T-k\right)$ where $\hat{\rho}_k^2$ is Autocorrelation Function (ACF) and T= sample size. Under the null hypothesis of no autocorrelation, it is distributed as $\lambda^2(k)$.

b. $Q^2(K)$ is the Ljung Box statistic identifying the presence of first order autocorrelation in the squared returns. Under the null hypothesis of no autocorrelation, it is distributed as $\lambda^2(k)$.

58 A sequence of random variables is independent and identically distributed if the random variables are mutually independent and they have same probability distribution.

59 Skewness is used to measure the asymmetry of a probability distribution. For normal distribution, the value of skewness is zero.

60 Kurtosis is used to measure the tail weight of a probability distribution. Large kurtosis means heavy tails. The value of kurtosis is three for normal distribution.

c. ARCH LM statistic is the Lagrange multiplier test statistic for the presence of ARCH effect. Under null hypothesis of no heteroscedasticity, it is distributed as . Critical value of at 1 per cent level of significance is 6.63 at 1 degree of freedom. Values for higher lags are also significant.

d. ACF is auto correlation function. ACF at lag k, denoted by is defined as = covariance at lag k/variance. The plot of against k is known as sample correlogram. Partial autocorrelation (PACF) measures correlation between time series observations Y_t and Y_{t-k} after removing the effect of the intermediate Y's.

Table 5-1 Descriptive Statistics of Daily Data

Statistic	Sensex	Nifty
Observation period	1st January 2000-3rd July 2008	1st January 2000-3rd July 2008
Number of observations	2111	2111
Mean	0.000422	0.000427
Standard deviation	0.01608	0.01607
Skewness	-0.5968	-0.6611
Kurtosis	6.7012	7.7056
Jarque-Bera Statistics	1329.97(2-tailed p=.000)	2101.45(2-tailed p=.000)
Q(1)[a]	9.57 (2-tailed p=.002)	11.75 (2-tailed p=.000)
$Q^2(1)$[b]	273.47 (2-tailed p=.000)	355.19 (2-tailed p=.000)
Q(12)	31.87 (2-tailed p=.001)	37.38 (2-tailed p=.000)
$Q^2(12)$	654.92 (2-tailed p=.000)	669.66 (2-tailed p=.000)
ARCH LM statistics[c] (at Lag =1)	287.63 (2-tailed p=.000)	373.18 (2-tailed p=.000)
ACF[d] at lag =1 for returns	0.064 (Asymptotic Bound=0.044)	0.075(Asymptotic Bound=0.044)
ACF at lag=1 for squared returns	0.360 (Asymptotic Bound=0.044)	0.410 (Asymptotic Bound=0.044)

Notes

a. Q(k) is the Ljung Box statistic identifying the presence of first order autocorrelation in the returns. It is defined as, $LB = T(T+2)\sum_{k-1}^{k}\left(\hat{p}_k^2/T-k\right)$ where

$\hat{\rho}_k^2$ is Autocorrelation Function (ACF) and T= sample size. Under the null hypothesis of no autocorrelation, it is distributed as $\lambda^2(k)$.

b. $Q^2(K)$ is the Ljung Box statistic identifying the presence of first order autocorrelation in the squared returns. Under the null hypothesis of no autocorrelation, it is distributed as $\lambda^2(k)$.

c. ARCH LM statistic is the Lagrange multiplier test statistic for the presence of ARCH effect. Under null hypothesis of no heteroscedasticity, it is distributed as . Critical value of at 1 per cent level of significance is 6.63 at 1 degree of freedom. Values for higher lags are also significant.

d. ACF is auto correlation function. ACF at lag k, denoted by is defined as = covariance at lag k/variance. The plot of against k is known as sample correlogram. Partial autocorrelation (PACF) measures correlation between time series observations Y_t and Y_{t-k} after removing the effect of the intermediate Y's.

The Ljung-Box LB (12) statistics (31.87 for Sensex and 37.38 for Nifty) for the cumulative effect of up to 12th-order autocorrelation indicates presence of serial correlation in the stock return series in both the indices that should be accounted for in the mean equation.

The Ljung-Box LB2 (12) statistical value 654.92 and 669.66 for BSE and NSE indices respectively which exceed 26.217 (1% critical value from a chi square distribution with 12 degrees of freedom) rejects significantly the zero correlation null hypothesis. It suggests that there is a clustering of variance. Thus, the distribution of square returns depends on current square returns as well as several periods' square returns, which will result in volatility clustering.

The daily returns and square return series show strong first order correlation. The correlations appear strongest in daily data with almost every coefficient of the returns and square returns series being outside the asymptotic bounds of 2T-0.5 which is equal to ±0.044 for Sensex and Nifty. The results clearly reject the independence assumption for the time series of daily stock return.

The Jarque-Bera[61] statistics reported in the Table 5-1 test the assumption of normality and it is an asymptotic or large sample test. The reported probability is the probability that a Jarque-Bera statistic exceeds (in absolute value) the observed value under the null hypothesis- a small probability value leads to rejection of the null hypothesis of normal distribution. For Sensex and Nifty, we reject the hypothesis of normal distribution at 1% significance level.

---

[61]The J-B teat statistic is T[skewness^2/6+(kurtosis-3)^2/24]

5.1.2 Unit root Test

Stationarity condition of the Sensex and Nifty daily return series were tested by Augmented Dickey-Fuller Test (ADF). It tests for a unit root in the univariate representation of time series. Unit root test is used to detect the presence of stationarity in the series. The discussion on unit root test is provided in the Section 4.10.2 of Chapter 4. The results of this test reported in the Table 5-2.

Table 5-2: Unit Root Testing of Daily Returns of Sensex and Nifty

Augmented Dickey-Fuller Tests **Number of Lags = 22**

Null Hypothesis	**Test statistics**				**Mackinnon Asymptotic**
Presence of Unit root	Level		First Difference		Critical value @ 1% level
	Sensex	Nifty	Sensex	Nifty	
Intercept	-0.45(0.89)	-0.49(0.89)	-42.86(0.00)	-42.56(0.00)	-3.13
Intercept coefficient	5.62(0.37)	1.83(0.36)	0.00(0.27)	0.00(0.28)	
Trend &Intercept	-2.26 (0.45)	-2.29(0.44)	-42.88(0.00)	-42.58(0.00)	-3.96
Trend coefficient	0.02(0.02)	0.00(0.02)	-0.00(0.18)	0.00(0.23)	
None	0.57(0.84)	0.57(0.84)	-42.84(0.00)	-42.54(0.00)	2.56

ADF statistics in level series shows presence of unit root in both the stock markets as their Mackinnon's values do not exceed the critical value at 1% level. It suggests that both the returns series are nonstationary. The trend coefficients of both the series are statistically insignificant suggesting absence of any trend in both the markets. It is, therefore, necessary to transform the series to make it stationary by taking its first difference.

ADF statistics reported in the Table 5-2 show that the null hypothesis of a unit root in case of both Sensex and Nifty is rejected. The absolute computed values for both the indices are higher than the MacKinnon critical value at 1% level. Thus, the results of both the indices show that the first difference series are stationary.

Application of Box-Jenkins methodology helps us to determine ARMA order. The details on ARMA identification is provided in the ensuing section. The findings presented in Table 5-1 also reveal the possible presence of ARCH effect which is indicated by the computed value of Lagrange Multiplier (LM). This finding suggests the clustering effect in daily returns, i.e., large shocks to the error process is followed by large one and small shock by small ones of either sign.

The analysis points out some evidences of dependence, non-normality, thick- tails, volatility clustering and changing conditional variance in the time series data of Sensex and Nifty daily stock returns. It means our next logical step in modeling exercise should be to express the conditional volatility as an ARCH or GARCH process with the mean return process as an AR process.

5.1.3 Model Estimation for Stock Return

There are two distinct steps in the estimation of the parameters of the model. The first is to estimate mean equation 2-8 with the help of Box-Jenkins methodology, and the second step is to estimate the parameters of variance equation of ARCH and GARCH class of models.

The general model introduced by Box and Jenkins (1976) includes autoregressive as well as moving average parameters, and includes differencing in the formulation of the model. The important three types of parameters in the model are: the autoregressive parameters (p), the number of differencing passes (d), and moving average parameters (q). In the notation introduced by Box and Jenkins, models are summarized as ARIMA (p, d, q); so, for example, a model described as (0, 1, 2) means that it contains 0 (zero) autoregressive (p) parameters and 2 moving average (q) parameters which were computed for the series after it was differenced once.

To estimate mean equation, The Autoregressive Integrated Moving Average (ARIMA) model, as developed by Box and Jenkins, has been widely applied in a variety of economic and financial time series. Box-Jenkins Methodology consists of four steps to estimate ARIMA-mean equation.

Box Jenkins methodology consists of the following steps:

1. **Identification:** Here appropriate values of p, d, and q are found out using autocorrelation (ACF) and partial autocorrelation (PACF) functions[62].

2. **Estimation:** Having identified the appropriate values of p and q, the next stage is to estimate the parameters of the autoregressive and moving average terms included in the model.

3. **Diagnostic Checking:** After choosing particular ARIMA model, and having estimated its parameters, the next step is to see whether chosen ARIMA model fits the data reasonably well. Residuals from this model are examined to see if they are white noise and if they are, then accept particular fit of model otherwise refine the model.

One constraint of the ARIMA model is the assumption that the disturbance term Σ_t in a model have a constant conditional variance through time. The studies of Mandelbrot (1965) and Fama (1965) have recognized that it is not valid to make this assumption when studying stock returns. A more flexible model is required to describe the volatility of the data.

---

62 ACF is correlation between observations of a stationary process as function of the time interval between them. PACF is also a measure of correlation used to identify the extent of relationship between current values of a variable with earlier values of that same variable while holding the effects of all other time lags constant.

Time varying volatility models have been popular since the early 1990s in empirical research in finance, following an influencing work by Engle (1982) and Bollerslev (1986). Models of this type are well known as generalized autoregressive conditional heteroscedasticity (GARCH) in the Time series econometrics literature. The data availability and strong empirical research interest in finance encouraged the application and facilitated the development of these models and their variations which have already been discussed in Chapter 2 in section 2.4.4.

5.1.4 Empirical results

In this section, we begin with a discussion on estimation of mean equations for stock markets followed by volatility model specifications for Sensex and Nifty. We try to check for asymmetry in both the stock markets using EGARCH and TARCH models. We, then, employed ARCH-M model for both indices.

5.1.4.1 Estimation of Mean Equations for Stock Markets

First, we estimate mean equation 2-8 for Sensex and thereafter for Nifty using Box-Jenkins (BJ) Methodology discussed earlier in the previous section 5.1.3. The steps involved in BJ methodology led us to identify ARIMA order for daily return series of BSE Sensex and NSE Nifty.

5.1.4.2 Application of Box-Jenkins Methodology in Sensex

Step 1. Identification

The input series for ARIMA needs to be stationary, before we can apply Box-Jenkins Methodology. The series first needs to be differenced until it is stationary. This requires log transforming the data to stabilize the variance. The step involves finding out the appropriate values of p, d and q. The Autocorrelation Function (ACF) and Partial Autocorrelation Function (PACF) aid in this task.

We plotted the first difference of LBSE (yt) as shown in Figure 5-1. We do not observe any trend in this series, perhaps suggesting that the first-differenced BSE time series is stationary. A formal application of Augmented Dickney Fuller Test (ADF) as shown in Table 5-1 rejects the null hypothesis of a unit root in the return series. There is rejection at the 0.01 level because absolute value of ADF statistics (42.84) exceeds McKinnon critical value (2.56). We can also see this visually from the estimated ACF and PACF correlogram given in the Table 5-3. We have a much different pattern of ACF and PACF.

The ACF at lags 1, 4 and 14 seem statistically different from zero. Almost all other lags are insignificant as they falls within the asymptotic bounds 2T-0.5 (±0.044). The PACF with spikes at lags 1, 4 and 14(shown with asterisk in Fig. 5-3) seem statistically significant but the rest are not statistically significant. From the partial correlogram, we know that only the AR terms at lag 1, 4 and 14 (shown with asterisk in Fig. 5-3) are significant.

Figure 5-3: Correlogram and Partial Correlogram of return series of BSE

<table>
<tr><th>Autocorrelation</th><th>Partial Correlation</th><th></th><th>AC</th><th>PAC</th><th>Q-Stat</th><th>Prob</th></tr>
<tr><td>|* |</td><td>|* |</td><td>1</td><td>0.067</td><td>0.067</td><td>9.5688</td><td>0.002</td></tr>
<tr><td>| |</td><td>| |</td><td>2</td><td>-0.019</td><td>-0.024</td><td>10.325</td><td>0.006</td></tr>
<tr><td>| |</td><td>| |</td><td>3</td><td>-0.013</td><td>-0.010</td><td>10.659</td><td>0.014</td></tr>
<tr><td>|* |</td><td>|* |</td><td>4</td><td>0.049</td><td>0.050</td><td>15.654</td><td>0.004</td></tr>
<tr><td>| |</td><td>| |</td><td>5</td><td>-0.032</td><td>-0.040</td><td>17.879</td><td>0.003</td></tr>
<tr><td>| |</td><td>| |</td><td>6</td><td>-0.042</td><td>-0.035</td><td>21.552</td><td>0.001</td></tr>
<tr><td>| |</td><td>| |</td><td>7</td><td>0.01</td><td>0.015</td><td>21.750</td><td>0.003</td></tr>
<tr><td>| |</td><td>| |</td><td>8</td><td>0.022</td><td>0.016</td><td>22.810</td><td>0.004</td></tr>
<tr><td>| |</td><td>| |</td><td>9</td><td>0.045</td><td>0.045</td><td>27.019</td><td>0.001</td></tr>
<tr><td>| |</td><td>| |</td><td>10</td><td>0.022</td><td>0.02</td><td>28.066</td><td>0.002</td></tr>
<tr><td>| |</td><td>| |</td><td>11</td><td>-0.038</td><td>-0.044</td><td>31.171</td><td>0.001</td></tr>
<tr><td>| |</td><td>| |</td><td>12</td><td>-0.018</td><td>-0.013</td><td>31.871</td><td>0.001</td></tr>
<tr><td>| |</td><td>| |</td><td>13</td><td>0.014</td><td>0.014</td><td>32.314</td><td>0.002</td></tr>
<tr><td>|* |</td><td>|* |</td><td>14</td><td>0.061</td><td>0.061</td><td>40.263</td><td>0.000</td></tr>
<tr><td>| |</td><td>| |</td><td>15</td><td>0.005</td><td>0.006</td><td>40.325</td><td>0.000</td></tr>
<tr><td>| |</td><td>| |</td><td>16</td><td>0.002</td><td>0.002</td><td>40.330</td><td>0.001</td></tr>
<tr><td>| |</td><td>| |</td><td>17</td><td>0.041</td><td>0.035</td><td>43.904</td><td>0.000</td></tr>
<tr><td>| |</td><td>| |</td><td>18</td><td>-0.008</td><td>-0.022</td><td>44.054</td><td>0.001</td></tr>
<tr><td>| |</td><td>| |</td><td>19</td><td>-0.054</td><td>-0.047</td><td>50.326</td><td>0.000</td></tr>
<tr><td>| |</td><td>| |</td><td>20</td><td>-0.036</td><td>-0.021</td><td>53.084</td><td>0.000</td></tr>
<tr><td>| |</td><td>| |</td><td>21</td><td>0.013</td><td>0.013</td><td>53.464</td><td>0.000</td></tr>
<tr><td>| |</td><td>| |</td><td>22</td><td>0.015</td><td>0.012</td><td>53.939</td><td>0.000</td></tr>
</table>

Step 2. Estimation of ARIMA Model

Let Yt denotes the first differenced logarithmic BSE Sensex series (DLBSE). Then tentatively identified AR model is

$$Y_t = \alpha_1 Y_{t-1} + \alpha_4 Y_{t-4} + \alpha_{14} Y_{t-14} + \varepsilon_t$$

Equation 5-1

Using Eviews 6, we obtained the following estimates:

$$Y_t = 0.000141 + 0.0752Y_{t-1} + 0.0442Y_{t-4} + 0.0602Y_{t-14} + \varepsilon_t$$

Equation 5-2

Table 5-3 Estimates of Parameters of Equation 5-2

Parameters	Coefficient	Std. Error	t-Statistic	Prob.
C	0.000141	0.000425	0.967550	0.3334
AR(1)	0.075166	0.021773	3.452272	0.0006
AR(4)	0.044191	0.021862	2.021310	0.0434
AR(14)	0.060243	0.021876	2.753904	0.0059

For the series, all the coefficients except constant term are statistically significant at the 5% level. Though coefficients are statistically significant, the size of coefficient is very small, indicating that the serial dependence of the series is weak.

Step 3. Diagnostic Checking

Having chosen the ARIMA model as specified in equation 5-2 and having estimated its parameters, we next see whether chosen model fits the data reasonably well. One simple diagnostic is to obtain residuals from equation 5-2 and obtain the ACF and PACF of these residuals up to lag 22 (Lags of upto 22 days have been considered since there were at the most 22 trading days in any month). The estimated ACF and PACF are shown in Figure 5-4.

The statistics presented in the Figure 5-4 shows that the autocorrelations and partial autocorrelations are not statistically significant-almost all of them lie between the asymptotic bounds of 2T-0.5 (±0.044). In other words, the Correlogram of both autocorrelation and partial autocorrelation give the impression that the residuals estimated from equation 5-2 are purely white noise. Hence, there may not be any need to look for another ARIMA model.

Figure 5.4 Correlogram of Residuals obtained from Equation 5-2

Autocorrelation	Partial Correlation		AC	PAC	Q-Stat	Prob
| |	| |	1	0.004	0.004	0.028	0.866
| |	| |	2	-0.023	-0.023	1.183	0.554
| |	| |	3	-0.013	-0.013	1.536	0.674
| |	| |	4	0.003	0.003	1.556	0.817
| |	| |	5	-0.033	-0.034	3.899	0.564
| |	| |	6	-0.043	-0.043	7.741	0.258
| |	| |	7	0.011	0.010	7.987	0.334
| |	| |	8	0.020	0.017	8.857	0.355
| |	| |	9	0.042	0.042	12.664	0.178
| |	| |	10	0.019	0.020	13.457	0.199
| |	| |	11	-0.040	-0.041	16.839	0.113
| |	| |	12	-0.010	-0.009	17.034	0.148
| |	| |	13	0.006	0.007	17.110	0.194
| |	| |	14	0.002	0.005	17.121	0.250
| |	| |	15	0.006	0.011	17.201	0.307
| |	| |	16	0.004	0.002	17.234	0.371
| |	| |	17	0.038	0.033	20.287	0.260
| |	| |	18	-0.013	-0.015	20.665	0.297
| |	| |	19	-0.050	-0.048	25.982	0.131
| |	| |	20	-0.034	-0.030	28.374	0.101
| |	| |	21	0.011	0.012	28.654	0.123
| |	| |	22	0.016	0.014	29.172	0.140

5.1.4.3 Application of Box-Jenkins Methodology in Nifty

The autocorrelation function (ACF) and partial correlation function (PACF) were computed. Ljung-Box-Pierce Q statistic is highly significant, as shown in Table 6-1 and it indicates the first order serial correlation in the return series. The correlogram and partial correlogram of the first differenced logarithm NSE presented in Figure 5-5. It suggests that the lags 1, 4 and 14 seem statistically significant (shown with asterisk). Almost all other lags are insignificant as they fall within asymptotic bounds. Therefore, the specification of AR model for Nifty is as follows:

$$X_t = \alpha_1 X_{t-1} + \alpha_4 X_{t-4} + \alpha_{14} X_{t-14} + \varepsilon_t$$

Equation 5-3

Where X_t denotes the first differenced logarithmic NSE Nifty series (DLNSE).

Figure 5-5: Correlogram and Partial Correlogram of return series of NSE

Autocorrelation	Partial Correlation		AC	PAC	Q-Stat	Prob
|* |	|* |	1	0.075	0.075	11.747	0.001
| |	| |	6	-0.033	-0.026	23.655	0.001
| |	| |	7	-0.004	-0.001	23.691	0.001
| |	| |	8	0.026	0.022	25.160	0.001
| |	| |	9	0.039	0.037	28.390	0.001
| |	| |	10	0.033	0.032	30.703	0.001
| |	| |	11	-0.045	-0.048	34.933	0.000
| |	| |	12	-0.034	-0.027	37.379	0.000
| |	| |	13	0.032	0.031	39.621	0.000
|* |	|* |	14	0.057	0.049	46.423	0.000
| |	| |	15	0.016	0.019	46.971	0.000
| |	| |	16	-0.006	-0.001	47.038	0.000
| |	| |	17	0.034	0.028	49.558	0.000
| |	| |	18	-0.008	-0.022	49.693	0.000
| |	| |	19	-0.045	-0.039	54.099	0.000
| |	| |	20	-0.037	-0.024	57.033	0.000
| |	| |	21	0.019	0.023	57.838	0.000
| |	| |	22	0.012	0.005	58.162	0.000

Using Eviews 6, we obtained the estimates and they are reported in Table 5-4.

Table 5-4 Estimates of Parameters of Equation 5-3

Parameters	Coefficient	Std. Error	t-Statistic	Prob.
C	0.000413	0.000423	0.975756	0.3293
AR(1)	0.080601	0.021779	3.700917	0.0002
AR(4)	0.04225	0.021852	1.933468	0.0533
AR(14)	0.053502	0.021881	2.445162	0.0146

Figure 5-6 Correlogram of Residuals obtained from Equation 5-4

Autocorrelation	Partial Correlation		AC	PAC	Q-Stat	Prob
| |	| |	1	0.005	0.005	0.050	0.823
| |	| |	2	-0.050	-0.050	5.383	0.068
| |	| |	3	-0.003	-0.002	5.397	0.145
| |	| |	4	0.003	0.000	5.412	0.248
| |	| |	5	-0.021	-0.021	6.326	0.276
| |	| |	6	-0.032	-0.032	8.507	0.203
| |	| |	7	-0.004	-0.006	8.540	0.287
| |	| |	8	0.027	0.024	10.057	0.261
| |	| |	9	0.031	0.030	12.073	0.209
| |	| |	10	0.033	0.035	14.391	0.156
| |	| |	11	-0.046	-0.045	18.939	0.062
| |	| |	12	-0.027	-0.024	20.436	0.059
| |	| |	13	0.026	0.023	21.898	0.057
| |	| |	14	0.000	0.000	21.898	0.081
| |	| |	15	0.018	0.024	22.593	0.093
| |	| |	16	-0.003	-0.003	22.614	0.124
| |	| |	17	0.031	0.028	24.616	0.104
| |	| |	18	-0.010	-0.014	24.820	0.130
| |	| |	19	-0.044	-0.040	28.851	0.068
| |	| |	20	-0.035	-0.032	31.453	0.049
| |	| |	21	0.020	0.021	32.319	0.054
| |	| |	22	0.009	0.005	32.496	0.069

All the coefficients are statistically significant at 5% level. AR coefficients of the fitted models are small, indicating that the serial dependence of the series is weak.

Thus, mean equation using BJ methodology for Nifty is presented below:

$$X_t = 0.000413 + 0.080601 X_{t-1} + 0.04225 X_{t-4} + 0.053502 X_{t-14} + \varepsilon_t$$

Equation 5-4

Box-Jenkins methodology test the model adequacy by examining Correlogram of both autocorrelation and partial autocorrelation Functions of AR model as specified in equation 5-4. The Correlogram is shown in the Figure 5-6.

It gives the impression that the residuals estimated from equation 5-4 are purely white noises as almost all ACF coefficients are not statistically significant and they lie between 2T-0.5 (±0.044). Hence, it can be said that this model is best fit for the Nifty daily return series-mean equation.

5.1.5 Volatility model Specifications

The purpose of this section is to choose an adaptive volatility model by comparing the GARCH, EGARCH, GJR-GARCH or TGARCH and GARCH-M models in both the stock markets. We apply GARCH models in both the stock markets. Using standard model selection criteria like Akaike Information Criteria (AIC), Schwartz Bayesian Criteria (SBC) and Logliklihood, We will select the most appropriate model to capture time varying volatility in the stock markets.

Existence of significant ARCH effect in the residuals of the fitted AR process to the return generating process and also the existence of volatility clustering led us to the next step of modeling. We model the conditional variance of the residuals as an ARCH(q) with the mean return being governed by the AR(1,4,14) for Sensex and Nifty.

1. Model Specification

a. BSE Sensex

Specifying mean equation for Sensex and Nifty, we now use ARCH-LM (Lagrange Multiplier) test to detect the presence of ARCH effect in the mean equation of Sensex. We tested for ARCH effect for higher order and found that coefficient of ε_{t-5}^2 and ε_{t-6}^2 found to be statistically insignificant as can be seen from the Table 5-5. We, therefore, restricted our ARCH-LM test upto lag 4 for Sensex.

ARCH-LM test is statistically significant which indicates the presence of ARCH effect in the residuals of mean equation of Sensex.

Table 5-5: ARCH-LM Tests Estimates for Sensex

Variable	Coefficient	Std. Error	t-Statistic	Prob.
C	0.000	0.000	7.305	0.000
	0.317	0.022	14.458	0.000
	0.049	0.023	2.117	0.034
	0.038	0.023	1.663	0.097
	0.146	0.023	6.303	0.000
	0.006	0.023	0.253	0.800
	-0.024	0.023	-1.044	0.297

Table 5-6: ARCH(4) Test

F-statistic	105.395	Probability	0.000
Obs*R-squared	351.6	Probability	0.000

The equation of residuals from the ARCH-LM test is given below:

$$\varepsilon_i^2 = 0.0001 + 0.317\varepsilon_{t-1}^2 + 0.0421\varepsilon_{t-3}^2 + 0.150\varepsilon_{t-4}^2$$

Equation 5-5

We now employ Akaike Information Criteria (AIC), Schwartz Bayesian Criteria (SBC) and Logliklihood to select ARCH (q) order. The result for different higher orders of ARCH (q) for Sensex is displayed in the Table 5-7.

Table 5-7: Comparison of AIC, SBC and Log Liklihood for the ARCH(q) Model with Different Combinations of q for Sensex

ARCH(q)	AIC	SBC	ARCH c-oefficient	Std. error	z-statistics	probability	Log likelihood
1	-5.565	-5.549	0.380	0.033	11.422	0.000	5840.616
2	-5.597	-5.578	0.190	0.028	6.820	0.000	5875.459
3	-5.636	-5.614	0.215	0.026	8.249	0.000	5917.307
4	-5.666	-5.641	0.143	0.025	5.632	0.000	5949.415

To select the order of ARCH model, we calculated the values of the Akaike Information Criteria (AIC), Schwartz Bayesian Criteria (SBC) and Logliklihood criteria as shown in the Table 5-7. All the standard model selection criteria presented in table 5-7 select ARCH (4) model. The mean equation and volatility model selection criteria select AR (1, 4, 14)-ARCH (4) process for Sensex.

b. Model Specification for Nifty

After specifying the mean equation for Nifty by Box Jenkins methodology, we now proceed to find out ARCH order. We now test for ARCH effect using LM test. The test is applied to high order of ARCH. The results are presented below in Table 5-8.

Table 5-8: Square Residuals Tests Estimates for Nifty

Variable	Coefficient	Std. Error	t-Statistic	Prob.
C	0.000	0.000	7.186	0.000
	0.388	0.022	17.688	0.000
	0.030	0.024	1.264	0.206
	0.032	0.024	1.269	0.205
	0.100	0.024	4.293	0.000
	-0.010	0.024	-0.420	0.675
	-0.018	0.024	-0.754	0.451
	0.026	0.024	1.113	0.266
	0.018	0.022	0.809	0.419

The coefficients of ε_{t-1}^2 and ε_{t-4}^2 are statistically significant while other higher orders are statistically insignificant. Therefore, we perform our ARCH-LM test with order four only.

The test result is presented below in Table 5-9.

Table 5-9: ARCH-LM(4) Test

F-statistic	125.120	Probability	0.000
Obs*R-squared	404.679	Probability	0.000

The test reveals the presence of ARCH effect. The linear regression of residuals from the ARCH-LM test is given below:

The equation of residuals from the ARCH-LM test is given below:

$$\varepsilon_t^2 = 0.0001 + 0.386\varepsilon_{t-1}^2 + 0.030\varepsilon_{t-2}^2 + 0.0322\varepsilon_{t-3}^2 + 0.100\varepsilon_{t-4}^2 + \mu_t$$

Equation 5-6

We now employ Akaike Information Criteria (AIC), Schwartz Bayesian Criteria (SBC) and Logliklihood to select ARCH (q) order. The result for different higher orders of ARCH (q) for Nifty is displayed in the Table 5-10.

Table 5-10: Comparison of AIC, SBC and Log likelihood for ARCH(q) Model with different combinations of q for Nifty

ARCH(q)	AIC	SBC	ARCH c-oefficient	Std. error	z-statistics	Probability	Log likelihood
1	-5.566	-5.550	0.334	0.031	10.606	0.000	5842.275
2	-5.600	-5.581	0.235	0.031	7.590	0.000	5878.372
3	-5.641	-5.620	0.201	0.024	8.515	0.000	5922.788
4	-5.669	-5.645	0.149	0.026	5.625	0.000	5953.183

All the standard model selection criteria presented in table 5-10 select ARCH (4) model. The mean equation and volatility model selection criteria select AR (1, 4, 14)-ARCH (4) process for Nifty.

2. Model checking for Sensex and Nifty

As a diagnostic check on the appropriateness of ARCH process for daily return series, the autocorrelation function (ACF) of the standardized residuals and standardized squared residual series are examined. The Correlograms of ACF of AR(1,4,14)-ARCH(4) of both Sensex and Nifty are presented below in Table 5-11 and Table 5-12 respectively.

From the results reported in Table 5-11 and Table 5-12, we found that the standardized residuals from the ARCH (4) models have ACF coefficients that are statistically significant-some of them lie beyond asymptotic bound. That is obvious in the case of square standardized residuals for both the return series

Table 5-11: Sensex Daily Series: ACFs of Standardized and Square Standardized Residuals from AR(1,4,14)-ARCH(4) process

Lags	Standardized Residuals	Probability	Square standardi zedResiduals	Probability
	$\varepsilon_t / \sqrt{h_t}$		ε^2 / h_t	
1	0.014	0.513	-0.012	0.590
2	-0.023	0.455	0.000	0.865
3	0.019	0.507	0.010	0.921
4	0.017	0.571	-0.018	0.886
5	-0.028	0.470	0.018	0.868
6	-0.039	0.256	0.005	0.928
7	0.024	0.253	0.031	0.781

8	0.013	0.314	0.012	0.829
9	0.034	0.223	0.037	0.619
10	0.001	0.296	0.017	0.647
11	-0.019	0.323	0.007	0.721
12	0.011	0.382	0.012	0.767
13	0.020	0.401	0.057	0.308
14	0.013	0.450	0.065	0.046
15	-0.016	0.484	0.008	0.063
16	0.007	0.549	0.016	0.075
17	0.039	0.397	0.107	0.000
18	-0.014	0.436	0.000	0.000
19	-0.033	0.355	0.045	0.000
20	-0.027	0.327	0.002	0.000
21	0.021	0.334	0.026	0.000
22	0.013	0.372	0.033	0.000

Note: Asymptotic bound for the daily data is 0.044.

Table 5-12: Nifty Daily Series: ACFs of Standardized and Square Standardized Residuals from AR(1,4,14)-ARCH(4) process

Lags	Standardized Residuals	Probability	Square standardized Residuals	Probability
1	0.025	0.258	-0.007	0.761
2	-0.036	0.139	-0.008	0.890
3	0.029	0.126	0.016	0.859
4	0.023	0.147	-0.024	0.735
5	-0.022	0.165	0.013	0.796
6	-0.030	0.133	0.001	0.882
7	0.012	0.181	0.026	0.803
8	0.008	0.247	0.011	0.851
9	0.023	0.251	0.007	0.900

10	0.008	0.320	0.035	0.748
11	-0.027	0.293	0.021	0.742
12	-0.009	0.356	0.005	0.806
13	0.035	0.258	0.059	0.310
14	0.011	0.309	0.094	0.002
15	-0.004	0.375	0.026	0.003
16	0.001	0.445	0.018	0.003
17	0.032	0.374	0.018	0.004
18	-0.003	0.438	-0.003	0.007
19	-0.030	0.387	0.031	0.005
20	-0.039	0.276	0.001	0.008
21	0.035	0.213	0.034	0.006
22	0.012	0.247	0.038	0.004

Note: Asymptotic bound for the daily data is 0.044.

Therefore, as far as the ACF of standardized residuals and square standardized residuals are concerned, the data do not fully conform to a pure ARCH process.

We now fit the GARCH models with different orders (up to 4) to the daily return series of BSE Sensex and NSE Nifty. The results are presented in the Tables 5-13 and 5-14.

Table 5-13: Comparisons of SBC for the GARCH(p,q) model with different combinations of p and q for Sensex

(p,q)	(1,1)	(2,2)	(3,3)	(4,4)
SBC	-5.67592	-5.67279	-5.66656	-5.66197

Table 5-14: Comparisons of SBC for GARCH(p,q) model with different combinations of p and q for Nifty

(p,q)	(1,1)	(2,2)	(3,3)	(4,4)
SBC	-5.67343	-5.6665	-5.66078	-5.65992

To select the appropriate model of GARCH, we used SBC criteria. The SBC value is lowest for p=1 and q=1 therefore, we select GARCH (1,1) model for our data set of Sensex and Nifty.

We find that GARCH (1, 1) is useful for explaining conditional volatility process for daily return series of Sensex and Nifty.

3.Model Selection

a. Sensex

As discussed earlier, diagnostic checking for model selection reveals that GARCH (1, 1) is a better fit. We now test the model adequacy using Ljung-Box statistics of standardized and squared standardized residuals for GARCH (1, 1). The results of Ljung-Box statistics are presented in Table 5-15.

Table 5-15: Ljung-Box Statistics of Standardized and Squared Standardized Residuals for Sensex

	AC	PAC	Q-Stat	Probability
JB 12	0.012	0.01	12.127	0.436
LB2 12	-0.025	-0.023	14.517	0.269

It is also seen that the standardized residuals from GARCH (1,1) have ACF coefficients LB(12) that are not statistically significant-as its value lie within asymptotic bound of ±0.044 and LB2(12) i.e. measure of standardized square residuals is lower than their critical value of 21.0926 at the 5% level from a chi-square distribution with 12 degrees of freedom.

Thus, we can say that GARCH (1, 1) explains return series data of Sensex well.

b. Model Selection for Nifty

Similarly, the diagnostic checks for GARCH (1, 1) of Nifty series are given in Table 5-16. The Ljung-Box Statistics of the series of standardized and squared standardized residuals denoted by LB (12) and LB2 (12), are lower than their critical value of 21.026 at the 5% level from a chi-square distribution with 12 degree of freedom. They fall within the asymptotic bound of ±0.044 meaning that GARCH (1,1) model is specified correctly.

Table 5-16: Ljung-Box Statistics of Standardized and Squared Standardized Residuals for Nifty

	AC	PAC	Q-Stat	Probability
JB 12	-0.008	-0.009	12.735	0.389
LB^2 12	-0.03	-0.028	12.2	0.43

The statistical analysis done so far shows that for the Sensex as well as Nifty, the conditional volatility of the daily return distribution follows GARCH (1, 1) process.

We now employ an autoregressive (AR) model- AR(1,4,14) for conditional mean in the return time series of Sensex and Nifty respectively and GARCH (1, 1), EGARCH (1,1), TGARCH (1,1) and ARCH-M (1,1) models for the conditional variance. The results are presented in the Table 5-17 for Sensex and Nifty respectively.

Table 5-17: Coefficients of Symmetric and Asymmetric Models

Sensex				Nifty				
Coefficients	GARCH (1,1)	EGARCH (1,1)	TARCH (1,1)	GARCH-M	GARCH (1,1)	EGARCH (1,1)	TARCH (1,1)	GARCH-M
a (0.000)	0.000-0.907 (0.000)	0.000 (0.000)	0.000 (0.000)	0.000 (0.000)	-0.998 (0.000)	0.000 (0.000)	0.000 (0.475)	
α	0.157 (0.000)	0.262 (0.000)	0.010 (0.489)	0.157 (0.000)	0.165 (0.000)	0.271 (0.000)	0.013 (0.418)	0.165 (0.000)
β	0.808 (0.000)	0.918 (0.000)	0.790 (0.000)	0.808 (0.000)	0.795 (0.000)	0.908 (0.000)	0.768 (0.000)	0.794 (0.000)
$\alpha_1 + \beta_1$	0.965				0.959			
b	-0.167 (0.000)				-0.179 (0.000)			
RESID<0)* ARCH(1)			0.263 (0.000)				0.284 (0.000)	
SQR(GARCH)				0.002 (0.97)				0.032 (0.67)
Log likelihood	5977.975	6004.624	6012.792		5975.364	6006.801	6010.933	
AIC	-5.695	-5.719	-5.727		-5.692	-5.721	-5.725	
SBC	-5.676	-5.698	-5.705		-5.673	-5.699	-5.704	

The ARCH and GARCH classes of models are tested for their fitness and adequacy using ARCH-LM test. The results are presented in the Table 5-18.

Table 5-18: ARCH-LM Test for Model Adequacy in Sensex and Nifty

ARCH-LM test for Model Adequacy in Sensex				Nifty		
Models	Tests	Value	Probability	Tests	Value	Probability
GARCH(1,1)	F-statistic	1.14524	0.2892	F-statistic	1.026217	0.4268
	Obs*Rsquared	25.16865	0.289	Obs*R squared	22.58138	0.4257
EGARCH(1,1)	F-statistic	1.361286	0.1215	F-statistic	1.251635	0.1934
	Obs*R squared	29.84834	0.1222	Obs*Rsquared	27.4759	0.1937
TARCH(1,1)	F-statistic	1.072544	0.3699	F-statistic	1.027854	0.4247
	Obs*R squared	23.58919	0.3691	Obs*R squared	22.61701	0.4236

The above findings indicate that there is no ARCH effect left after estimating the models because the results of F-statistics or ARCH-LM test after fitting the model are statistically not significant as its probability value is higher than 0.05. It, therefore, suggests that the estimated models are better fit. All models can capture time varying volatility.

The parameters estimates of the GARCH (1, 1) models in Tables 5-17 are all statistically significant. The estimates of β_1 are always markedly greater than those of a1 and the sum a1+β_1 is very close to but smaller than unity. It is observed that a1+ β_1 is equal to 0.965 for Sensex and 0.959 for Nifty. This is less than unity indicating that the stationarity condition is not violated. The sum is closer to one, which indicates a long persistence of shocks in volatility. As the lag coefficient of conditional variance a1 is higher than the error coefficient a1 implying that volatility is not spiky. It also indicates that the volatility does not decay speedily and tends to die out slowly.

Lamoureux and Lastrapes (1990) have proposed a half-life period of a shock to the variance. Half-life period is that period in which the shock diminishes to half of its original size. The half life for GARCH (1, 1) process is $1+\left[\log^2{}_e/\log_e{}^{(\alpha_1+\beta_1)}\right]$. In our study, this is coming out to be 20.46 days for Sensex and 17.56 days for Nifty. Thus, the effects of shock to the volatility process of daily return of Sensex and Nifty take about 21 and 18 days to diminish by half its original impact. It appears that any bad news or good news does have a significant impact on volatility of the stock prices. Persistence of volatility is higher and has long memory in Sensex than in Nifty. A large body of literature has mentioned about this persistence effect of volatility in US and Japanese Market (for instance Porterba and Summers, 1986, Lamoureux and Lastrapes, 1990, Andersen and Bollerslev, 1997).

5.1.5.1 Testing for Leverage (Asymmetry) Effect: EGARCH and TARCH models

Conditional volatility of returns may not only be dependent on the magnitude of error terms but also on its sign. It is known as leverage or asymmetry effect. We checked for the asymmetry in both the stock markets using EGARCH and TARCH models. The results are presented in the Table 5-17.

The analysis of this EGARCH model suggests that all the coefficients are significant both in case of Sensex (-0.167) and Nifty (-0.179). The leverage effect term y is negative and statistically different from zero, indicating the existence of leverage effect in the stock market returns during the sample period.

Similarly, results of TARCH model estimation are listed in Table 5-17. Most importantly, the leverage term (γ), represented by (RESID<0)* ARCH(1) is here greater than zero and highly significant. Their values are 0.263 for Sensex and 0.284 for Nifty. This reinforces the assumption that negative and positive shocks have different impact on the volatility of daily returns. Here good news has an impact of a1 = 0.10 and 0.013 in BSE and NSE stock Markets but these values are not statistically different from zero as can be seen from the Table 5-17. The bad news has an impact of which are equal to 0.263 and 0.284 for Sensex and Nifty respectively. Thus, it can be said that negative or bad news create greater volatility than positive or good news in both the stock markets.

The values of AIC, SBC and Log likelihood suggest that EGARCH and TARCH models outperform the GARCH class of models. The improvements in model fitting signify the fact that returns respond differently to the arrival of negative and positive shocks unlike the GARCH. However, when we compare the EGARCH and TARCH models, we find that, for Sensex and Nifty, TARCH model is a better fit. The values of AIC, SBC and log likelihood suggest TARCH model over other ARCH/GARCH class of models in the stock markets to capture the volatility for the kind of high frequency data used in this study.

The model is presented below:

$$\sigma_t^{\,2} = 1.53E-05 + 0.010\varepsilon_{t-1}^2 + 0.263\varepsilon_{t-1}^2 d_{t-1} + 0.790\sigma_{t-1}^2 \quad \textbf{for Sensex}$$

Equation 5-7

$$\sigma_t^{\,2} = 1.76E-05 + 0.013\varepsilon_{t-1}^2 + 0.284\varepsilon_{t-1}^2 d_{t-1} + 0.768\sigma_{t-1}^2 \quad \textbf{for Nifty}$$

Equation 5-8

The y coefficient in above TARCH model is 0.263 for Sensex and 0.284 for Nifty which is greater than 0 and is significant as can be seen from Table 5-17. This indicates the presence of leverage effect in both stock markets

5.1.5.2 GARCH-M Model

It can be seen from the Table 5-17 that the coefficients of variance in the mean equation SQR (GARCH) in both the stock markets are not statistically significant as their probability values exceed 0.05. Therefore, we see no strong evidence that there are higher returns during the time of higher volatility in Sensex as well as Nifty.

The volatility in the Indian stock markets exhibits the persistence of volatility, mean reverting behavior and the asymmetric impact of return innovations. We have used Box-Jenkins methodology to identify ARMA structure for Sensex and Nifty. It is AR (1,4,14) for both the stock markets. The conditional volatility of the Sensex was found to be quite persistent, with a volatility half-life of about 20.46 days than Nifty with volatility half-life of about 17.56 days.

The key finding is that asymmetrical GARCH models outperform the conventional symmetrical GARCH models. Various diagnostic tests indicate volatility clustering and the response to news arrival is asymmetrical, meaning that impact of good and bad news is not the same. By the application of asymmetrical GARCH models, EGARCH and TARCH, we can say that there is a presence of leverage effect in both the stock markets. These models suggest that the volatility appears to be more when price decline than that when price increases. Formal application of ARCH-M reveals that there is no strong evidence that the periods of high volatility always caused high returns.

5.2 Stock Market Interactions

The section discusses how much of the movements in one stock market is explained by innovations in other markets with the help of a five-market vector-autoregressive system using daily rates of return on the stock market indices from the period 3rd January 2000 through 3rd July 2008. Section 5.2.1 presents empirical results. VAR results including variance decomposition and impulse response analysis are presented in section 5.2.2. Section 5.2.3 summarizes.

5.2.1 Empirical Results

We offer preliminary discussion on results of unit root test and Langrange multiplier[63] test of residual autocorrelation in section 5.2.1.1. Section 5.2.1.2 discusses the results of Granger causality test.

5.2.1.1 Preliminary Discussion

The information regarding stock indices and their opening and closing times of the stock exchanges are given in Table 5-19. We have included both major stock indices of India to study the interactions of world stock markets with them.

Table 5-19: Market indices' opening and closing times

Country	Index	Local Time	Greenwich mean time
USA	Standard and Poor's 500 Index.	09:30-16:00	14.30-21.00[a]
China	Shanghai Stock Index	09:30-15:00	01:30-07:00
Hong Kong	Hang Seng Index	09:45-12:30 14:30-16:15	02:00-4.30 06:30-08:15
India	Bombay Stock Exchange	09:55-3.30	04:25-10.00
	Standard and Poor CNX Nifty	09:55-3.30	04:25-10.00

[a] Times corresponds to previous day

The VAR model assumes that all variables should be stationary. The present study uses Augmented Dickey Fuller (ADF) unit root test to verify whether the variables possess

unit root or not. The next step is to decide the ordering of the variables used in VAR as per earlier opening time. The final step is to fix the lag-length of variables in the

63 The null hypothesis of the test is that there is no serial correlation in the residuals up to the specified order.The testreports a statistic labeled F-statistic and an Obs*R-squared (NR^2-the number of observations times the R-square) statistic. The statistic has an asymptotic distribution under the null hypothesis.

system through Akaike Information Criteria (AIC), Schwarz Bayesian Criteria (SBC), Final Prediction Error(FPE), Modified Liklihood Ratio (L)R, Log Liklihood (LogL) and Hannan-Quinn(HQ). It is then further tested for residual autocorrelations using VAR residual serial correlation Langrange Multiplier test to judge the adequacy of the selected model. It is imperative to note that the coefficients obtained from the VAR regression cannot be interpreted directly (Eun and Shim, 1989). Hence, the present study uses Innovation Accounting Techniques, which contains both impulse response functions and variance decomposition. The impulse response functions trace out the dynamic responses of the endogenous variables to one standard deviation innovation in each of the variables in the system. On the other hand, variance decomposition shows the extent to which a variable is explained by the innovations or shocks in all the variables in the system. It could be explained by the forecast error variance decomposition, which is the proportion of the movements in the sequence due to its 'own' shocks versus shocks to the other variable.

The estimation of VAR results is suitable only if variables included in the system are stationary. The results of the Augmented Dickey Fuller test for unit root test are given in Table 5-20. It shows that all the variables are non-stationary at their log level. However, they are stationary at their first difference and are integrated of order one. Confirming the variables are stationary at their first difference, the VAR model is estimated with the first difference of all variables.

Table 5-20: Unit root Test

Stock markets	Level	First Difference of Logarithmic series
S&P500	-1.901(0.332)*	-48.451(0.000)
Shangai	(-0.970)0.760	-45.900(0.000)
Heng Seng	-0.817(0.814)	-45.920(0.000)
BSE	-0.450(0.898)	-42.855(0.000)
NSE	-0.491(0.891)	-42.560(0.000)

*Figures in the parenthesis indicate probability values.

We reported the results of various lag length selected by Schwarz and Akaike Information Criteria, LR, HQ in Table 5-21 to decide the lag length of the variables for VAR analysis.

Table 5 -21: VAR Lag Order Selection Criteria

Lag	LogL	LR	FPE	AIC	SC	HQ
0	32514.42	NA	2.09E-20	-31.1244	-31.1109	-31.1194
1	32634.65	239.7826	1.91E-20	-31.2156	-31.13450*	-31.1859
2	32688.84	107.7992	1.86E-20	-31.2435	-31.0949	-31.1891
3	32742.72	106.9307	1.81E-20	-31.2712	-31.055	-31.19196*
4	32765.74	45.57912	1.81E-20	-31.2693	-30.9856	-31.1653
5	32805.95	79.41547	1.78E-20	-31.2838	-30.9326	-31.1551
6	32832.33	51.98676	1.78E-20	-31.2851	-30.8663	-31.1317
7	32850.96	36.6253	1.79E-20	-31.2791	-30.7927	-31.1009
8	32883	62.80836	1.78e-20*	-31.28578*	-30.7319	-31.0828
9	32903.94	40.95921	1.79E-20	-31.2819	-30.6604	-31.0542
10	32926.5	44.02617	1.79E-20	-31.2796	-30.5906	-31.0271
11	32941.76	29.70587	1.81E-20	-31.2702	-30.5137	-30.9931
12	32963.4	42.01546	1.81E-20	-31.267	-30.4429	-30.9651
13	32980.71	33.52365	1.83E-20	-31.2597	-30.368	-30.933
14	32998.3	33.98311	1.84E-20	-31.2526	-30.2934	-30.9011
15	33013.49	29.27044	1.86E-20	-31.2432	-30.2164	-30.867
16	33029.24	30.27618	1.87E-20	-31.2343	-30.14	-30.8334
17	33048.96	37.82424*	1.88E-20	-31.2293	-30.0674	-30.8036
18	33066.08	32.74296	1.90E-20	-31.2217	-29.9923	-30.7713
19	33083.35	32.96153	1.91E-20	-31.2143	-29.9174	-30.7392
20	33100.5	32.63031	1.93E-20	-31.2068	-29.8423	-30.7069
21	33112.19	22.19676	1.95E-20	-31.1941	-29.762	-30.6694
22	33126.96	27.9651	1.97E-20	-31.1843	-29.6847	-30.6349

* indicates lag order selected by the criterion

LR: sequential modified LR test statistic (each test at 5% level)

FPE: Final prediction error

AIC: Akaike information criterion

SC: Schwarz information criterion

HQ: Hannan-Quinn information criterion

It can be seen from the Table 5- 21 that LR, FPE, AIC, SC and HQ select lag length of 17, 8, 8, 1 and 3 respectively. We proceed to check for residual correlation at various lag length suggested by the criteria. We choose the lag length where residual serial autocorrelations are zero. We use VAR residual serial correlation Langrange Multiplier[64] test to check the null hypothesis that all residual covariances are zero against the alternative that at least one autocorrelation is nonzero. The result of the test is presented in Table 5-22 with different VAR lags suggested by various selection criteria.

Table 5-22: Autocorrelations LM Test

Criteria	Lags	LM-stats	Probability
LR	17	20.55047	0.7174
FPE	8	49.06711	0.0028
AIC	8	49.06711	0.0028
SC	1	119.9501	0.0000
HQ	3	83.70874	0.0000

The autocorrelation test for the lags other than 17 reveals statistically significant autocorrelation in residuals. The value of LM-stats at lag length of 17 is not statistically significant as its associated probability value is greater than 0.05. The results reported in Table 5-22 suggest the residual autocorrelations are zero at lag length of 17. Thus, all the statistical results presented in this section are based on the VAR with a lag of 17 trading days.

Now, we carry out correlation analysis between the stock markets of USA, Hong Kong, China and India. Table 5-23 reports correlations of the residuals returns among the stock markets. The residuals represent abnormal stock market returns that were not predicted on the basis of information reflected in past returns. It also reflects the degree to which new information producing an abnormal return in one market is shared by the other market during the period under study.

64 It reports the multivariate LM test statistics for residual serial correlation up to the specified order. The test statistic for lag order h is computed by running an auxiliary regression of the residuals on the original right-hand regressors and the lagged residual.Under the null hypothesis of no serial correlation of order, the LM statistic is asymptotically distributed with Chi-square degrees of freedom.

Table 5-23: The correlation matrix of returns

	DLSP500	DLHANGSENG	DLSSE	DLBSE	DLNSE
DLSP500	1	0.08266403	-0.00707	0.013763	0.015888
DLHANGSENG		1	0.006317	0.007653	0.000813
DLSSE			1	0.02423	0.022496
DLBSE				1	0.974299
DLNSE					1

Table 5-23 indicates the correlations between the stock markets are low. Developments in these markets do not appear to create much impact in each other's market. The strong correlation is observed between BSE and NSE of India while relatively high correlation is found between HANG SENG of Hong Kong and S&P 500 of USA and between S&P 500 and BSE and NSE of India.

5.2.1.2 Granger Causality

The granger causality tests are conducted in order to test for the existence of possible causality between the two markets and the results are reported in Table 5-24.

Table 5-24 Granger Causality Test

Null Hypothesis: Lag length 2	Obs	F-Statistic	Probability
DLHANGSENG does not Granger Cause DLSP500	2109	11.9155	7.10E-06
DLSP500 does not Granger Cause DLHANGSENG		8.28266	0.00026
DLSSE does not Granger Cause DLSP500	2109	0.74349	0.47558
DLSP500 does not Granger Cause DLSSE		0.20871	0.81165
DLBSE does not Granger Cause DLSP500	2109	0.45771	0.63279
DLSP500 does not Granger Cause DLBSE		15.4171	2.30E-07
DLNSE does not Granger Cause DLSP500	2109	0.60194	0.54784
DLSP500 does not Granger Cause DLNSE		15.0629	3.20E-07
DLSSE does not Granger Cause DLHANGSENG	2109	5.5197	0.00407
DLHANGSENG does not Granger Cause DLSSE		6.35062	0.00178
DLBSE does not Granger Cause DLHANGSENG	2109	6.58	0.00142
DLHANGSENG does not Granger Cause DLBSE		3.14329	0.04334

DLNSE does not Granger Cause DLHANGSENG	2109	5.39317	0.00461
DLHANGSENG does not Granger Cause DLNSE		2.10172	0.1225
DLBSE does not Granger Cause DLSSE	2109	0.32559	0.72214
DLSSE does not Granger Cause DLBSE		0.05743	0.94419
DLNSE does not Granger Cause DLSSE	2109	0.54792	0.57824
DLSSE does not Granger Cause DLNSE		0.17691	0.83787
DLNSE does not Granger Cause DLBSE	2109	4.36288	0.01286
DLBSE does not Granger Cause DLNSE		8.88084	0.00014

Note: The test for causality is based on an F-statistic that is calculated by using unconstrained and constrained forms, $F= \{SSE_r - SSE_f /m\} / \{ SSE_f / (T-2m-1)\}$, where SSE_r and SSE_f = residual sum of squares of the reduced and full models, respectively; T= total number of observations, and m= number of lags.

We find bidirectional causality between Hang Seng and S&P 500, SSE and Hang Seng, BSE and Hang Seng and between NSE and BSE stock markets at 5 % significant level. The results in the Table 5-24 reveal one-way causality between S&P 500 and BSE, S&P 500 and NSE and between NSE and Hang Seng. We find no evidence of causality between SSE and S&P 500, BSE and SSE and between NSE and SSE.

Correlations alone do not indicate whether there are any links between any pair of markets. Although there may not be a link among stock markets, such markets may simultaneously respond to global shocks (Soydemir, 2000). For this purpose a VAR model is needed to investigate the existence of stock market linkages.

5.2.2 VAR Estimates

The analysis included computation for the 15-step ahead impulse responses and variance decomposition for the VAR system.

5.2.2.1 Impulse Response Analysis

To obtain additional insight into the mechanism of transmission of stock price movements, we now examine the pattern of dynamic responses of each of the five stock markets to innovations in a particular market using the stimulated responses of the estimated VAR system. We report the results for the Impulse Response Functions (IRFs) in Table 5-25 through Table 5-29.

Table 5-25 Impusle Response of S&P500 to other stock markets

Period	DLSP500	DLSSE	DLHANGSENG	DLBSE	DLNSE
1	1.10E-02	0	0	0	0
2	-0.00091	-0.000148	0.000881	0.000129	1.93E-04
3	-0.00032	3.56E-04	0.001167	-0.000263	1.64E-04
4	-0.0002	0.00033	0.00123	-8.07E-05	0.00037
5	-4.19E-05	-3.39E-05	3.17E-04	-2.54E-05	-0.000517
6	-0.00052	-0.000149	0.000124	-0.000171	2.23E-05
7	-0.00037	-0.000201	-2.15E-05	-4.52E-04	4.91E-04
8	-0.00012	0.000237	0.000308	-0.000233	-0.000377
9	-1.58E-04	1.29E-04	-1.40E-04	-1.44E-05	0.000497
10	4.80E-05	-6.11E-05	0.000233	-0.000458	-2.67E-05
11	1.19E-04	4.99E-04	0.000219	2.67E-04	-1.22E-04
12	0.000207	-1.33E-04	-0.000104	0.000146	-0.000106
13	0.000709	-2.53E-04	1.68E-05	0.000138	3.09E-04
14	2.27E-04	-9.74E-05	1.69E-05	-7.15E-05	-1.91E-04
15	-3.86E-04	-2.33E-04	-0.000223	2.89E-05	2.23E-04

Table 5-26 Impusle Response of SSE to other stock markets

Period	DLSP500	DLSSE	DLHANGSENG	DLBSE	DLNSE
1	2.70E-05	0.015678	0	0	0
2	-0.00034	-0.00024	0	0	0
3	0.000164	-6.74E-05	-0.000738	-0.00011	-2.50E-05
4	-0.00035	-0.00035	-0.00035	-0.00035	-0.00035
5	0.000107	-0.000341	4.94E-04	-0.000169	-0.000669
6	-0.00035	-0.00035	-0.00035	-0.00035	-0.00035
7	-0.00051	0.000882	4.80E-04	5.02E-04	3.50E-04
8	-0.00035	-0.00035	-0.00035	-0.00035	-0.00035

9	-3.07E-05	6.01E-04	9.79E-05	-1.36E-05	-0.000145
10	-3.50E-04	-3.50E-04	-0.00035	-0.00035	-3.50E-04
11	-1.41E-05	-5.44E-05	-0.000654	4.65E-06	-1.43E-04
12	-0.00035	-3.50E-04	-0.00035	-0.00035	-0.00035
13	0.000505	-4.92E-04	4.97E-04	0.000175	-3.31E-04
14	-3.50E-04	-0.00035	-0.00035	-0.00035	-3.50E-04
15	-0.00013	0.000451	-0.000653	5.69E-04	-4.95E-05

Table 5-27 Impulse Response of Hang Seng to other stock markets

Period	DLSP500	DLSSE	DLHANGSENG	DLBSE	DLNSE
1	0.001492	0.000237	0.013926	0	0
2	-0.00031	-0.0003	-0.00022	0	0
3	0.00092	0.000294	-0.000163	0.000331	0.000196
4	-0.00031	-0.00031	-0.00031	-0.00031	-0.00031
5	0.000906	0.000855	-8.30E-04	0.001002	-0.000406
6	-0.00031	-0.00031	-0.00031	-0.00031	-0.00031
7	0.000205	-0.000216	4.23E-04	-2.49E-04	2.06E-04
8	-0.00032	-0.00031	-0.00031	-0.00032	-0.00031
9	8.45E-04	-8.56E-05	0.000252	-1.07E-04	0.000185
10	-3.20E-04	-3.10E-04	-0.00031	-0.00032	-3.10E-04
11	0.000296	4.67E-04	-0.00126	0.000537	2.66E-04
12	-0.00032	-3.20E-04	-0.00032	-0.00032	-0.00031
13	0.000674	9.49E-06	5.62E-04	-0.000859	8.89E-05
14	-3.20E-04	-0.00032	-0.00032	-0.00032	-3.10E-04
15	0.00036	-0.000205	0.000207	-1.04E-04	0.000465

Table 5 -28 Impulse Response of BSE to other stock markets

Period	DLSP500	DLSSE	DLHANGSENG	DLBSE	DLNSE
1	-1.22E-04	0.000387	-0.000182	0.015414	0
2	-0.00034	-0.00034	-0.00034	-0.00024	0
3	0.001051	-3.41E-04	0.000352	0.000486	-1.56E-04
4	-0.00034	-0.00034	-0.00034	-0.00034	-0.00034
5	0.001185	0.000162	7.26E-04	-0.001019	-0.000885
6	-0.00035	-0.00034	-0.00035	-0.00035	-0.00034
7	0.001239	0.000599	1.64E-03	-6.34E-04	5.57E-04
8	-0.00035	-0.00035	-0.00035	-0.00035	-0.00035
9	7.69E-04	7.20E-05	1.58E-03	4.05E-04	-0.000208
10	-3.50E-04	-3.50E-04	-0.00035	-0.00035	-3.50E-04
11	6.72E-04	-5.32E-05	0.001441	-9.70E-04	1.88E-05
12	-0.00035	-3.50E-04	-0.00035	-0.00035	-0.00035
13	0.000395	4.39E-04	4.89E-04	-0.000951	2.55E-04
14	-3.60E-04	-0.00035	-0.00035	-0.00036	-3.50E-04
15	5.54E-05	1.70E-05	0.00059	-1.85E-04	-1.53E-04

Table 5-29: Impulse Response of NSE to other stock markets

Period	DLSP500	DLSSE	DLHANGSENG	DLBSE	DLNSE
1	-1.28E-05	0.000317	-0.00025	0.015004	0.003379
2	-0.00034	-0.00034	-0.00034	-0.00024	-5.20E-05
3	0.001063	-1.61E-04	0.000273	0.000826	-1.03E-03
4	-0.00034	-0.00034	-0.00034	-0.00034	-0.00034
5	0.001125	4.44E-05	5.68E-04	-0.001274	-0.000768
6	-0.00035	-0.00034	-0.00035	-0.00035	-0.00034
7	0.001161	0.000641	1.67E-03	-5.86E-04	2.68E-04
8	-0.00035	-0.00035	-0.00035	-0.00035	-0.00035.

9	8.24E-04	8.14E-05	1.74E-03	4.27E-04	-0.000184
10	-3.50E-04	-3.50E-04	-0.00035	-0.00035	-3.50E-04
11	7.34E-04	9.51E-05	0.001378	-7.24E-04	-3.64E-06
12	-0.00035	-3.50E-04	-0.00035	-0.00035	-0.00035
13	0.000261	3.78E-04	5.88E-04	-0.000837	1.88E-04
14	-3.50E-04	-0.00035	-0.00035	-0.00036	-3.50E-04
15	4.33E-05	3.87E-05	0.000743	-3.08E-04	-1.48E-04

To facilitate the interpretations of Table 5-25 through 5-29, we plot the time paths of the impulse responses of five stock markets in Figure 5-7.

Figure 5. 7 Impulse Responses of Stock Market

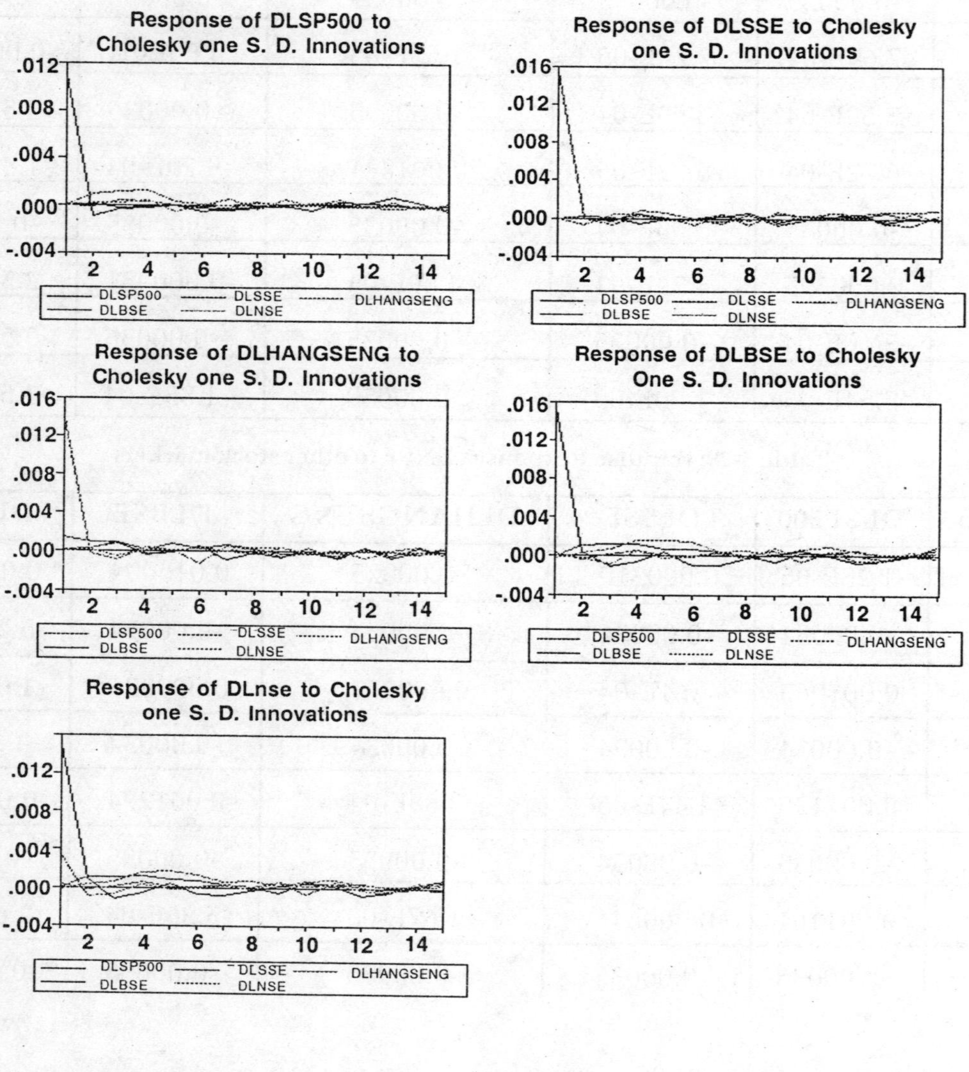

As can be seen from the Figure 5-7, the magnitudes of the innovations among the stock markets are very low. The response of each stock market to its own shocks is higher on first day. It gradually dies out thereafter.

Similarly, we investigated the dynamic response of S&P500 of USA to other stock markets. We can see from Figure 5-7 that its responses to other stock markets are weak. The responses of S&P500 to the shocks from SSE, Hang Seng, BSE and NSE are zero on first day. The stock market is more responsive to Hang Seng than other stock markets. The highest response of 0.001167 was detected with Hang Seng followed by the responses with magnitudes of 000499, 0.000497 and 0.000317 with SSE, NSE and Hang Seng on 11, 7 and 5 days respectively. The impulse responses of Hong Kong stock market to other stock markets are weak. The Chinese stock market seems to be less responsive to the shocks of other stock markets as can be seen from the Figure 5-7.

Although the responses of the Indian stock markets to a shock in other stock markets are weak, they show some interactions with all the stock markets except SSE whose interactions are weak with rest of the stock indices. Higher interactions of NSE ad BSE with S&P500 and Hang Seng are found during first few days but thereafter the responses die out. BSE and NSE show interactions with each other. The response of BSE to the shock of NSE is found to be zero on first day while NSE is responsive to the unit shock of BSE. The response of NSE is 0.01504 on first day. Thus, we can say that BSE seems to be influential in explaining movements of stock return of NSE.

5.2.2.2 Decomposition of Forecast Error

The results of variance decomposition are reported in Table 5-30. The table presents the decomposition of 5-day, 10-day and 15-day ahead forecasts of stock market returns into fractions that are accounted for by innovation of different markets. Table 6-30 can be viewed as a summary that is useful in identifying the main channels of influence in the five stock markets dynamic system. The decomposition of variance of the forecast errors of the returns of a given market indicates the relative importance of the various markets in causing the fluctuations in returns of that market. A leading market is one which explains a large percentage of the error variance of other markets while its own forecast error is not explained by innovations in other markets.

Table 5 30: Variance decomposition of Forecast Error term

		By Innovations in				
Market	**Horizon (days)**	**SP500**	**SSE**	**Hang Seng**	**BSE**	**NSE**
Explained						
SP500	5	96.3681	0.2054	2.9806	0.0739	0.3721
	10	95.2851	0.3112	3.0811	0.4625	0.8600
	15	94.7022	0.6125	3.1275	0.5478	1.0100

Hang Seng	5	2.3019	0.4588	96.5127	0.5880	0.1386
	10	2.5849	0.6667	95.0505	1.3302	0.3677
	15	2.9407	0.9455	93.7426	1.7893	0.5820
SSE	5	0.1193	99.1127	0.4130	0.1174	0.2376
	10	0.3766	97.9043	1.0705	0.3332	0.3153
	15	0.5157	96.8084	1.6582	0.5395	0.4782
BSE	5	1.8469	0.2609	2.3336	95.0974	0.4611
	10	2.1789	0.5874	3.5051	92.9843	0.7444
	15	2.5015	0.7223	3.8934	91.8913	0.9915
NSE	5	1.7524	0.2165	2.4849	90.3278	5.2184
	10	2.1834	0.5440	3.7112	88.3419	5.2195
	15	2.4036	0.7201	3.9940	87.4011	5.4813

The Table 5-30 indicates that no stock market is exogenous in that a market's own innovations largely account for its variance. The analysis of forecast error variance decomposition of China shows that it is largely explained by its own shocks. Chinese stock market innovations account for about 99 percent of its own variance. No other stock market is so nearly exogenous in this regard. Table 5-30 shows that Hongkong stock market accounts for near 4% of the forecast error variance of the Indian stock markets represented by BSE and NSE whereas S&P500 of USA explains about 2.5% variance of the Indian Stock Markets. BSE explains about 90% variance of NSE which suggests that BSE is exogenous market significantly impacting the stock price movements of NSE. Shanghai stock market explain less than 1 percent variance of Indian stock markets. Hong Kong has more impact on return of Indian and USA stock markets than any other markets. Hong Kong explains nearly 4 percent variance of return of S&P500 and S&P500 explains approximately 3 percent variance of Hong Kong. S&P500 explains around 2.5% return variance of Indian stock markets while Indian stock markets collectively explain less than 1.5 percent variance of it. Table 6-30 provides that the innovations in Chinese stock market do not explain any substantial part of error variance of other markets. Our analysis suggests some interactions between Indian, Hong Kong and USA stock markets. Innovations in these stock markets have some repercussions in every other market except Chinese stock market whose return variance of 1.5 percent is explained by Hong Kong stock market. The results reveal that Hong Kong stock market is highly interactive and having greater interactions between American and Indian stock markets.

The study provides an analysis of the co-movements of returns of the major stock markets. Using Granger Causality test and Vector Autoregression (VAR) analysis, the study examines an interdependence structure of the stock markets. Test results of Granger Causality suggest bi-directional causality in returns between the stock markets of Hong Kong, China and USA, between Hong Kong and BSE of India and between NSE and BSE of India. The analysis indicates unidirectional causality from NSE to Hang Seng, S&P 500 to NSE and S&P 500 to BSE.

A VAR analysis is performed on the full sample from 2000-2008. The impulse response analysis was used to investigate the pattern of dynamic impulse response the stock markets. The stock markets' responses to the shocks of other stock markets are not substantial. Our analysis suggests that each stock market is more sensitive to its own shocks.

The variance decomposition results show that Chinese stock markets have very little control over other stock markets. The analysis of forecast error variance decomposition of SSE of China shows that it is largely explained by its own shocks. The results indicate that the Hong Kong stock market accounts for about 4% of the forecast error variance of Indian stock markets. The findings suggest that Hong Kong stock market is highly interactive having greater comovements with American and Indian stock markets.

5.3 Analysis of Return and Volatility Spillover

In this study, we use stock markets in India and China to represent the emerging markets. The stock markets in Hong Kong and USA are considered to serve well as proxies for the regional and global developed markets respectively and are expected to play an influential role in the emerging markets in Asia. The inclusion of the stock markets in Hong Kong and USA, therefore, permits us to investigate the regional and global integration of the emerging markets in Asia in terms of return and volatility spillover. This section discusses the results of return and volatility spillover using Multivariate GARCH(MGARCH) model. This section is organized into three subsections. Subsection 5.3.1 provides preliminary analysis of statistical properties of return series of various stock markets. Subsection 5.3.2 presents empirical results on unit root tests and MGARCH model.

5.3.1 Preliminary Analysis

For diagnostic checking, visual inspection of the plots of daily return series of the stock markets will be very useful. The stock prices are in local currency terms and their changes are restricted to the movements in the stock process solely, avoiding any distortions induced by the currency devaluations of the countries.

Figure 5-8 presents the time plots of the price series, which fluctuate on a daily and long term basis. It can be seen from the Figure 5-8 that Indian stock markets indices and Hang Seng follow similar pattern after year 2003. It can also be seen that the indices of the two emerging markets of Asia namely India and China follow similar pattern in the most recent time i.e. after year 2006. The most developed stock markets of the world i.e.

Hang Seng and S&P 500 have similar trend. Overall, all the stock markets indices are trending upward in recent times. The rise in the stock indices may be due to the increased interest of foreign investors due to the policy of less restrictions and more deregulations for their participations.

Figure 5. 8 : Stock indices during year 2000 to year 2008.

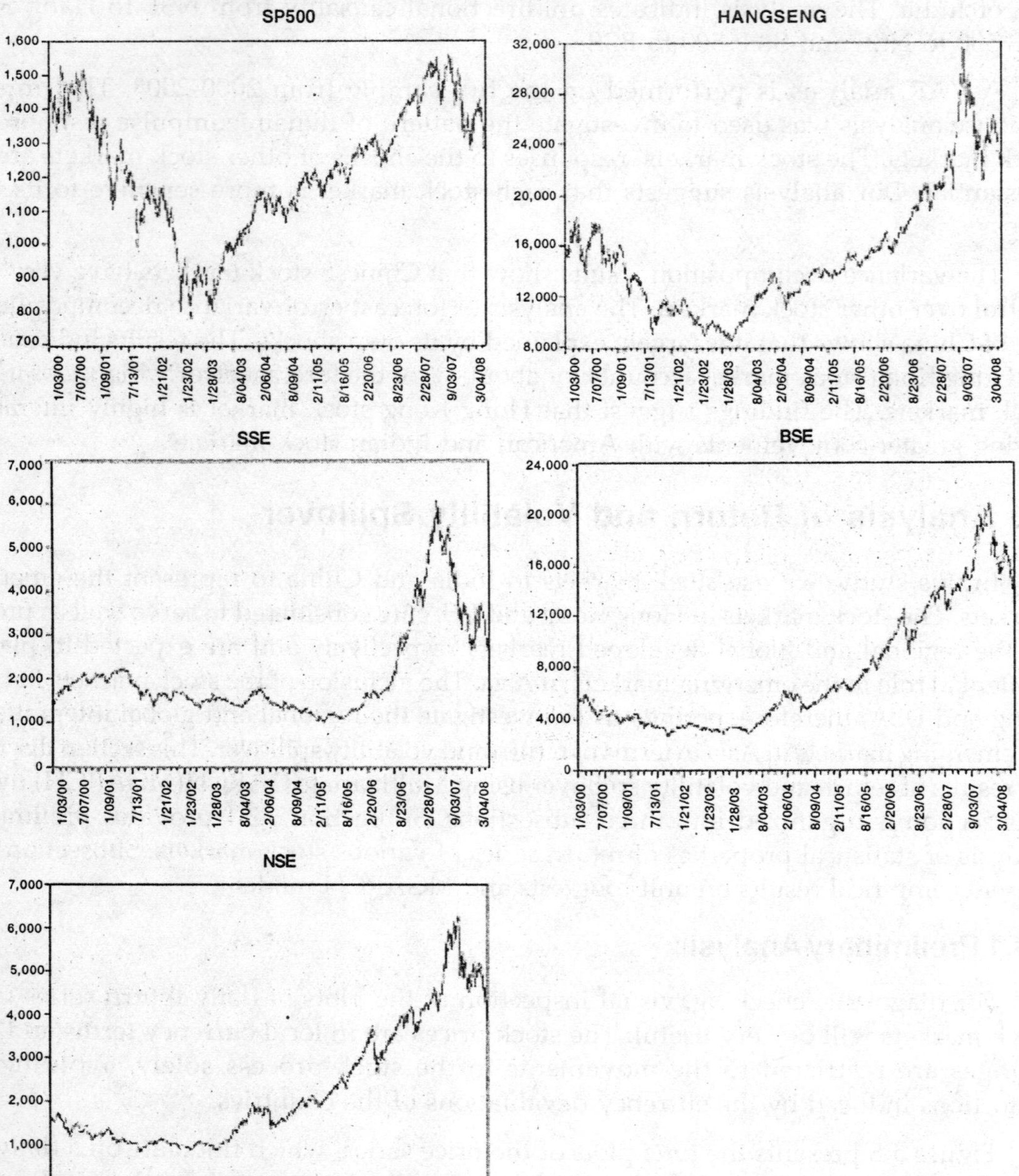

Figure 5-9 indicates that the returns of the share price indices defined as the first differences of the natural logarithm of the share price indices during the period under study. Indian stock markets have high volatility during the year 2004 and thereafter, the magnitude of volatility is in line with the volatility of the developed markets. Indian stock markets display higher volatility than any other stock markets under study. Furthermore, all five indices are characterized by volatility clustering, i.e. large (small) volatility followed by large (small) volatility. As the cluster tends to occur simultaneously, between the indices of emerging markets and between the indices of the developed markets, volatility must be modeled systematically.

Figure 5-9: Returns of Stock Market Indices during year 2000 to year 2008.

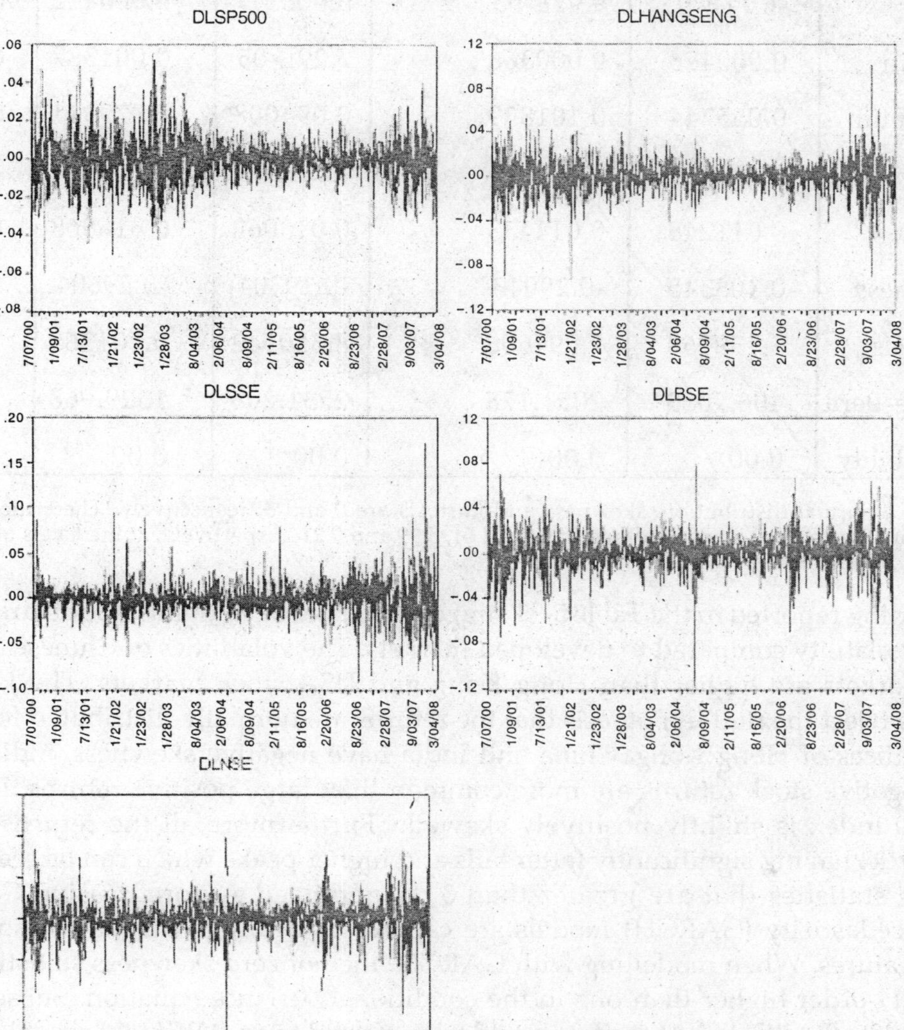

Note: The stock indices of DLBSE, DLHANGSENG, DLNSE, DLSP500 and DLSSE correspond respectively to the stock markets in India, Hong Kong, India, US and China.

Table 5-31 reports summary statistics for the returns series. During the period under study, the performance of the shares, measured by the average returns, in emerging stock markets, especially of India is better than other stock markets.

Table 5.31 : Summary statistics of returns during January 2000 to July 2008

Descriptive Statistics	DLSP500	DLHANGSENG	DLSSE	DLBSE	DLNSE
Mean	-6.71E-05	9.94E-05	0.00031	0.000422	0.000427
Median	0.000426	0.000366	7.29E-05	0.001387	0.001462
Maximum	0.055744	0.101839	0.094008	0.079311	0.079691
Minimum	-0.05047	-0.09285	-0.09256	-0.11809	-0.13054
Std. Dev.	0.011248	0.014433	0.016062	0.016068	0.016073
Skewness	0.108345	-0.29043	-0.19304	-0.59604	-0.66114
Kurtosis	5.139368	7.794006	8.350542	6.701265	7.70563
Jarque-Bera	406.7063	2051.178	2531.208	1329.968	2101.447
Probability	0.00	0.00	0.00	0.00	0.00

Note: For a normal distribution, skewness and kurtosis are 0 and 3, respectively. The critical values for Jarque-Bera with 2 degrees of freedom are 4.61, 5.99 and 9.21, respectively, at the levels of significance 10%, 5% and 1%.

Finding reported in the Table 5-31 suggests that the developing stock markets exhibit greater volatility compared to developed markets. The volatilities of Chinese and Indian stock markets are higher than Hong Kong and USA stock markets. The Jarque-Bera statistics reject the null hypothesis that the returns are normally distributed for all cases. Stock indices of Hong Kong, China and India have negative skewness, indicating that large negative stock returns are more common than large positive returns. In contrast, S&P 500 index is slightly positively skewed. Furthermore all the returns series are leptokurtic, having significantly fatter tails and higher peaks which can be seen from the kurtosis statistics that are greater than 3. Generalized Autoregressive Conditional Heteroscedasticity (GARCH) models are capable of dealing with data displaying the above features. When modelling with GARCH, the nonzero skewness statistics indicate an ARCH order higher than one in the conditional variance equation. Subsequently, a Multivariate GARCH (1, 1) model should be preferred to an ARCH (*p*) model to examine volatility spillover effects for the sake of parsimony (Li, 2007).

In the study, we use Multivariate GARCH to examine the impact of volatility and return spillover among Asia's emerging stock markets and developed stock markets of the world. The discussion on MGARCH is provided in the Chapter 2.

5.3.2 Empirical Results

In this section, we perform unit root test to check for nonstationarity of the stock markets series. we report the estimated results about market linkages. We will look for any statistically significant cross-market effects as evidence of linkages and measures the extent of the linkages by the estimated time-varying covariances and the decomposition of forecast error variances. We organize the section as follows. In section 5.3.3, we discuss Augmented Dickey Fuller Test (ADF) results. In section 5.3.4, we report the evidence of market linkages in the estimated five-variable asymmetric GARCH-BEKK model. Section 5.4 summarizes.

5.3.3 Unit root test results

Stationarity conditions of the stock market indices are tested by Augmented Dickey-Fuller Test (ADF). The results of this test are reported in Table 5-20.

ADF statistics reported in the Table 5-20 show that the null hypothesis of a unit root in case of all five indices is rejected. The absolute computed values for all the indices are higher than the MacKinnon critical value at 1% level. Thus, the results show that the return series are stationary. As the results suggest that the underlying return series are stationary, our next step is to examine the stock markets' linkages.

5.3.4 The evidence of market linkages

The mean Equation 2-19 and time-varying variance-covariance Equation 2-22 are estimated simultaneously by the maximum likelihood method. Note that the stock exchanges in S&P 500,Hang Seng, SSE, BSE and NSE are indexed 1, 2, 3, 4 and 5 respectively. We first look at the matrix in the mean equation, Equation 2-19 captured by the parameters $\gamma_{ij.}$ in Table 5-32, in order to see the relationship in terms of returns across the five indices. As the diagonal parameters $\gamma(2,2)$ and $\gamma(3,3)$ are statistically insignificant, the returns of Hang Seng and Shanghai (SSE) do not depend on their first lag while the other diagonal parameters are statistically significant suggesting that the returns of S&P500, BSE and NSE depend on their first lags. The cross market return linkages are represented by off-diagonal parameters and they are evident in the following pattern. Firstly, the off-diagonal parameters $\gamma(1,4)$ and $\gamma(4,5)$ are statistically significant at 5% level while their counterparts $\gamma(4,1)$ and $\gamma(5,4)$ are also statistically significant at 5% and 10% level indicating that there are bi-directional return spill over from S&P500 to BSE and from BSE to NSE respectively. The parameter $\gamma(1,2)$ and $\gamma(2,1)$ are found to be statistically significant at 10% level, implying that there is a bi-directional return linkage between S&P500 and Hang Seng. These results do not find any return spillover from Chinese stock market to other stock markets and vice versa. We can corroborate that the BSE of India and Hang Seng of Hong Kong are linked to the global developed stock market namely S&P500.

Table 5-32: Estimated coefficients from mean equation 2-22

Return	S&P500	Prob	Hang Seng	Prob	SSE	Prob	BSE	Prob	NSE	Prob
	0.049	0.023	0.047	0.061	-0.039	0.246	0.052	0.073	0.012	0.672
	0.030	0.079	-0.001	0.951	-0.014	0.582	0.007	0.770	-0.005	0.821
	-0.016	0.265	-0.010	0.597	0.014	0.525	0.000	0.990	0.005	0.803
	0.033	0.042	0.005	0.796	0.001	0.969	0.049	0.017	0.159	0.012
	0.010	0.539	-0.003	0.874	0.007	0.779	0.337	0.000	0.338	0.000

Note: i=1 ,2,3, 4 and 5 stands for S&P 500, Hang Seng, SSE, BSE and NSE respectively.

Now, we examine the estimated results of the time varying variance-covariance Equation 2.25 (p. 31) in the system. The results of five-variable asymmetric GARCH model are reported in Table 5-33.

Table 5-33: Estimated coefficients for four variable asymmetric MGARCH

	SP500(i=1)	SSE(i=2)	Hang Seng (i=3)	BSE(i=4)	NSE(i=5)
a_{i1}	0.200(0.00)	-0.081(0.00)	-0.120(0.00)	0.045(0.00)	-0.071(0.00)
a_{i2}	0.020(0.32)	0.196(0.00)	0.056(0.00)	0.015(0.56)	0.046(0.01)
a_{i3}	-0.177(0.00)	-0.076(0.00)	0.276(0.00)	-0.051(0.01)	-0.041(0.00)
a_{i4}	0.058(0.00)	-0.013(0.50)	0.005(0.71)	-0.001(0.05)	0.022(0.12)
a_{i5}	-0.131(0.00)	0.197(0.00)	0.191(0.00)	-0.135(0.00)	-0.372(0.00)
g_{i1}	0.093(0.00)	0.401(0.01)	0.914(0.00)	-0.009(0.62)	-0.041(0.07)
g_{i2}	0.060(0.00)	0.971(0.00)	-0.058(0.00)	-0.007(0.47)	0.033(0.11)
g_{i3}	0.944(0.00)	0.009(0.59)	-0.084(0.00)	0.012(0.56)	-0.032(0.19)
g_{i4}	-0.014(0.31)	0.001(0.84)	0.008(0.58)	0.968(0.00)	0.015(0.33)
g_{i5}	-0.039(0.28)	-0.048(0.15)	0.021(0.59)	-0.027(0.52)	0.267(0.00)
d_{i1}	0.125(0.00)	0.076(0.02)	0.224(0.00)	-0.105(0.01)	0.027(0.33)
d_{i2}	-0.003(0.89)	-0.004(0.00)	-0.063(0.00)	-0.042(0.28)	0.030(0.29)
d_{i3}	0.197(0.00)	0.084(0.00)	0.133(0.00)	-0.096(0.02)	0.008(0.73)
d_{i4}	0.048(0.01)	-0.036(0.14)	0.041(0.04)	-0.330(0.00)	-0.007(0.75)
d_{i5}	0.185(0.00)	0.059(0.00)	-0.102(0.00)	-0.064(0.20)	-0.143(0.00)
Portmanteau tests for autocorrelations					
	Q statistics(5)	183.96			
	Probability	0.108			

Notes

a. Figures in the parenthesis indicate probability values.

b. Coefficients a, g and d captures ARCH, GARCH and asymmetric GARCH effects in the markets.

c. Q(k) is the Ljung Box statistic identifying the presence of first order autocorrelation in the returns. It is defined as, $LB = T(T+2)\sum_{k=1}^{k}(\hat{\rho}_k^2 / T-k)$ where $\hat{\rho}_k^2$ is Autocorrelation Function (ACF) and T= sample size.Under the null hypothesis of no autocorrelation, it is distributed as $\lambda^2(k)$. Portmanteau autocorrelation test computes multivariate Ljung-Box Q-statistics for residual serial correlation up to the specified order

It can be noted that the Ljung-Box *Q* statistics for the fifth orders in the squared standardized residuals shows that there is no series dependence in the squared standardized residuals, indicating the appropriateness of the fitted variance-covariance equations by the five-variable asymmetric BEKK model. The matrices *A* and *G* reported in Table 5-33 help examine the relationship in terms of volatility as stated in Equation 2-22.The diagonal elements in matrix A capture the ARCH effect, while the diagonal elements in matrix *G* measure the GARCH effect. As shown in Table 5-33, the estimated diagonal parameters a_{11} through a_{55} and g_{11} through g_{55} are all statistically significant , indicating a strong GARCH (1,1) process driving the conditional variances of all the indices. Own past shocks and volatility affect the conditional variance of the S&P 500, SSE, Hang Seng, BSE and NSE indices.

The off-diagonal elements of matrix A and G capture the cross-market effects such as shock spillover and volatility spillover among the four stock exchanges. Firstly, we find evidence of bidirectional shock transmissions between S&P 500 and Hang Seng, between S&P500 and NSE, SSE and Hang Seng, SSE and NSE, Hang Seng and NSE and between S&P500 and BSE as the pairs of off-diagonal parameters a_{13} and a_{31}, a_{15} and a_{51}, a_{23} and a_{32}, a_{25} and a_{52}, a_{35} and a_{53} and a_{14} and a_{41} are statistically significant. The two way shock spillover indicates strong connection between the stock markets. The bidirectional shock spillover indicates the news about shocks in one stock exchange affect the volatility of other stock exchange and vice-versa. Secondly, there are bidirectional volatility linkages between S&P500 and SSE and between S&P500 and Hang Seng as g_{12} and g_{21} and g_{13} and g_{31} are statistically significant. It indicates that the conditional variance of one index depends on past volatility of the other index, implying strong connection between them. However, the magnitude of coefficients g_{13} (0.944) and g_{31} (0.914) are highest between S&P500 and Hang Seng while all other values of the coefficients are relatively small, suggesting that the extent of the volatility linkages between other stock exchanges. Thus, we can say that the magnitude of volatility spillover from S&P500 of USA to Hang Seng is the highest among all the spillover effect. Thirdly, the significant a_{21}, a_{43} and a_{45} and insignificant a_{12}, a_{34} and a_{54} indicate unidirectional shock spillover from SSE to S&P 500, BSE to Hang Seng and from BSE to NSE. In the meanwhile, the statistically significant g_{32} and insignificant g_{23} indicates unidirectional volatility spillover from Hang Seng to SSE.

As far as matrix D is concerned, we find evidence of asymmetric responses to negative shocks of own markets for all the stock markets as the diagonal parameters, D1(1,1) D1(2,2), D1(3,3), D(4,4) and D(5,5) are statistically significant. The sign of the own past shocks affects the conditional variance of these indices. We also find the evidence of bidirectional cross-market asymmetric responses across the indices of USA and Hong Kong, China and Hong Kong, USA and BSE of India and Hong Kong and BSE of India as the coefficients d_{13} and d_{31}, d_{23} and d_{32}, d_{14} and d_{41} and d_{34} and d_{43} of D matrix are statistically significant. The statistically significant values of d_{15}, d_{35} and d_{45} and insignificant values of d_{51}, d_{53} and d_{54} indicate unidirectional asymmetric cross market responses spillover from S&P500 to NSE, Hang Seng to NSE and from BSE to NSE.

5.4 Summary

The key finding is that asymmetrical GARCH models outperform the conventional symmetrical GARCH models. By the application of asymmetrical GARCH models, EGARCH and TARCH, we can say that there is a presence of leverage effect in both the stock markets.

VAR analysis suggests that each stock market is more sensitive to its own shocks. The variance decomposition results show that Chinese stock markets have very little control over other stock markets. The findings suggest that Hong Kong stock market is highly interactive having greater comovements with American and Indian stock markets.

The study investigates the return and volatility spillover effect between the emerging stock markets in India and China and the developed markets in Hang Seng and USA. Summary statistics of returns series of all the stock exchanges suggest that they are leptokurtic, having significantly fatter tails and higher peaks. Generalized Autoregressive Conditional Heteroscedasticity (GARCH) models are capable of dealing with the property of the data.

By applying a multivariate asymmetric GARCH approach to the daily stock indices from January 1, 2000 to July 3, 2008, we found evidence of linkages in terms of return and volatility. There is a bidirectional return spillover from S&P500 to BSE, between BSE to NSE and between S&P500 to Hang Seng stock markets.

Results of time varying variance-covariance equation of MGARCH suggest that own shocks and volatility affect the conditional variance of all the stock markets under study. We found evidence of bidirectional shock transmissions between S&P 500 and Hang Seng, between S&P500 and NSE, SSE and Hang Seng, SSE and NSE, Hang Seng and NSE and between S&P500 and BSE. There is also unidirectional shock spillover from S&P500 to Hang Seng, BSE to Hang Seng and from BSE to NSE. There are bi-directional volatility linkages between S&P500 and SSE and between S&P500 and Hang Seng. The extent of volatility linkages between S&P 500 and Hang Seng is highest among all the stock exchanges. There is also unidirectional shock spillover from S&P500 to Hang Seng,

BSE to Hang Seng and from BSE to NSE. We find evidence of asymmetric responses to negative shocks in all the stock market indices. The results reveal that the past shocks affect the conditional variance of these indices. We find the evidence of cross market asymmetric responses to volatility between stock markets of USA and Hong Kong, China and Hong Kong, USA and BSE of India and Hong Kong and BSE of India.

***

CHAPTER 6

Summary and Policy Recommendations

Volatility is a known phenomenon in the stock markets around the world. Excess volatility is harmful which is caused by irrational behavior of the traders and investors, trading mechanism imperfections and lack of information transparency (Kaur, 2001). Investors are always concerned about present and future value of their investments.

Volatility in equity markets has become a matter of mutual concern in recent years for all the participants in stock markets across the globe. Their concern centres on the perception that high levels of volatility can lead to a general erosion of investor confidence in capital markets and a flow of capital away from equity markets. It is perceived as an indicator of market inefficiency and a potential threat to the very integrity of market mechanism. When the stock price takes a sharp nose-dive, investors see the value of their assets rapidly dissipating. When the asset price exhibits significant volatility over a time, investors loose confidence in the market. They begin to see financial markets as the province of the speculator and the insider, not of the rational long-term investor. If this view becomes pervasive, investors may simply withdraw from the market. The widespread concern in the marketplace has underlined the importance to market participants to measure and analyze stock market volatility. It will assist to put effective monitoring mechanism which will help in the prevention of such aberration.

Despite stock market volatility being a vital issue, few significant efforts have been made in India to examine it empirically and adequately. Reasonable numbers of researches have been taken place in developed countries such as USA, UK, and other European markets. However a systematic study on magnitude and pattern of volatility in the Indian stock markets, their interactions with world stock markets and examination of their return and volatility spillover effects is lacking in numbers. The present study has attempted to empirically investigate volatility in India and its relation with other stock markets of the world. The objectives of the study are:

(1) To investigate the nature and pattern of volatility of Indian stock markets namely S&P CNX nifty of NSE and BSE Sensex.

(2) To model the volatility of Indian Stock markets with ARCH, GARCH, EGARCH, TARCH and ARCH-M models.

(3) To examine the interactions of Indian Stock markets with world stock markets using Vector Autoregression.

(4) To analyze the return and volatility spillover effects among the stock markets of the world with MGARCH-BEKK model.

The study spans over more than eight year period from 3rd January, 2000 to 3rd July, 2008. The period was chosen due to the fact that the major market upheavals, regulatory activity and changes in market's institutional structure took place during this period. The sample of the study consists of the two most prominent indices of India namely BSE Sensex and S&P CNX Nifty of NSE, S&P500 of USA, Shanghai of China and Hang Seng of Hong Kong.

The results of the analysis show that the volatility in Indian stock market exhibits volatility clustering. The analysis finds that interactions among the stock markets are weak. The analysis further finds the evidence of return and volatility spillover among the stock markets of the world.

6.1 Key Findings of the Study

(1) The volatility in the Indian stock markets exhibits the persistence of volatility, mean reverting behavior and the asymmetric impact of return innovations. The volatilities of Indian stock markets are time varying. The conditional volatility of the Sensex was found to be quite persistent, with a volatility half-life of about 20.46 days than Nifty with volatility half-life of about 17.56 days.

(2) Asymmetrical GARCH models outperform the conventional symmetrical GARCH models. By the application of asymmetrical GARCH models namely EGARCH and TARCH, we can say that there is a presence of leverage effect in both the stock markets. These models suggest that the volatility appears to be more when price decline than that when price increases. The results of ARCH-M reveal that there is no strong evidence that the periods of high volatility always caused high returns.

(3) Using Granger Causality test and Vector Autoregression (VAR) analysis, the study examines an interdependence structure of the stock markets. The results of Granger Causality test suggest bi-directional causality in returns between the stock markets of Hong Kong, China and USA, between Hong Kong and BSE of India and between NSE and BSE of India. The analysis indicates unidirectional causality in returns from NSE of India to Hang Seng of Hong Kong, S&P500 of USA to NSE and BSE.

(4) The impulse response analysis of VAR suggests that stock markets are most sensitive to their own shocks. Own stock market responses to other stock markets are not substantial. The variance decomposition analysis reveals that Chinese stock market has very little control over other stock markets of the world. The results indicate that the Hong Kong stock market is highly interactive stock markets than any other stock markets.

(5) Summary statistics of return series of the stock markets of the world suggest that the return series are leptokurtic, having significantly fatter tails and higher peaks. Generalized Autoregressive Conditional Heteroscedasticity (GARCH) models are capable of dealing with the property of the data.

(6) Results suggest that the developing stock markets exhibit greater volatility compared to developed markets. The volatilities of Chinese and Indian stock markets are higher than Hong Kong and USA stock markets. Indian stock markets display higher volatility than any other stock markets under study.

(7) Average stock return of Indian stock market is better than any other stock markets under study but they also carry high risk.

(8) Stock indices of Hong Kong, China and India have negative skewness, indicating that large negative stock returns are more common than large positive returns. In contrast, S&P 500 index is slightly positively skewed.

(9) By applying a multivariate asymmetric GARCH model to the daily stock indices from January 3, 2000 to July 3, 2008, we found evidence of linkages in terms of return and volatility. There is a bidirectional return spillover from S&P500 to BSE, between BSE to NSE and between S&P500 to Hang Seng stock markets.

(10) Results of MGARCH suggest that own shocks and volatility affect the conditional variance of all the stock markets under study. We found evidence of bidirectional shock transmissions between S&P 500 and Hang Seng, between S&P500 and NSE, SSE and Hang Seng, SSE and NSE, Hang Seng and NSE and between S&P500 and BSE. There are also evidences of unidirectional shock spillover from S&P500 to Hang Seng, BSE to Hang Seng and from BSE to NSE.

(11) There are bi-directional volatility linkages between S&P500 and SSE and between S&P500 and Hang Seng. We found evidences of unidirectional shock spillover from S&P500 to Hang Seng, BSE to Hang Seng and from BSE to NSE.

(12) The findings suggest that the extent of volatility linkages between S&P 500 and Hang Seng is highest among all the stock exchanges. We found evidences of asymmetric responses to negative shocks in all the stock market indices. The results reveal that the past shocks affect the conditional variance of these indices. We found the evidence of bidirectional cross-market asymmetric responses across the indices of USA and Hong Kong, China and Hong Kong, USA and BSE of India and Hong Kong and BSE of India. The results reveal that there are unidirectional asymmetric cross market responses spillover from S&P500 to NSE, Hang Seng to NSE and from BSE to NSE.

6.2 Area of Further Research

The subject of volatility has been extensively researched in the developed and some of the developing countries. However, not much work has been done on the Indian stock market from the volatility perspective. The present study attempts to carry out somewhat comprehensive analysis of the stock market volatility of stock markets. But, there are some avenues of research hitherto unexplored. It would be worthwhile to do meaningful research in these areas and make useful contributions to the stakeholders of the capital markets. Research can be pursued in any of the following areas:

(1) The present study has restricted itself to two major stock market indices. Now a days, numerous indices are constructed to track the performance of specific industries. Further studies on volatility analysis can be conducted involving these indices.

(2) There are number of interesting issues concerning modeling stock market volatility. Firstly, most of the studies focus on aggregate stock market index. It would be therefore an interesting exercise to investigate applicability of GARCH models to individual company's share price data.

(3) Applicability of GARCH model can be extended to derivative markets. GARCH model can be used to study the impact of various factors namely margin trading, introduction of derivatives, introduction of circuit filter etc. on conditional volatility.

(4) Market co-integration study can be undertaken to find out the level of integration of Indian stock market with other developing and developed stock markets. This facet has special appeal in the context of increasing globalization of Indian capital markets and listing of Indian companies on US, European and other stock markets.

(5) Cointegration studies of Indian stock markets with other financial markets like money market, forex market could be undertaken.

(6) Attempts can be made to explain intra-day, weekly and monthly behavior of volatility by means of GARCH models. A study of this issue may provide important insights into the factors that influence stock market volatility and consequently an insight into the true nature of the stock market.

(7) Forecasting of volatility is important in various applications related to risk management. Forecasting performance of various conditional volatility models can be compared to arrive at the best model in terms of forecasting accuracy which could be helpful to investors.

(8) Stochastic autoregressive volatility models are considered to be appropriate for modeling volatility as stochastic process. ARCH and GARCH processes are not stochastic, rather they are deterministic. A use of GARCH model is thus

restrictive. Stochastic volatility models can be used to model volatility.

(9) Recent developments in time series analysis allow proper modeling of nonlinearities in economic and financial variables. Various nonlinear time series models like Logistic Smooth Transition autoregressive (LSTR), Exponential Smooth Transition autoregressive (ESTR) and Threshold Autoregressive Models (TAR) can be used to investigate nonlinearities in stock markets.

6.3 Policy Recommendations

(1) Investing in Indian stock market is riskier than developed and developing stock markets of the world. The investor need to take cognizance of the fact as well before investing in the stock market. Steps need to be taken for increasing the depth of the markets by encouraging more participation of reputed firms and curbing excessive speculation.

(2) Excessive volatility is not desirable. The widespread concern of the stock exchange management, brokers, investors and regulators alike has focused upon the need for measuring and predicting stock market volatility. The policy makers and stock exchange regulatory authorities should frame appropriate policy guidelines for the benefit of investors and for smooth working of the stock markets.

(3) Volatility is central to many investment decisions in new financial product areas and is the critical variable in option pricing in derivative markets. The cost of many sophisticated hedging strategies depends on the level of market volatility. The present study attempted to estimate a volatility model for BSE Sensex and S&P CNX Nifty and found that the asymmetric TARCH (1, 1) specification fits both the stock market return time series quite well. Such model can be used while designing advance financial products such as derivatives.

(4) Application of GARCH-M model suggests that the risk and return relationship is not proper in both the stock markets of India. The policy makers should ensure that the proper risk-return relationship because without it, educated and institutional investors will keep on turning away from capital markets. Even if they participate, they will resort to other sources of profit making opportunities like inside information and other unethical way.

(5) The foreign investors obviously avoid the stock markets due to information asymmetry. Policy makers and regulator should take steps to make the stock markets such that economic fundaments are the basis of asset valuation and information about the market is efficiently disseminated so that investors cannot make abnormal gains.

* * *

BIBLIOGRAPHY

Agmon. T (1972), "The relations among Equity Markets: A Study of Share Price Comovements in the United States, United Kingdom, Germany and Japan", Journal of Finance, Vol.27 (4), pp. 839-855.

Ahmad, Ashraf and Ahmed (2005), "Is the Indian stock market integrated with the US and Japanese stock markets?: An empirical analysis"' South Asia economic journal, 193-206.

Akgiray, V (1989), "Conditional Heteroscedasticity in Time Series of Stock Returns:Evidence and Forecast," Journal of Business, 62(1), 55-80.

Allen D. E and Rachim U. S (1996), "Dividend policy and stock price volatility: Australian Experience", Applied Financial Economics, Vol. 6, No.2,pp.175-188.

Amihud,Y. and Mendelson, H(1987),"Trading Mechanism and Stock Market Returns:An Empirical Investigation, The Journal of Finance,533-55.

Amihud,Y. and Mendelson, H(1991),"Volatility, Efficiency and Trading :Evidence from Japanese Stock Market, The Journal of Finance,1765-1789.

Andersen, T G and Bollerslev, T (1998), "Answering the Skeptics: Yes, Standard Volatility Models Do Provide Accurate Forecasts, " International Economic Review, 39(4), 885-905.

Baillie, R T and Bollerslev, T (1991), "Intra-day and Inter-market Volatility in Foreign Exchange Rates," Review of Economic Studies, 58(3), 567-585.

Bakaert, Harvey (1995), "Time varying world market integration, Journal of finance, 50(2), 403-444.

Ballie, R T and DeGennaro, R P (1990), "Stock Returns and Volatility," Journal of Financial and Quantitative Analysis, 25(2), 203-214.

Basher, Hassan and Islam (2007), "Time-varying volatility and equity returns in Bangladesh stock market", Applied Financial Economics, Vol. 17, pp. 1393-1407.

Beckers, S (1983), "Variances of Security Price Returns Based on high, Low and Closing Prices", Journal of Busiess, Vol.56, No. 1, pp. 97-112.

Bera, A., and M. Higgins, (1993), "ARCH Models: Properities, Estimation and Testing," Journal of Economic Surveys,. 305-362.

Bhattacharya and Samanta (2001), "A tale of two indices: the story of the NASDAQ and The Sensex", Journal of Quantitative Economics, Vol.1(1), pp. 89-102.

Bhole L. M., (2005), *Financial Institutions and Markets-structure, growth and innovations*, Tata McGraw-Hill Publishing Company Limited, New Delhi.

Biswal and Kamaiah (2001), "Stock Market Development in India: Is There Any Trend Break?", Institute for Social and Economic Change, Working Paper no. 62.

Black (1986), "Noise", The Journal of Finance, no. 41, 529-44.

Black,F(1976), "Studies of Stock Price Volatility Changes," Proceedings of 1976 Meetings of the American Statistical Association, Business and Economics Statistics Section, Washington, DC, American Statistical Association, 177-181.

Bollersflev T., Chou R.Y., and Kroner K.F., (1992), "ARCH modeling in finance: A review of the theory and empirical evidence," Journal of Econometrics, 52, 5-59.

Bollerslev, Engle and Wooldridge (1988), "A capital asset pricing model with time-varying covariances", Journal of political economy, 96, 116-131.

Bollerslev,T.(1986), "Generalised Autoregressive Conditional Heteroscedasticity", Journal of Econometrics,. 307-327.

Box, G E P and Jenkins, G M (1976), *Time Series Analysis: Forecasting and Control*, revised edition, California: Holden-Day.

Brooks Chris(2008),*Introductory Econometrics for Finance*, Cambridge University Press, UK.

Campbell John, Lo Andrew and Mackinlay (2006), *The Econometrics of Financial Markets*, New Age International Publishers.

Chelley-Steeley (2005), "Modeling equity market integration using smooth transition analysis: a study of eastern European stock markets", Journal of International money and finance, 24, 818-831.

Chen Y.M, (1993), "Price Limits and Stock Market Volatility in Taiwan", Pacific Basin Journal,139-153.

Chodhury Abdur R (1997), "Margin Requirements and stock market volatility in Thailand" Applied Economics Letters, Vol. 4, No.2, pp. 83-87.

Chou, Lin and Wu(1999), "Modeling the Taiwan stock market and international linkages", Pacific Economic Review, vol 4, 305-320.

Chung Yin-Wong and Ng Lillian (1992), Interactions Between the U.S. and Japan Stock Market Indices, Journal of International Financial Markets, Institutions and Money, Vol.2, No.2, pp. 51-69.

Colm Kearney and Kevin Daly (1998), The causes of stock market volatility in Australia", Applied Financial Economics, Vol.8, pp. 597-605.

Cooray T.M.J.A., (2008), *Applied Time Series Analysis and Forecasting*, Narosa Publishing House, India.

Corhay, A and Rad T (1994), " Statistical Properties of Daily Return: Evidence from European Stock Markets," Journal of Business, Finance and Accounting, 21(2), 271-282.

Corhay, A and Tourani, A.R. (1994), Statistical Properties of Daily Stock Returns: Evidence from European Stock Markets, Journal of Business Finance and Accounting, 21(2), 271-282.

Damodar Gujarati (2004), *Basic Econometrics*, PHI, fourth Edition.

Dickey D. and Fuller W, (1979), "Distribution of the estimators for Autoregressive time series with a unit root", Journal of American Statistical Association, Vol. 74, pp. 427-31.

Dickey, David & Fuller (1981), "Likelihood Ratio Statistics for for Autoregressive Time Series with a Unit Root." Econometrica, 49, 1057 – 72

David Rupport,(2006), *Statistics and Finance:An Introduction*, Second Edition, Springer, New York.

Dimitar Tonchev and Tae-Hwan Kim (2004), Calendar effects in Eastern European financial markets: evidence from the Czech Republic, Slovakia and Slovenia Applied Financial Economics, Volume 14, Issue 14, 1035 1043.

Eliseabete Mendes Duarte and Jose Alberto Da Fonseca (2001), Volatility Analysis of Portugese Stock Market,1-17

Engle and Kroner(1995), Multivariate simultaneous generalized ARCH, Econometric theory, 11, 122-150.

Engle R.F. and Ng V. K., (1993), Measuring and testing the impact of news on volatility, Journal of Finance, 48, 1749-1778.

Engle, R (2001), GARCH 101: The use of ATCH/GARCH models in Applied Econometrics, Journal of Economic Perspective, Vol.15, No.4, pp. 157-168.

Engle, R (2003), Risk ad Volatility Econometric models and financial practice, Nobel lecture, pp. 326-349.

Engle, R ad Patton, A (2001), What Good is a volatility model?', Quantitative Finance, Vol. 1, 237-45.

Engle, R F and Susmel, R (1993), Common Volatility in Internatioal Equity Markets," Journal of Business and Economic Statistics, 11(2), 167-176.

Engle, R. (1982), Autoregressive Conditional Heteroscedasticity with Estimates of the Variance of UK Inflation, Econometrica, 50(4), 987-1008.

Engle, R. (1982), Autoregressive Conditional Heteroscedasticity with Estimates of the Variance of UK Inflation," Econometrica, 50(4), 987-1008.

Eun C., and Shim S, (1989), "International Transmission of Stock Market Movements", Journal of Financial and Quantitative Analysis, Vol. 24(2), 241-255.

Fama, E (1965), "The Behaviour of Stock Market Prices," Journal of Business, 38(1), 34-105.

French,K,Schewert, G and Stambaugh, R (1987), "Expected Stock Returns and Volatility," Journal of Financial Economics, 19(1), 5-26.

French,K.R. and Roll, R., (1986), "Stock Return Variances-The Arrival of Information and Reaction of Traders," Journal of Financial Economics, 17, 5-26.

Frenkel and Rose (1997), " Is EMU more justifiable ex post than ex ante", European Economic Review,. 41, 753-760.

Garner A.C., (1988), "Has Stock Market Crash Reduced Customer Spending?" Economic Review, Federal Reserve Bank of Kanas City, April, 3-16.

Gertler, M. and Hubbard, R.G.,(1989)," Factors in Business Fluctuations, Financial Market Volatility", Federal Reserve Bank of Kanas City, 33-72.

Gilmore C., and McManus G, (2002), International portfolio diversification: US and Central European equity markets, Emerging Markets Review Vol.3, pp. 69–83.

Glosten, L, Jagannathan, R and Runkle, D (1993),"On the Relation Between the Expected Value and Volatility of the Nominal Excess Returns on Stocks," Journal of Finance, 48(5), 1779-1801.

Goldsmith W (1969), *Financial Structure and Development*, New Haven Conn. Yale University Press.

Gourieroux Christian and Jasiak Joann (2005), *Financial Econometrics*, New Age International Publishers.

Goyal, R(1995), "Volatility in Stock Market Returns,"Reserve Bank of India Occasional Paper, 16(3), 175-195.

Gurley and Shaw (1955), "Financial Aspects of Economic Development", American Economic Review, 45, pp. 515-38.

Harris and Pisedtasalasai (2006), "Return and volatility spillovers between large and small stocks in the UK", Journal of business finance and accounting, 1-16.

Harris and Sollis (2006), *Applied Time Series Modelling and Forecasting*, John Wiley and Sons, Singapore.

Heimonen (2002), "Stock market integration: evidence on price integrating and return convergence", Applied financial economics, vol.12, 415-429.

Heins and Allison (1966), "Some factors affecting stock price volatility", Journal of Business, January, pp.19-23.

Hilliard. J,(1979), "The Relationship between Equity Indices on World Exchanges", Journal of Finance, Vol. 34(1), pp.103-114.

Ho, R and Cheung, Y (1994)," Seasonal Pattern in Volatility in Asian Stock Markets," Applied Financial Economics, 4(1), 61-67.

Hogue (2007), "Co-movement of Bangladesh stock market with other markets: cointegration and error correction approach", Managerial finance, vol.33, no.10,810-820.

Hsieh, D.A. and Miller (1990), "Margin Regulation and Stock Market Volatility," The Journal of Finance,Vol. XLV(2),3-29.

Islam (2007), "Asymmetric volatility and stochastic behavior of the Bombay stock exchange", Asian-African Journal of Economic and Econometrics, Vol.7, No.1-2, pp. 33-43.

Jamshed Y. Uppal, (1998), " Stock Return Volatility in an emerging market: A case study of the Karachi Stock Exchange" Managerial Finance, 24, pp 34-51.

Jiangang Xu (1999), "Modeling Shanghai stock market volatility", Annals of Operations Research, Vol.87, pp.141-52.

Jones and Wilson (1989), "Is stock price Volatility Increasing?,"Financial Analysts Journal,20-26.

Kaplanis, E.C.,(1988), "Stability and forecasting of the comovement measures of international stock returns", Journal of International Money Finance, Vol. 14, No.1, pp. 63-75.

Karmakar M, (2005), "Modeling Conditional Volatility of the Indian Stock Markets", Vikalpa, 30. 21-37

Karmakar M,(2006), "Stock Market Volatility in the Long Run, 1961-2005," Economic and Political Weekly, 1796-2000.

Karolyi (1995), "A Multivariate GARCH model of international transmissions of stock returns and volatility: The case of the United States and Canada", journal of business and economic studies, vol.13, no.1, 11-24.

Karolyi and Stulz(1996), "Why do markets move together? An investigation of US-Japan stock return co-movements", The Journal of finance, LI, 951-956.

Karpoff, J.M (1987), "The Relation between price changes and Trading volume: A survey", Journal of Financial and Quantitative Analysis, Vol. 22, No.1, 109-23.

Kaur, H (2002), "Time varying volatility in the Indian stock market", Vikalpa, Vo. 29, No.4, pp. 25-42.

Kevin S (2004), *Portfolio Management*, Prentice-Hall of India Pvt. Ltd.

Khan M Y (2005), *Indian Financial System,* Tata McGraw-Hill Publishing Company Limited, New Delhi.

King and Levine (1993), "Finance and Growth: Schumpter might be Right", Quarterly Journal of Economics, 717-37.

Knight Frank (1921), *Risk, Uncertainty and Profit,* Houghton Mifflin Co., Boston.

Kumar (2004), Comparative performance of volatility forecasting models in Indian markets, Decision, Vol. 33, No. 2, pp. 25-40.

Kumar and Sumanjeet (2006), Is Indian stock market more volatile in reform period? Evidence from E-GARCH model, International Jouranl of Applied Business and Economic Research, Vol. 4, No.2, pp.147-163.

Lamoureux, C G and Lastrapes, W D (1990), Persistence in Variance, Structural Change and the GARCH Model Journal of Economic and Business Statistics, 8(2), 225-233

Lee and Yool, (1991), Time Varying Volatilites and Stock Market Returns:International Evidence, Pacific Basin Capital Markets Research,261-81.

Levin and Zervos (1996), Stock Market Development and Long Run Growth, World Bank Economic Review

Levin and Zervos (1998), Stock Markets, Banks and Economic Growth, American Economic Review, June 88(3), 537-58.

Li (2007), International Linkages of the Chinese stock exchanges: a multivariate GARCH analysis, Applied financial economics, vol.17, 285-295.

Li and Lam (1995), Modelling asymmetry in stock returns by threshold autoregressive conditional heteroscedastic model", The Statistics, Vol.44, No. 3, pp.333-341.

Li and Majerowaska (2007), " Testing stock market linkages for Poland and Hungary: A Multivariate GARCH approach", Research in international business and finance, 1-20.

Ljung L. G. M. and Box G. E. P., (1978),"On a measure of lag fit in time series models," Biometrica 67, 397-303.

Lo, A.W., and MacKinlat,(1988), "Stock Market Prices do not Follow Random Walk: An Evidence from a Simple Specification Test." Review of Financial Studies, 41-66.

Lockwood,L.J. and Linn,(1990), "An Estimation of Stock Price Return Volatility During Overnight and Intra-Day Periods-1984-1989",The Journal of Finance,Vol.XLV(2), 591-601.

Longin and Solnik (1995), "Is the correlation in international equity returns constant:1960:1990?", Journal of international money and finance, 14(1), 3-26.

Longjam, (2001), "An index for Financial Sector Development of India", India Development Report, 45-60.

Magdy Farag, Aiman Ragab, Ayman EL-Temsahy(2000), "Controlling the Volatility in the Egyptian Stock Market: The Case of ARCH and GARCH Models", Arab Academy for Science & Technology,1-23.

Mandelbrot, B (1963), "The Variation of Certain Speculative Prices," Journal of Business, 36, 394-419.

Marko S. Maukonen (2002), "On the predictive ability of several common models of volatility: an empirical test on the FOX Index" Applied Financial Economics, 12, 813-826.

Markowitz Harry (1952), "Portfolio Selection", The Journal of Finance, Vol. VII, pp. 77-91.

Mills T C and Markellos Raphael (2008), *The Econometric Modeling of Financial Time Series*, Cambridge University Press, UK.

Minho Kim, Gyeong Rok Kim, and Mincheol Kim (2004), "Stock market volatility and trading activities in KOSPI 200 derivative markets", Applied Economic Letters, Volume 11, no.1, pp. 49-53.

Mohanty and Kamaih (2000), "Volatility and its persistence in Indian stock market: A case of 30 scrips", working paper 53, Institute for Social and Economic Change.

Nelson, D (1991), "Conditional Heteroscedasticity in Asset Returns: A New Approach," Econometrica, 59(2), 347-370.

Nicholls, D and Tonuri, D (1995), "Modelling stock market volatility in Australia" Journal of Business Finance and Accounting, No.22(3), pp.377-95.

Nickolaos V. Tsangarakis(2007), "The day-of-the-week effect in the Athens Stock Exchange (ASE)", Applied Financial Economics, Volume 17, Issue 17, 1447 – 1454

Padhi Puja (2004), "Persistence and Asymmetry volatility in Indian Stock Market", Journal of Quantitative Economics, pp. 103-113.

Pagan (1984), "Econometrics issues in the analysis of regression with generated regressor", International economic review, 25, 221-247.

Pagan A. R and Schewert G.W (1990), "Alternative models for conditional stock volatility," Journal of Econometrics, 45, 267-290.

Pagan, A. R. and Sabau(1987), " On the inconsistency of the MLE in certain heteroskedastic regression models,", Mimeo, 1987.

Pandey, A., (2002), "Modeling and Forecasting Volatility in Indian Capital Markets," Paper published as part of the NSE Research Initiative, available at www.nseindia.com.

Patell, J M and Wolfson, M A (1981), "The Ex-Ante and Ex-Post Price Effects of Quartely Earnings Announcement Reflected in Option and Stock Price," Journal of Accounting Research, 19, Autumn, 434-458.

Poon, S H and Granger, C (2003), "Forecasting Financial Market Volatility: A Review," Journal of Economic Literature, 41(2), 478-539.

Poshakwale, S (1996), "Evidence on Weak Form Efficiecy and Day of the Week Effect in the Indian Stock Market," Finance India, 10(3), 605-616.

Poshakwale, S and Murinde V (2001), "Modelling volatility in East European emerging markets: evidence on Hungary and Polland", Applied Financial Economics, Vol. 11, No. 4, pp. 445-456.

Prabir Mohanty (2006), "A study of Asymmetric volatility in Indian Equity Market: A GARCH approach", Decision, Vol. 33, No. 1, pp. 121-134.

Raju, M.T. and Ghosh, Anirban (2004),"Stock Market Volatility: An International Comparision"-Working Paper Series no.8, SEBI.

Reddy, Y S (1997), "Effects of Microstructure on Stock Market Liquidity and Volatility," Prajan, 26(2), 217-231.

Reserve Bank of India, Annual Reports, Various Issues.

Robert Engle and Andrew Patton (2001), "What Good A Volatility Model?, "Working paper, Department of finance, NYU Stern School of Business and Economics.

Roll (1989), "Price Volatility, International Market Links and their implications for regulatory policies", Journal of Financial Services Research, 3, 211-246.

Roll, R., (1988), "R2", The Journal of Finance, Vol. XLII, No.3, 541-66.

Roll, R., (1988), "The International Crash of October 1987", Financial Analysts Journal, September-October, 19-35.

Roy M. K. and Karmakar M, (1995), "Stock Market Volatility: Roots and Results,"

Roy M. K. and Karmakar M, (1995), "Stock Market Volatility: Roots and Results," Vikalpa,37-48.

Ruey S. Tsay (2005), *Analysis of Financial Time Series*, 2nd Edition, John Wiley and Sons, New York.

Sasidharan and Mathews (2008), *Financial Services and Systems,* The McGraw Hill Companies, New Delhi

Scheicher(2001), "The comovements of stock markets in Hungary, Poland and the Czech republic", International journal of finance and economics, vol.6, 27-39.

Schwert, G W (1990), "Stock Volatility and the Crash of 87," Review of Financial Studies, 3(1), 77-102.

Schwert, G.W(1989), "Why does Stock Market Volatility Change Over time?" Journal of Finance, 54, 1115-1153.

Security and Exchange Board of India, Annual Reports, Various Issues.

Sen and Ghosh (2006), "Relationship between stock market liquidity and Volatility at an aggregate level: A case study on NSE, ICFAI journal of Applied Finance, Vol. 12, No.2, pp.25-32.

Shah Saeed and Iqbal (2005), "Volatility and stock returns in Dhaka stock exchange: An empirical evidence using ARCH models", International journal of Applied Business and Economic Research, Vol. 3, No. 1, pp. 1-17.

Sims. C,(1980), "Macroeconomics and Reality", Econometrica, Vol.48, pp. 1-48.

Singh Ajit (1997), *The Stock Market Industrial Development and the Financing of Corporate Growth in India*, ed. By Deepak Nayyar, Oxford University Press.

Singh Y. P. and Bhatia Shalini (2006), "Does Futures Trading Impact Spot Market Volatility? Evidence from Indian Financial Markets", Decision, Vol.33, No. 2, pp. 41-62.

Sioud Benouda and Hmaied Dorra (2003), "The effects of Automation on liquidity, volatility, stock returns and efficiency: Evidence from the Tunisian stock market", Review of Middle East Economics and Finance, Vol. 1, No.2, pp. 141-154.

Siourounis, G. D. (2002), "Modelling volatility and testing for efficiency in emerging capital markets: the case of the Athens stock exchange", Applied Financial Economics, 12, pp. 47–55.

Stephen P. Keef and Melvin L. Roush (2005), "Day-of-the-week effects in the pre-holiday returns of the Standard & Poor's 500 stock index", Applied Financial Economics, Volume 15, Issue 2, 107 – 119.

Tan III (1998), "Contagion effects during the Asian Financial crisis:some evidence from stock price data", working paper no. PB98-06, Federal reserve bank of San Franscisco.

Theierry Ane, (2006), "Short run and long term component of volatility in Hong Kong Stock return " Applied Financial Economics, 16, 439-460.

Thiam Ng., (2002), "Stock Price Movements in South-East Asia", Asian Economic Journal, Vol.16(4), pp.353-77.

Voronkova (2004), "Equity market integration in Central European stock markets: A cointegration analysis with shifting regimes", International review of financial analyst, 13, 633-647.

Wagmare (1998), *The future of India's Stock Market,* Tata-Mcgraw Hill.

Walter Enders, (1995), *Applied Econometrics Time Series,* John Willey and Sons, New York.

Wing-Keung Wong & Aman Agarwal & Jun Du, (2005), "Financial Integration for India Stock Market, a Fractional Cointegration Approach," Departmental Working Papers wp501, National University of Singapore, Department of Economics.

Worthington and Higgs (2004), "Transmission of Equity returns and volatility in Asian developed and emerging markets: A multivariate GARCH analysis", International journal of Finance and Economics, vol. 9, 71-80.

Yang and Wang (2006), "The emerging market crisis and stock market linkages: further evidence", Journal of applied econometrics, 21, 727-744.

Zakoian, J. M., (1994), Threshold Heteroskedastic Models, Journal of Economic Dynamics and Control, 18, 931-55.

Zikmund, W. G., (2003), *Business Research Methods,* Thomson South-Western, Bangalore.

* * *